Beyond the Family Romance

The Legend of Pascoli

MARIA TRUGLIO

In *Beyond the Family Romance*, Maria Truglio offers fresh insight into the writing of Giovanni Pascoli (1855–1912), one of Italy's most celebrated and innovative poets. While tracing Pascoli's major influences, Truglio offers a psychoanalytic perspective of his work, focusing on his conceptions of childhood and his preoccupation with formative, primary experiences. Drawing on some of Freud's theories, Truglio examines themes of regression, memory, and other manifestations of 'origins' in Pascoli's poetry. In addition to the Freudian comparison, Truglio also explores parallels between Pascoli's work and that of such writers as Tarchetti, Boito, Poe, and Invernizio.

Pascoli's poetry is noted for its refined, lyrical style and its melancholy, evocative qualities. An eminent classical scholar, Pascoli had a tragic childhood, marked by the death of both parents (his father was assassinated) and five of his siblings. Truglio reveals the ambivalence with which images of the home are fraught in Pascoli's poetry, and examines the dichotomy between 'safety within the home' and the 'threatening outside world.' Exploring Pascoli's fascination with the uncanny and his particular use of imagery, she shows that his poetry bridges the logic of the rational modern adult and the mythic vision of the child. However, she firmly situates Pascoli's work in its larger social, historical, and literary context, thus moving beyond the biographical interpretations which have hitherto dominated criticism of his poetry.

MARIA TRUGLIO is an assistant professor in the Department of Spanish, Italian, and Portuguese at Pennsylvania State University.

MARIA TRUGLIO

Beyond the Family Romance

The Legend of Pascoli

UNIVERSITY OF TORONTO PRESS
Toronto Buffalo London

© University of Toronto Press Incorporated 2007
Toronto Buffalo London
Reprinted 2017

ISBN-13: 978-0-8020-9191-8 (cloth)
ISBN-13: 978-1-4875-8723-9 (paper)

Printed on acid-free paper

Toronto Italian Studies

Library and Archives Canada Cataloguing in Publication

Truglio, Maria
  Beyond the family romance : the legend of Pascoli / Maria Truglio.

(Toronto Italian studies)
Includes bibliographical references and index.
ISBN-13: 978-0-8020-9191-8 (bound)
ISBN-13: 978-1-4875-8723-9 (pbk.)

1. Pascoli, Giovanni, 1855–1912 – Criticism and interpretation.
2. Psychology and literature. 3. Freud, Sigmund, 1856–1939.
I. Title. II. Series.

PQ4835.A3Z865 2006   851'.8   C2006-904173-3

This book has been published with the assistance of a grant from the Research and Graduate Studies Office of the Pennsylvania State University.

University of Toronto Press acknowledges the financial assistance to its publishing program of the Canada Council for the Arts and the Ontario Arts Council.

University of Toronto Press acknowledges the financial support for its publishing activities of the Government of Canada through the Book Publishing Industry Development Program (BPIDP).

Contents

Acknowledgments vii

Introduction: Nesting Instincts 3
1 Foreshadowing: The *Scapigliati* and Psychoanalysis 24
2 Returning: The *Poemi conviviali* and the Uncanny 57
3 Positioning Pascoli in the Fin de Siècle: The Case of Infanticide 83
4 Envisioning Childhood: Memory, Desire, *Pietas*, and Play 107
5 Remembering the Golden Age 135
Conclusion: Reading beyond the Family Romance 159

Notes 161
Bibliography 191
Index 199

Acknowledgments

Many colleagues and friends have contributed to this project, both in its early form as my doctoral dissertation (Yale 2001) and throughout the extensive process of revision and expansion. My first word of thanks goes to my dissertation adviser, Paolo Valesio, for his mentorship, insights, and, not least of all, encouragement. I acknowledge with gratitude Giuseppe Mazzotta, Olivia Holmes, and Mary Ann Carolan for their valuable constructive criticism. Ernesto Livorni kindly provided detailed comments on several chapters, and Michael Levine generously shared his expertise in psychoanalytic methodology. I have enjoyed insightful mentorship and kind support from my colleagues at the Pennsylvania State University: John Lipski, Bob Blue, Sherry Roush, Chip Gerfen, Paola Gambarota, and Heather McCoy. I thank Scott Surrency for his work on the index.

The Paul Gignilliat fellowship at Yale provided financial support. I thank the anonymous readers and the Manuscript Review Committee at University of Toronto Press for their excellent and insightful advice. The manuscript benefited greatly from the meticulous work of Margaret Allen, copy editor, and Anne Laughlin, managing editor. My heartfelt thanks go to Toronto Italian Studies series editor Ron Schoeffel, with whom it has been a pleasure to work, for his guidance and expertise.

My discussions of 'La voce' (in the introduction) and 'Antìclo' (in chapter 2) are reprinted with kind permission of the *Romance Review*. A slightly modified version of chapter 2 has appeared as an article. It is reprinted with permission from the *Romanic Review*, volume 97, number 2, March, 2006. Copyright by the Trustees of Columbia University in the City of New York. I thank Professor Umberto Sereni, mayor of Barga, Italy, for his kind permission to use the photograph of Giovanni Pascoli that appears on the jacket.

I could not have made it through the challenging years of graduate school without the truly overwhelming support of friends. In spite of their own strenuous schedules, they found time to proofread, baby sit, substitute teach, return library books, and pick up groceries. I am profoundly grateful to Sherry, Scott, Paola, Hilary Link, Arielle Saiber, Joe Luzzi, Jason Houston, Silvia DiPierdomenico, Francesca Seaman, Mike Mirabile, Ed Lintz, and James Lavino. I thank David Karp, Jon Bernhard, Donna Haverty-Stacke, and Joe Truglio for their untiring support. I dedicate this book, with deepest gratitude and love, to my amazing parents, Rosemary and Mario, and to Anthony Michael and Thomas Santino, *i miei fanciullini.*

BEYOND THE FAMILY ROMANCE

Introduction: Nesting Instincts

[I]mages like the cypress tree, the nest, the isolated house or the sound of bells [become] ... 'private symbols': [they] relate to an inner world of anxieties, preoccupations, and fears.
          P. R. Horne, Introduction to *Selected Poems of Giovanni Pascoli*, 37

For the critic, there is no such thing as private symbolism, or if there is, it is his job to make sure it does not remain so.
          Northrop Frye, *Anatomy of Criticism*, 111

The myth of Orpheus, as recounted in Ovid's *Metamorphoses*, warns against the temptations of looking back. As the beloved Eurydice slips 'back into the depths,' we are reminded of the dangers of nostalgia and the consequences of turning our gaze from the path ahead to the path behind. Yet such a backward turn and, more precisely, a desire to retrace and examine origins, defines the projects of both Giovanni Pascoli and Sigmund Freud. Both these turn-of-century writers attempt to lay hold of – to define and depict – an originating moment that, like Eurydice, proves to be slippery, intangible, and, in many respects, infernal. Freud's early paper on the etiology of hysteria, for example, proudly asserts the discovery of a 'source of the Nile,' positing infantile sexual abuse as the origin at 'the bottom of every case of hysteria.' The bottom, of course, would later fall out in Freud's revisions of the seduction theory.[1] Whether as poetic images of maternity, theorizations of the 'pre-Oedipal,' ideological constructions of childhood, or evocations of the golden age myth, the writings of Pascoli and Freud persistently address the question of origins, a question as elusive as it is seductive. In Pascoli's poetry, the image of the nest emerges as the emblem of origins.

In his extensive study *Simboli e strutture della poesia del Pascoli*,[2] Giorgio Bàrberi Squarotti establishes, along the lines explicitly described by Pascoli himself in poems such as 'La siepe,'[3] a psychical schema whose most pervasive and central metaphor is the *nido* or nest. According to this schema, the contents of the nest (most often the family, and particularly the ghosts of deceased family members) are characterized as good, safe, and desirable. Images of birds' nests appear with notable frequency throughout Pascoli's poems, which are celebrated for their detailed depiction of rustic country life. Populated with flowers and birds, the poetry associates the nest with the idea of 'home,' warmth, and security. When one ventures out of the nest, argues Bàrberi Squarotti, one encounters the threatening and cold world. Relationships with people outside the family circle are portrayed as undesirable and even dangerous. Bàrberi Squarotti elaborates this basic schema through readings of a vast number of Pascoli's poems culled from the full range of his Italian collections. More recently, Steno Vazzana has elaborated a similar dialectic, using the terms 'romantic' and 'classical' to distinguish the concrete, small, safe phenomena of the 'inside' from the vast, vague, noumena of the 'outside.'[4]

One of Pascoli's most famous poems, 'X agosto' (in the collection *Myricae*), enacts quite emphatically the dichotomies articulated by these critics. In the poem, Pascoli dramatizes one of the most formative events of his life – the assassination of his father, Ruggero Pascoli, on 10 August 1867 – and describes the emotional effect this trauma had on himself and his family.[5]

> San Lorenzo, io lo so perché tanto
>   di stelle per l'aria tranquilla
> arde e cade, perché sì gran pianto
>   nel concavo cielo sfavilla.
>
> Ritornava una rondine al tetto:
>   l'uccisero: cadde tra spini:
> ella aveva nel becco un insetto:
>   la cena de'suoi rondinini.
>
> Ora è là, come in croce, che tende
>   quel verme a quel cielo lontano:
> e il suo nido è nell'ombra, che attende,
>   che pigola sempre più piano.

Anche un uomo tornava al suo nido:
  l'uccisero: disse: Perdono;
e restò negli aperti occhi un grido:
  portava due bambole in dono...

Ora là, nella casa romita,
  lo aspettano, aspettano in vano:
egli immobile, attonito, addita
  le bambole al cielo lontano.

E tu, Cielo, dall'alto dei mondi
  sereni, infinito, immortale,
oh! d'un pianto di stelle lo inondi
  quest'atomo opaco del Male! (*Opere*, 140)

[Saint Lawrence, I know why so many stars burn and fall through the tranquil air, why such a great cry glitters in the domed sky. A swallow was returning to its home: they killed it: it fell among the thorns: it had an insect in its beak: dinner for its little ones. Now it is there, as if on a cross, holding that worm towards that far-off sky; and its brood is in the shadows, waiting, chirping ever more faintly. There was also a man returning to his family: they killed him: he said: Pardon; and a scream remained in his open eyes: he was carrying two dolls as a gift ... Now there, in the solitary house, they wait for him, they wait in vain: immobile, astonished, he shows the dolls to the far-off sky. And you, Heaven, from the infinite, immortal heights of the serene worlds, Oh! you flood with a cry of stars this opaque atom of Evil. (my translation)]

The title of the poem records the date of his father's assassination, and the first line repeats this gesture, this time by referring to the saint whose feast is observed on 10 August. The feast of San Lorenzo is the 'night of the shooting stars,' and Pascoli, straightforwardly employing the 'pathetic fallacy,' asserts that the unusually high number of stars that 'burn and fall' on that night do so as a demonstration of cosmic grief for the evil that has befallen on that day. From this boldly hyperbolic gesture – the claim that the very heavens are lamenting the death of a single man – Pascoli abruptly switches to its opposite: in a kind of litotes or understatement, he compares the man to a little swallow returning to its nest with a worm for its offspring. In these central stanzas of the poem we see clearly the functioning of the image of the nest, where it appears both literally (in stanzas two and three) as the home of the swallow and figuratively (in stanzas three and four) as the home of the man. Through a metonym, in fact, the *nido* is not merely the physical structure in which the family lives, but also the family itself: the *nido* 'waits' and 'chirps.' The man, like the swallow, has left the nest for the benefit of the family – to bring back food. But having left the security of the family, he is killed by an unnamed 'them' – culprits all the more threatening for their anonymity. The staccato-like narrative and the use of the *passato remoto* enforce the sudden and unexpected nature of the assassination. The baby swallows that chirp 'sempre più piano' and the children that wait for their father's return 'in vano' are depicted as bereft and helpless as a result of this act of pure evil. The last stanza returns to the hyperbole of cosmic grief, announcing the profound and absolute evil encapsulated in this assassination, the 'atomo opaco del Male.' The double gestures of hyperbole and litotes are complementary strategies for eliciting the reader's compassion: the metaphor of the swallows underscores the helplessness and fragility of the victims, and the references to the annual feast day of the saint, the sky, and the stars underscore the universality of the loss. The act of violence harms not only those directly affected but mars all humanity – indeed, all life – through its participation in pure evil. Although this poem does not represent Pascoli's best poetic achievement (in fact, I think he is here somewhat too saccharine in his depiction of the tragedy: the evocation of dolls that never make it home to his sisters, for instance, seems to me a bit heavy-handed), it provides a strikingly clear example of the outside/inside dichotomy centred on the nest that I have been summarizing. Furthermore, many critics have identified the tragic event commemorated by this poem as the origin of Pascoli's poetic voice. 'X marks the spot,' as it were: the loss of the father giving birth to the conflicts and grief elaborated in the orphan's poems.

Bàrberi Squarotti himself, however, suggests various complications in the dichotomy he posits. The consoling mother, he notes, seems almost always to appear in conjunction with evocations or dramatizations of some form of 'auto-annullamento.'[6] He points out a similar complication in the representation of the father. Because of his assassination, the father cannot fulfil his paternal role as protector and defender of the 'nest.' While, clearly, it is utterly illogical to foster resentment towards the father for having been killed, such ambivalent emotions are a well-known psychological phenomenon and, in this context, help constitute what Bàrberi Squarotti terms the 'mito del padre' [the myth of the father] in Pascoli's poetry: 'il padre è il segno della sicurezza, della difesa dei piccoli' [the father is the sign of safety, of the defence of the children]. But he is represented 'non senza una punta di rancore, quasi, contro il padre che ha tradito, ha abbandonato, sia pure contro la sua volontà, la famiglia, provocando la dissoluzione' [not without a hint of rancour, almost, against the father, who has betrayed and abandoned – albeit against his will – the family, provoking its dissolution].[7]

I suggest, through a focus on the *Poemi conviviali*, that the haunting poetic experience created by Pascoli derives from an essential ambiguity within the psychic framework. Specifically, I argue that the poetry does not sustain the inside/outside distinction, and that the image of the nest itself and its plethora of significations are always already fraught with ambivalence: that they are desired, comforting, and homey, and at the same time threatening, dangerous, and 'unhomey.' In short, Pascoli's poetry deploys the 'uncanny,' as adumbrated by Freud, as both its effect and agenda.[8]

In Freud's account, the experience of the 'uncanny' is triggered by an encounter with something intimately familiar that is, however, perceived as something strange because it has undergone repression. Where many of Freud's major works describe the unconscious generation or *expression* of repressed material (dreams, parapraxes, jokes, neurotic symptoms), the 'uncanny' explores the unconscious *recognition* of repressed fears and desires. Freud published this suggestive essay in 1919, while he was in the process of formulating his theories of repetition compulsion and the death drive, theories he would articulate in a boldly speculative manner in *Beyond the Pleasure Principle* of 1920.[9] I privilege this essay not as a statement of Freudian doctrine that explains Pascoli's poetry but as another, nearly contemporary text that elaborates and in some ways dramatizes the same issues that concern Pascoli's writing. The dialogue I am opening between these two independently developed discourses will free our understanding of Pascoli's work from the biographical boundaries that have hitherto determined it.

Freud's introductory foray into dictionary definitions of *heimlich* demonstrates that this word potentially coincides in meaning with its opposite, *unheimlich*, noting that 'What interests us most in this long extract is to find that among its different shades of meaning the word "*heimlich*" exhibits one which is identical with its opposite, "*unheimlich*" ... on the one hand it means what is familiar and agreeable, and on the other, what is concealed and kept out of sight' (224–5). This insight provides the first intersection with Pascoli's poetic enterprise, namely, the gesture of locating the eerie, frightening, and uncanny not in foreign objects but nestled deep within the most familiar and intimate aspects of the self.

Freud then moves to analyses of both literary and experiential examples of the uncanny in an attempt to define the origins and 'common core' of this particular class of the frightening. His strategy, like Pascoli's, entails turning back to infantile thought processes, thought processes marked by ambivalence and the coexistence of logical contraries. Freud posits initially that 'the uncanny is that class of the frightening which leads back to what is known of old and long familiar' (220), and later in the essay, more specifically, that 'an uncanny experience occurs either when infantile complexes which have been repressed are once more revived by some impression, or when primitive beliefs which have been surmounted seem once more to be confirmed,' qualifying this definition with the caveat that 'the distinction is often a hazy one' (249). The inescapable *haziness* that emerges in the search for the 'core' of the uncanny, in fact, motivates the movement of Freud's essay. While the piece is punctuated (at least six times) by tentative definitions of the uncanny (like the two cited above), none of these formulations remains adequate as the definitive definition. The essay moves from one example to the next (the most well known of which is the analysis of Hoffmann's 'The Sandman'), each discussion in some way not quite hitting the mark dead on, each one generating yet another example in a series of narrative detours. As one of these examples, Freud narrates an autobiographical anecdote of an uncanny experience in Italy. Finding himself unexpectedly in the local red-light district, he attempts to walk elsewhere, but after strolling away (or so he thought) he finds himself again in the same spot. He attempts several times to escape, but somehow always repeats his return. This vignette, I think, reproduces the movement of the essay as a whole: repeated wanderings and returns to the same spot (the Italian prostitutes, the definition of the uncanny), a destination that is both desired and feared, both seductive and disreputable. The essay ends rather abruptly, not coming to rest in any summation or conclusion, but rather referring the reader 'elsewhere.'[10] Freud's suggestive piece, then, demonstrates that the evocation of the uncanny is linked to the impossibility of locating definitively its source or origin. The larger implications of the haziness and mobility of the 'core' of the uncanny emerge in a letter Freud wrote concerning the degrees to which psychoanalysis could sustain dissent and differences of opinion. In discussing the possible threat of essential, fundamental difference, Freud writes that, while a certain level of theoretical diversity can be tolerated, 'one must hold on to the homogeneity of the core, otherwise it is something else.'[11] And yet the uncanny, in many respects a 'core' concept of psychoanalysis, is by definition heterogeneous, by definition indefinable. The 'core' (or indeed the *nido*), in other words, is always 'something else,' always 'elsewhere.' Pascoli's poetry, I will show, dramatizes the anxiety elicited by this irreducible haziness.

The significance of 'Das Unheimliche' remains neither static nor self-evident, and the text has been a site of fruitful examinations by critics who rearticulate and remobilize it through Derridean and Lacanian modes of reading, among others. Hélène Cixous, for example, has argued that Freud's text exemplifies what it purports to describe, that is, 'Das Unheimliche' is itself an 'uncanny' text, one that proceeds through 'a game of infinite substitutions' and 'echoes.'[12] She proposes that in Freud's piece, the 'truth of the uncanny,' simultaneously pursued and avoided by Freud, remains a 'concept without any nucleus,' one 'whose entire denotation is a connotation.'[13] She proposes that Freud here betrays a kind of envy of literary authors (such as Hoffmann, his 'double') who can conjure up the uncanny at will, and she emphasizes the place of fiction in the theorization of the uncanny. Indeed, for Cixous, the uncanny derives from the process of representation (hence Freud's heavy dependence on literary examples), a process that announces death, which alone is unrepresentable. Thus, she critiques Freud's reading of 'The Sandman,' in which he analyses *themes* and establishes *identities* (eyes = penis, Coppola = Coppelius) where he should have examined narrative *structure* and textual *ambiguities*. The intrusion of death into life, spread out in fiction (as representation) emerges in Cixous's reading as the uncanny.[14] Cixous's emphasis on death and particularly the image of the ghost will illuminate my readings of the Gothic-like poetry of the *scapigliatura*, as well as the representations of the living dead, the *cari morti*, that haunt so many of Pascoli's compositions.

The image of the ghost as a marker of temporal and spatial disruption emerges in Ruth Parkin-Gounelas's recent piece on the uncanny.[15] Gounelas, who brings the Freudian uncanny to bear on an analysis of Coleridge's 'Cristabel,' synthesizes Derrida's reading of Freud's work. The ghost (specifically, Hamlet's father), 'like the repetition compulsion ... returns over and over to disturb the concept of an original origin or cause.'[16] Gounelas points out that 'Derrida paid tribute to Freud for his recognition of *différance* (difference/deferral) at the origin, his challenge to the concept of primariness.'[17] This deconstruction of origins informs my questioning of the inside/outside dichotomy described above. Instead, I show how Pascoli's lyrics meditate on originary (homey, maternal) moments, revealing their constitutive ambiguities and fractures.

Samuel Weber centres or, better, decentres the uncanny around 'castration,' insisting that castration be understood 'not as an event or mere fantasy but as a structure.' He codes castration as 'a restructuring of experience ... in which the narcissistic categories of identity and presence are riven by a difference they can no longer subdue or command.'[18] Weber underscores the particular capacity of the grammatical present participle to designate 'those activities and processes that are going on around us all the time,' yet 'never come full circle, never come "home."'[19] Thus, for example, Weber suggests a translation of the famous 'primal scene' not as 'primal,' which suggests a single, discrete event, but as '*originating*.'[20] The concepts Weber explores of process, substitution, repetition, and incomplete return structure the dialogue I open in these pages between Freud's essay and Pascoli's literature. Like Pascoli's poetry, Freud's 'Das Unheimliche' not only reveals the surprising conflation of the familiar and the strange but also stages an encounter with repetition and difference as it rearticulates its own originating scene.

Many critics have described Pascoli's poetry as a kind of evocation of lost, infantile, or, more precisely, 'primary' experiences. Descriptive terms such as 'infantile regression,' 'primordial drive,' 'Edenic desire,' and 'return to the maternal womb' regularly appear in the criticism, but the profoundly ambivalent and conflicted nature of this nostalgia has not been sufficiently emphasized. Though Pascoli celebrates the purity of the child's vision and claims that such vision is the very heart of all true poetry, we find that in his poetic practice the return to the wonder of the *fanciullino* always entails a concomitant self-negation or 'autoannullamento.'[21] Pascoli's poetry enacts the uncanny, realizing it in both its sublime and its horrific aspects.

This study has three main objectives. First, it traces the influence of the *scapigliatura* – the surprisingly little studied, Gothic-like movement in northern Italy – on the subtly haunting lyrics of Giovanni Pascoli. Second, it offers new readings of Pascoli's writings in light of Freud's articulation of the uncanny, insisting on the essential ambiguity of the maternal and of the recurrent imagery of the *nido*. Finally, this study compares in a sustained manner this body of late nineteenth-century Italian literature and Freudian psychoanalysis, juxtaposing these two contemporary discourses and using each to shed light on the other. The final chapters give particular attention to Freud and Pascoli's conceptions of childhood, their constructions of a modern-day 'golden age' myth, and their visions of the moral and social goals and implications of their undertakings.

Pascoli, to my knowledge, was not a reader of Freud; nor was Freud a reader of Pascoli. Thus, the study does not suggest either as a source for the other. Rather, a comparative look at the rhetorical strategies and thematic preoccupations of these writers reveals a shared ambition to create a universalizing discourse that would intervene in the public sphere by speaking to and conditioning personal memory and desire. Throughout this work, and most rigorously in these introductory pages, I consider various ways in which psychoanalysis has been employed as a method of literary criticism, and assess their advantages and shortcomings.

Pascoli's representations of such themes as infanticide (in 'Il ceppo') and abortion (in 'L'etèra') are indebted to the earlier literary experiments of the *scapigliatura*. In my first chapter, I explore the works of the *scapigliati*, particularly I.U. Tarchetti and Arrigo Boito, as a literary precedent for Pascoli's deployment of his uncanny poetic. The ghostly appearances that haunt Pascoli's work often have a touch of the macabre, and their chilling effects, though subtle, are reminiscent of the more explicitly grotesque sensibility of the Gothic movement of the 1860s and 1870s. In the chapters that follow, I move to a psychoanalytically informed reading of Pascoli's works, taking into account various examples of readings already undertaken in this methodology. Chapter 2 focuses on the moving and evocative *Poemi conviviali*. The poems in this volume are inspired by such classical writers as Hesiod, Homer, and Plato, and thus offer another re-elaboration of the investigation of origins: here, the origins of the Western literary tradition.[22] Chapter 3 considers the theme of infanticide as portrayed in the short story 'Il ceppo,' an example of Pascoli's critically neglected prose fiction. The renegotiation of laws concerning inheritance, legitimacy, and adoption, the efforts of state welfare to join with private and religious charities in curtailing abortion and infanticide by facilitating abandonment, plus the scientific community's discussions of telegony, all bespeak a cultural anxiety of origins in this period, particularly in terms of locating and asserting paternal identity. I situate Pascoli's story in the context of contemporary representations of infanticide, particularly the criminological inquiries of Cesare Lombroso and the popular fiction of Carolina Invernizio, in order to articulate his unique contribution to this issue. Together, chapters 2 and 3 revise the dominant paradigms within which Pascoli's work has been classified and interpreted. Finally, I move to a comparison of Pascoli and Freud as contemporary turn-of-the-century thinkers. In the fourth chapter, I analyse each writer's characterization of childhood and show how the emphasis given to the earliest stages of life serves each writer's universalizing aspirations. In this undertaking, I compare Freud's *Three Essays on the Theory of Sexuality* and Pascoli's *Il fanciullino*, because both these works deploy theories of childhood. Freud's claim that even infants possess sexuality and aggression, as is well known, uprooted contemporary conceptions of human development. Pascoli's articulation of poetics, instead, embraces and furthers the romantic notion of childhood innocence and asexuality. Despite this fundamental difference, points of convergence emerge. Chapter 5 interrogates the critique of religious faith offered by Freud in his *Future of an Illusion* and by Pascoli in his 'L'era nuova,' with particular attention to rhetorical strategies. This critique opens the way for an examination of the classical myth of the golden age, another manifestation of 'origins.'

Though not the dominant critical approach in Pascoli scholarship, as underscored by a recent article in Italy's *La Repubblica*, psychoanalytically informed criticism has yielded several fascinating interpretations.[23] Bàrberi Squarotti's study, discussed above, has been perhaps the most extensive undertaking in this camp. More recently, critics such as Patrizio Rossi, Stefano Agosti, Fausto Curi, and Elio Gioanola have made further contributions in this arena. I consider their studies at some length here because my book concerns itself explicitly with methodology. Before turning to a description of my own methodological approach, then, I offer here a critical evaluation of alternative though related paths of inquiry.

Rossi, Gioanola, and Curi share an interest in the clandestine erotics of Pascoli's poetry, and their criticism proposes an unmasking or decoding of the latent (sexual) meaning behind the manifest content. These critics take on the role of the analyst who interprets dreams. Curi quite explicitly adopts this role, for example, when he argues that the character of 'Rosa' and the appearances of Homer's 'Nausicaa' are 'really' Pascoli's sister Ida, whose marriage Pascoli saw as a betrayal of his jealously guarded nest.[24] He further argues that the long poem 'L'ultimo viaggio,' which dramatizes Ulysses' final sea voyage, and which serves as the centrepiece to the *Poemi conviviali*, is 'nothing but the story of an erotic failure, disguised as a quest for knowledge.' Curi is explicit in his assumption that the poems unconsciously express the author's repressed sexual libido, which, given his choice of lifestyle, had no other outlet.[25] According to Curi, the poems do not directly describe sexual desire or eroticism because Pascoli's strong superego acted as a censor, thus giving rise to various 'displacements,' such as the white arms of the 'little queen' (i.e., Ida), and to what Curi calls 'masks.' He focuses his analysis on the mask of old age (*senilità*) which, he claims, functions as a vehicle for safely meditating on eroticism while simultaneously denying it.[26] This classically psychoanalytic interpretation relies on the mutual explanation of the author's life events and literary texts, and assumes the unconscious nature of literary production.

Bàrberi Squarotti shares an interest in both the dreamlike quality of Pascoli's poetry and the erotic elements at play in specific poems. His study, however, seems to me more descriptive than interpretive in that it does not posit a secret sexual meaning under the words, as it were, but rather elucidates the way in which eroticism is portrayed and staged: namely, as 'infantile sexuality.' Here, the adjective 'infantile' recalls both the *fanciullino* of Pascoli's poetics and the earliest stages of sexuality explored by Freud in his *Three Essays*. Although Bàrberi Squarotti does not cite this specific essay among the works of Freud that inform his reading,[27] the concept of 'infantile sexuality' seems to be at work in his account. The sexuality he describes is not that of an adult relationship for the purpose of procreation under the primacy of the genitals but rather various forms of 'perversity,' such as autoeroticism and voyeurism, along the lines delineated by Freud in his account of infantile sexuality. At the same time, Bàrberi Squarotti maintains the general sense of 'wonder' that most strongly characterizes the child in Pascoli's prose account. He writes, for example, that the 'curiosità pascoliana ... ha sempre in sé, infatti, un aspetto di partecipazione, di immedesimazione che oscilla fra la fantasia onanistica dell'infanzia e un certo gusto della dissacrazione, della violenza come senso dei rapporti umani' [Pascolian curiosity ... always has within it, in fact, an aspect of participation, of identification that oscillates between infantile onanistic fantasy and a certain taste for desecration, for violence as the meaning of human relationships].[28]

In his analysis of the epithalamium 'Gelsomino notturno,' Elio Gioanola undertakes an excursus into the author's biography in order to establish a symbolic association between the floral imagery of the text and female genitalia. In the course of his analysis, Gioanola offers not merely biographical data but a kind of psychological diagnosis, suggesting that Pascoli suffered from a 'marriage phobia.' This diagnosis, in fact, is rendered in French and thus printed in italics. As such, the phrase immediately claims the reader's attention, standing out as the focal point of the analysis. At the same time, the foreign language serves to distance the critic from his subject, reinforcing the image of Pascoli as 'other' and deviant.[29]

Patrizio Rossi offers close readings of two of Pascoli's most striking poems, 'Digitale purpurea' and 'Gelsomino notturno,' in the context of what he terms the 'ethics of the nest.'[30] Synthesizing observations by Bàrberi Squarotti, Gioanola, and Goffis, Rossi analyses the origins of this ethic and the double-bind situation that inevitably arises from it. Briefly, the loss of Pascoli's original family fostered resentment towards the responsible parties of the outside world and a regression in search of comfort and protection to a re-created 'maternal womb' (imagined in the poetry variously as nests, cradles, and ghosts of *cari morti*). Fidelity to the re-created nest, consisting of himself, Ida, and Maria, elicits fears of lack of progeny: Pascoli will never be able to become the protective father of his own nest without breaking faith with this one. The dialectic of 'Eros' and 'Thanatos' arises from this ethic: sexuality, while seductive both for its mysterious pleasures and for its offer of progeny, nevertheless requires an intimate encounter with someone outside the nest, and thus its seduction is also threatening. The tension of this dialectic fuels the poetry. In his discussion of 'Digitale purpurea,' Rossi insists that the characters of Maria and Rachele should be seen as personifications of two attitudes towards sexuality (represented by the beautiful yet poisonous plant) and not as masks for specific people in Pascoli's life.

These psychoanalytically minded critics share an interest in the contents and themes of Pascoli's poetry. The questions they raise – Which characters are really Ida? How is eroticism portrayed? – examine how Pascoli works his alleged neuroses into, and out in, the poetry. Biographical data unmask the latent and sexually transgressive meanings unconsciously encoded in the texts.

The Lacanian critic Stefano Agosti follows a different path. His brief piece on Pascoli focuses on the use and effects of language per se. Agosti is, of course, not the first to underscore and to submit to analysis the verbal texture of Pascoli's poetry. Indeed, Pascoli's revolutionary *linguaggio*, characterized by its heavy use of onomatopoeia, repetitions, and strong assonance, its scientifically precise terminology (especially ·in the domains of botany and ornithology), and its employment of dialect terms, has been the object of many insightful studies, most of which cite Gianfranco Contini's 'Il linguaggio di Pascoli' as the foundational work in this camp. Agosti, however, is unique in his insistence upon the signifier's independence from and supremacy over the signified. In his analysis of 'La via ferrata' (in *Myricae*), Agosti argues that the extreme complexity of the phonic fabric goes beyond word painting, onomatopoeia, or enhancement of meaning (here the vibration of telegraph lines) and instead becomes a transcendent non-significance: the signifiers do not mean, they are. He concludes that

> gli effetti a-significanti che coronano il testo poetico non sembrano saturabile da nessun senso: oserei dire, nemmeno da quello – mimetico – dell'onomatopea, ne' da quei sensi che, al di là delle articolazioni significative, 'riproducono' (o riduplicano) determinati contenuti deposti negli enunciati ... il testo poetico sembra indicare il punto di fuga del linguaggio, il luogo del suo non-ritorno, o – il che è lo stesso – della dissipazione inesausta del senso: della sua non-inscrivibilità in un sistema di valori e di scambi. Il sole e la morte ne potrebbero essere, allora, le metafore più adeguate.[31]

> [the non-signifying effects that crown the poetic text do not seem able to be saturated by any meaning: I dare say, not even by that – mimetic – of onomatopoeia. Nor are they saturated by those meanings that, beyond significant articulations, 'reproduce' (or reduplicate) determined contents set down in the enunciated terms ... the poetic text seems to indicate the locus of the flight of language, its point of no return, or – which amounts to the same thing – the point of the unexhausted dissipation of meaning: of its unwritability in a system of values and of exchanges. The sun and death, then, might be its most appropriate metaphors.]

Agosti's approach (at the same time its strength and its weakness, as is often the case in a rigorous implementation of a specific methodology) subordinates all other potential issues to the linguistic: language replaces sexuality as the master code.

The methods exemplified in the studies I have summarized here, while offering valuable insights, at times risk portraying the poetry either as an outlet of libidinal energy or as a pleasurable play of signifiers. More significantly, this summary suggests that Pascoli's work itself generates a certain critical stance. Much criticism, psychoanalytically informed or based in other methodological approaches, adopts the position exemplified in a marked way by Gioanola's essay described above. That is, Pascoli's biography is both privileged as an interpretive lens and simultaneously disowned as exceptional, deviant, and even perverse. Thus, the critics seek to establish a safe distance between themselves and their object and create a stable, spectator-like position from which they may judge the poetry. I suggest that the uncanniness of Pascoli's poetry itself elicits this kind of performance. For, as Weber asserts, the uncanny 'confounds prediction, judgment, and lets a certain form of "constative" discourse [in this case, critical assessments] reveal itself as always already "performative"' (21) because 'there is no longer the possibility of a stable separation from that which is under consideration' (19). Weber's remarks pertain to his reading of Hoffmann's 'The Sandman,' but I invoke them here as a way to understand the dominant critical scenario played out vis-à-vis Pascoli's work.

My own use of psychoanalysis has in many respects been informed by the work of Francesco Orlando.[32] Orlando argues that only in *Jokes and Their Relation to the Unconscious* and in the essay 'The "Uncanny"' does Freud provide a formal model for a fruitful study of literature, because the models set forth in these works can accommodate literature's role as meaningful communication rather than reducing it to an unconsciously expressed symptom. In the notion of the compromise formation (most succinctly embodied in the basic negation 'I do not like it,' where the analyst knows simply to ignore the 'not'), the 'repressed' element can be understood to include the socially unacceptable and/or the rationally 'surmounted' – to use Freud's term from 'The "Uncanny."' In other words, the model itself does not force us to limit our conception of the 'repressed' to sexual desires driven into the unconscious. The model becomes one of the juxtaposition and interaction of two forces, both of which are given voice in the text. The compromise formation, which Orlando often represents by the fraction 'repression/repressed' (the former over the latter, with the bar between them), provides the structural blueprint whose specific contents are determined by the particular text being analysed.[33] Such an approach, he argues, avoids the vicious circularity of biographical psychoanalytic criticism in which the text is used to understand or even diagnose the author, while the facts of the author's life (gathered from letters, other historical documents, and indeed the literary texts themselves) are used to understand the text. In the chapters that follow, I employ this structure to elucidate and explore many manifestations of conflicting yet mutually enabling forces at work in Pascoli's texts. For example, chapter 2 discusses the tensions between barbarity and civilization as dramatized in the long poem 'Gog and Magog,' while chapter 5 examines the dialogue between faith and science in Pascoli's speech 'L'era nuova.'

This structural model allows Orlando to articulate a definition of literature as a unique use of language that has the ability to sustain and convey the voices of both the 'repression' and the 'repressed.' Julia Kristeva develops a similar model in her groundbreaking study *Revolution in Poetic Language*.[34] Her insights, based on the Freudian concept of the primary processes (condensation, displacement) and illustrated by Mallarmé's work on poetic musicality, illuminate my readings of Pascoli's Italian symbolist poetry. Kristeva shares with Orlando an emphasis on poetry's ability to embody conflicting yet interdependent processes. She articulates 'a dialectical notion of the signifying process as a whole, in which signifiance puts the subject in process/on trial [*en procès*].'[35] The modalities of this dialectic, the 'semiotic' and the 'symbolic,' relate in language as repressed and repression. The symbolic here refers to the social practice of signification, the 'law' by which meaning is stabilized in and by language, the most basic of which is the implied copula of the sign. The 'semiotic,' which precedes and enables the symbolic, refers to ambiguous, non-signifying drives based in the corporeal experiences of the pre-linguistic subject. The 'musicality' of modern poetry, argues Kristeva, allows the semiotic to erupt into and via the symbolic, thus 'pluraliz[ing] signification or denotation.'[36] But while the semiotic disrupts the very basis of the symbolic, it cannot signify without it. The dynamic that Kristeva postulates between the repressing 'symbolic' and the repressed 'semiotic' can enlighten our understanding of Pascoli's poetic practice. As I develop in the present study, Pascoli gives voice to 'infantile' linguistic play within the logical system of rational adult language, creating a poetics in which the former both disrupts and depends on the latter.

To articulate in detail the dynamics of Pascoli's revolutionary poetic practice, and because Pascoli's linguistic innovations had foundational importance for subsequent Italian poetry, I will review the major and most recent criticism that highlights the issue of language per se. Many critics have characterized Pascoli's innovative linguistic techniques as a poetics of evocation rather than description, and they delineate two linguistic tendencies in the poetry: one towards extreme precision and accuracy of imagery, and another towards a shadowy or hazy continuum.[37] Gianfranco Contini, for example, argues that Pascoli synthesizes concrete, autosufficient images with a melodious continuum, and further characterizes his poetic project as a juxtaposition of the determinate with the indeterminate; precision with *inquietudine*; foreground with background.[38] Similarly, Francesco Flora writes that 'egli aveva bisogno di un'immagine concreta nella quale riposarsi, non di un termine più o meno riflesso ... Il Pascoli è un poeta della immagine esattissima' [he needed a concrete image on which to rest, not a term more or less reflected ... Pascoli is a poet of extremely precise images].[39] He goes on to argue that this precision of the word combines with a musicality and an impressionism of overall effect, pointing out the contemporaneity of

Pascoli's poetry with the impressionist school of painting. More recently, this descriptive term has been taken up and elaborated by Katja Liimatta, who compares Pascoli's poetry (particularly the *Myricae* collection) with the painting of the French impressionists and the music of Debussy.[40] Enumerating and giving examples of several specific techniques (the predominance of nouns and adjectives over action verbs; the proliferation of adjectives denoting colour; the propensity for describing scenes surrounded by fog, haze, and smoke; and the frequent use of sound-images), Liimatta, too, underscores the evocative nature of the 'impressionist-symbolist' poems and their power to offer the reader a 'reality more suggested than defined or drawn.'[41] It is, I think, not coincidental that Freud makes a similar comparison between his own conception of the psyche and impressionist painting: 'We cannot do justice to the characteristics of the mind by linear outlines like those in a drawing or in primitive painting, but rather by areas of colour melting into one another as they are presented by modern artists.'[42]

Guido Guglielmi, in an insightful study of the *Poemi conviviali*,[43] has characterized Pascoli's poetic project as 'una fenomenologia di nomina. Le cose ci sono, ma prendono vita dai nomi ... e quanto più i nomi sono specifici e locali, e tanto più si fanno indeterminati, allusivi a mondi inespressi e nascosti' [a phenomenology of naming. Things are there, but they take life from their names ... and the more precise and local the names are, the more they become indeterminate, allusive to unexpressed and hidden worlds].[44] He goes on to point out the thematic relevance of this stylistic technique: 'Pascoli è un poeta visionario; un poeta di ombre e non di cose. Egli rifiuta il presente – si rifiuta ad esso – e lo popola di immagini oniriche, di voci e suoni ossessivamente ritornanti' [Pascoli is a visionary poet; a poet of shadows and not of things. He rejects the present – he refuses it – and he fills it with dreamlike images, with obessively returning voices and sounds].[45] Though Guglielmi does not explicitly propose a psychoanalytic reading, his suggestions of 'dreamlike images' and 'obsessively returning' voices and sounds, as well as his observation of the dominance of the past over the present in the poetry, certainly recall key Freudian concepts. The 'return of the repressed' enacted through the compromise formation comes to life in Pascoli's poetry precisely as, to borrow Guglielmi's formulation, the 'voci e suoni ossessivamente ritornanti' both linguistically and thematically.

Bàrberi Squarotti, in an essay on Pascoli's syntax, argues that the clear, evocative, carefully arranged images provide a structure but not temporal or causal relations or a logical narrative. Thus the 'impressionist' effect is created not so much linguistically but rather through a kind of breakdown of syntax. He argues that a radical disquiet, an anxiety, pervades the fragmented reality evoked in atomized detail, and he underscores the poetry's inability to comprehend reality. Along these lines, Bàrberi Squarotti argues that Pascoli's true innovation is not linguistic but syntactic.[46] I submit that Pascoli's 'other' syntax – analogical rather than logical, described in this essay as 'non-causal, non-temporal, non-hierarchical' – could be characterized in positive terms. Rather than gathering up the discrete images under a single, synthesizing purview, Pascoli offers a free, even playful, opening up of these images, though I would not deny (but rather would underscore) the strong presence of a tone of anxiety in the poems.

Pascoli's playful use of language and his emphasis on phonics and graphics (as in the examples of Greek onomatopoeia) recall Freud's observation that children treat words like things. Freud writes, 'It is also generally acknowledged that rhymes, alliterations, refrains, and other forms of repeating similar verbal sounds which occur in verse, make use of the same source of pleasure [as do some techniques of jokes] – the rediscovery of something familiar.'[47] Pascoli's very use of language becomes a return of the repressed: a return to and of the familiar but estranged childlike delight in the materiality of language and sounds that is 'repressed' by the demands of adult rationality and logic, a process Francesco Orlando has termed 'regressione ludica.' Indeed, Pascoli's linguistic experimentations with words melting into onomatopoeia ('anch'io ... chio ... chio'), and the delight in the invention of exotic-sounding names, are very reminiscent of childhood games. Pascoli explicitly connects childhood and onomatopoeia in the *Conviviali*'s 'La civetta.' Here, the owl with which the young boys had been playing flies upward at the moment of Socrates' death:

Ed i compagni del morto ed i fanciulli
scosse un subito fremito, uno strillo
di sopra il tetto, *Kikkabau* ... dall'alto,
Kikkabau ... di più alto, *Kikkabau* ...
dal cielo azzurro dove ardean le stelle.   (lines 182–6)

[A sudden trembling shook the dead man's friends and the boys, a shriek from o'er the roof, 'Tu whit! Tu whoo!,' from on high, '*Tu whit!*' from higher still, '*Tu whit! Tu whoo!*'][48]

These departures from the 'normal' use of language refute the adult demands on language as a tool to persuade, to convey meaning, to 'comprehend reality' (in both senses of comprehension). Instead, we are invited to encounter and to marvel at reality, and at language itself as a part of rather than a representation of (or substitute for) reality.

Pascoli's relinquishing of the comprehensive demands of language constitutes the sublime aspect of the uncanny. At the same time, his quasi-Gothic preoccupation with death constitutes the horrific aspect of the infantile regression, the fear that is elicited in the encounter with the grandeur and power of the 'other,' which is first of all the 'mother.' Where the writers of the romantic sublime incorporate other into self to master the agonistic situation, the subject of a Gothic anti-sublime finds (or imagines) himself incorporated and mastered by the other. Pascoli leads us to the doorstep, as it were, of this Gothic gesture but retains an uncanny ambivalence and does not cross the threshold to complete Gothic horror, as did his *scapigliatura* predecessors.

Pascoli's moving poem 'La voce,' from his *Canti di Castelvecchio* (1903), demonstrates the effectiveness of his subtle deployment of Gothic-like imagery. The poem narrates how, on several occasions, the despairing speaker was rescued from his suicidal thoughts by the reassuring voice of his deceased mother. In the poem, Pascoli explicitly draws from events of his own life, including his father's assassination, his time as a university student at Bologna, and his brief imprisonment for his involvement in a socialist uprising. 'La voce' dramatizes the affinity suggested by Freud between the fantasy of being buried alive and the fantasy of intrauterine existence, as the speaker envisions his deceased mother calling to him from within her grave.[49]

This poem registers the familiar desirable qualities of the mother in her encouragement of her son to goodness and prayer, and in her role as life giver and sustainer. The deathly, fearful, and strange aspect of the uncanny derives not merely from the fact that his mother is dead, but from the vivid and horrifying image, repeated twice and then a third time with a change, of the mouth (then the eyes) full of dirt. In and of itself the image horrifies, especially because the mouth is such a sensitive organ and, to draw on Georges Bataille's reflections, because the mouth is the body's centre of emotional expressiveness. The image becomes even more uncanny if we consider the metaphoric evocation of the mother's reproductive organs through the references to her lips and mouth – in which case we are presented with both a blockage, by the 'bad earth,' of the life-sustaining voice through the organ of the literal mouth and a blockage of the original life-giving birth canal or metaphorical mouth. I would draw a parallel here with Edgar Allan Poe's 'Bernice,' in which the protagonist's simultaneous fear of and fascination with his fiancé's teeth seems to displace his conflicting feelings about the radical otherness of the female sexual organs.[50]

The mouth is subtly fetishized in this poem, as evidenced by the several repetitions of 'bocca,' 'boccone,' and 'baci.' Particularly in lines 68 to 72, the triple repetition of 'bocca,' 'baci,' and 'quei dì' dramatizes the protagonist's psychological fixation on the memory of his mother's sad kisses:

> ma piena di terra ha la bocca:
>   la tua bocca! con i tuoi baci,
> già tanto accorati a quei dì!
>   a quei dì beati e fugaci
> che aveva i tuoi baci ... *Zvanì!* ...

[but the mouth is full of dirt: your mouth! with your kisses, already so sorrowful in those days! in those blessed and fleeting days when your kisses were given to ... Johnny! (my translation)]

As a fetish, this fixation functions as a sort of defence against or mitigation of the actual beloved or desired object. We might think of a fetish, as described by Freud, as a sort of psychological synecdoche – it stands in for the desire for the whole, in this case for the consolatory and lifegiving presence of the mother. Specifically, it signals a desire for the original home of the womb through the metaphoric displacement of the vagina on to the image of the mouth. At the same, the desire for pre-Oedipal nearness to the mother need not be represented through a neat, metaphorical substitution of mouth for vagina. On the contrary, because of the polymorphous and strongly oral nature of infantile sexuality, the image of the mouth itself 'bespeaks' such regressive desire.[51]

The poem reveals suggestive moments of slippage or syntactic ambiguity between the subjectivity of the mother and that of the speaker. This ambiguity is especially pronounced in lines 25 and 26: 'Oh! la terra, com'è cattiva! / la terra, che amari bocconi!' [Oh! the earth, how bad it is! / the earth, what bitter mouthfuls!]. Given the context of this exclamation, the 'bitter mouthfuls' may refer to the imaginary food about which the starving and poverty-stricken poet dreamt, only to awaken at the first mouthful and remember his real hunger. Following this reading, the world is called 'bad' because it leaves the speaker in financial hardship. At the same time, however, the 'bitter mouthfuls' could signify the mouthful of dirt that prevents his buried mother from speaking to him, in which case the earth is bad because it blocks their verbal interaction. This syntactic slippage is suggestive of the overall thematic shift in subjectivity that we witness in the poem. The mother, in fact, does not have her own voice – she does not *generate* any of the words attributed to her. Instead, the speaker expressly states that he 'understands' what he does not actually hear. The poem develops in a hypothetical space: the speaker knows what the mother would have said, and so he puts words into her fetishized mouth – going so far as actually to quote her. In this way, the speaker reanimates or resurrects his mother. In short, he appropriates for himself the generative, procreative powers of the desired maternal womb, becoming the life-giving and, through the durability of the poem, the life-sustaining mother, thus completing the slippage of subjectivity suggested earlier.

However, this ventriloquism is a retroactive, or backward-turning, animation: the speaker is not giving birth to a new being but rather reanimating the mother so that she, in turn, can repeatedly name and animate him. That is, he resurrects her so that she may continue to keep him alive by calling him away from his suicide. The reciprocal generation of mother and son creates an echo-chamber effect, in which the voices of the dead resonate with the voices of the living, each vanishing into the other. We are confronted with a 'breathless' poem that seems constantly on the verge of vanishing into silence. Pascoli creates this effect through an assortment of repetitions, the most notable of which is the inscription of his own dialect nickname, 'Zvanì,' which resonates with the word *svanì* (he/she vanished). In addition, we see the repeated trailing off of the ellipses into a nothingness; the repetition of the description of the mother as 'breathless'; the assertions by the speaker that he could not hear her; and finally the speaker's position as being twice on the verge of death by suicide. The poem, then, and indeed much of Pascoli's poetry, positions itself on this brink of silence, in a sort of echo chamber that blurs the distinctions between the dead and the living, where the dead cannot be laid to rest and the living continue to be bound to them. The force of the poem is economically localized within the uncanny image of the mouth, and sustained by the dramatization of the irresolvable ambiguity of 'home.' The circularity of the mother-son relationship resists linear temporality grounded in a single point of origin and moving forward in time. In other words, the poem questions the logic of turning to biographical data as a stable source for the generation (and interpretation) of poetry.

The title of this introduction and its epigram play on the acknowledged importance of nest imagery in Pascoli's opus. I would suggest that this symbol's recurrence, that is, the *repetition in and of itself*, bespeaks the repeated image's inherent instability and ambiguity. In his analysis of the myth of Medusa, Freud has argued that the subject's recognition of the missing maternal phallus motivates the perception of the many writhing snakes.[52] By means of this *multiplicity* of images (here, snakes) the petrified subject attempts to (over)compensate for the one desired but missing object (the maternal phallus). The *proliferation* of nests and similar womb imagery in Pascoli's poetic production suggests not only that these images are inadequate substitutes for the missing home but that this home itself (like the maternal phallus compensated for by the snakes) is always imaginary. The seemingly infinite rearticulations of nest imagery reveal a desired wholeness, presence, and stability that, rather than having been lost only with the assassination of the father, are always lost and always being reconstituted.[53] Many readings of Pascoli's work, as we have seen, focus on his biography and attempt to locate there the real, historical events that spawned and explain the poetry. Such readings reenact, I suggest, Freud's early attempts to trace the cause of hysteria by fixing its origins in real childhood experiences of sexual abuse.[54] Freud's later revisions of the 'seduction theory' turn away from a grounding in a specific, traumatic event.[55] Similarly, Pascoli's poetry, marked by relentless repetitions, haunted by ghostly images and echoes of voices, and perforated by ambivalence, questions the linear temporality and stable origins posited by biographically grounded readings. Indeed, it is the very lack of stable origins that engenders the poetry, poetry that, in turn, envisages and laments its missing 'mother.'

1 Foreshadowing: The *Scapigliati* and Psychoanalysis

> More than the analysis of an affection, more than the story of a passionate affair, what I offer here is perhaps the diagnosis of an illness.
>
> I.U. Tarchetti, *Passion*, 8

The literature of the *scapigliatura* – an artistic movement in northern Italy that was productive during the 1860s and 1870s – has been one of the less recognized and less critically treated bodies of literature in the Italian tradition. This group of writers, christened by Cletto Arrighi in the preface to his novel *La scapigliatura e il 6 febbraio*, included Arrigo Boito, his brother Camillo, Emilio Praga, and Igino Ugo Tarchetti.[1] Dissatisfied with the developing capitalism of the parliamentary monarchy, the *scapigliati* self-consciously resisted and opposed themselves to the dominant bourgeois values of the industrializing north.[2] Much of the criticism that has been undertaken on the *scapigliatura* focuses on its 'dualismo' – the title of a programmatic poem by Arrigo Boito. Disillusioned idealists, these young writers turned to and appropriated the realist ideology of contemporary science, most notably the sordid bodily reality of the anatomist. As Boito writes, 'non trovando il Bello, ci abbranchiamo all'Orrendo' [not finding the Beautiful, we reach out to the horrendous]. The *scapigliati*, in resistance to polite bourgeois society, cultivated a macabre literature populated with 'worms and abortions.'

Arrighi's title refers to the Mazzinian uprising in Milan in February of 1852. The culminating pages of the novel depict this rebellion, in which the protagonists participate. As is well known, the political fruit of such mid-century revolutionary activities was ultimately the constitutional monarchy, with its extremely limited franchise, leaving many Mazzinians disillusioned. Resistance to the newly constructed nation and to its social and civic agenda in part motivated the *scapigliati*. This agenda, I believe, can be articulated through the lens of the two most influential and popular children's books of the period, Collodi's *Pinocchio* and De Amicis' *Cuore*. The values these stories impart to their young readers – the first 'Italians' – include thrift, hard work, honesty, loyalty, and respect for authority. The civic values modelled in these texts may to some degree be summarized under the rubric of boundaries. Following the hard-won establishment of the country's geographic boundaries, the work of cultivating strong civic values and respect for social boundaries begins and finds expression in these children's novels. Respect for others' property, restraint of appetites to what is appropriate, and understanding of one's proper place (in these instances as a child vis-à-vis parents and teachers) constitute many of the lessons to be appropriated by the novels' protagonists and readers. This admittedly cursory overview of the dominant social values expressed in *Pinocchio* and *Cuore* provides a language with which to characterize the literature of the *scapigliatura*. The *scapigliati* disrupt and destabilize boundaries and consequently the notions of property, propriety, and the 'self' that they engender. These pages will explore the works of the *scapigliatura* as a borderline site in which the distinctions between health and illness, life and death, body and mind, self and other are transgressed, producing effects of *disagio* – horror and anxiety. I will further suggest deep affinities between the writings of the *scapigliati* and Freudian psychoanalysis.

The relative obscurity of the *scapigliati* derives partly from their historical position, overshadowed by the two great triumvirates of Foscolo, Leopardi, and Manzoni, who usher in the century, and Carducci, Pascoli, and d'Annunzio, who bring it to a close. Emilio Praga's poem 'Manzoni,' demonstrates the ambivalent attitude of admiration and envy of the *scapigliati* towards the monumentality of this paternal figure: 'oh! eran belli i tuoi tempi, / Goethe, Foscolo, ... Porta, / Una falange di sublimi esempi, / una olimpica scorta. / Noi vaghiam nell'Ignoto. I figli siamo / del Dubbio' [oh! your times were beautiful, Goethe, Foscolo, ... Porta! / A phalanx of sublime examples, an Olympic stock./We wander in the Unknown. We are the sons of Doubt]. I.U. Tarchetti's critique of Manzoni's *I promessi sposi* attempts to deflate the prestige of this novel by depicting the author as the big fish in a little pond: Italians admire his novel because it appeared at a moment of severe paucity in Italian letters, but the work pales in comparison to the masterpieces of European fiction.[3] Tarchetti even asserts that Manzoni 'togliesse dal celebre scozzese la forma e lo stile del suo libro' (528) [took from the famous Scotsman [Sir Walter Scott] the form and the style of his book]. Though he praises Manzoni's desire to depict 'gli uomini quali sono, non quali dovrebbero essere' (529) [men as they are and not as the ought to be], he does not disagree with those who criticize the novel as having 'little heart' and the characters as less than inspiring. In contrast, Tarchetti's various nods to Ugo Foscolo, including the appropriation of his name and the reference in *Fosca* to the protagonist's admiration of 'l'uomo antico' [that venerable man], indicate that he chooses to trace his literary genealogy to the exiled romantic.[4]

In spite of Tarchetti's attempts to create a romantic lineage, subsequent literary criticism has not deemed him the equal of his self-appointed forefather. Carducci levels harsh criticism against both Praga and Tarchetti. He attacks the alleged originality of Praga, claiming him to be entirely derivative of Hugo, Heinz, and, from the metre and refrains to the 'stupid uglinesses,' of Baudelaire.[5] Tarchetti's work, he claims, lacks form and is badly written. Any esteem for his work is merely a symptom of the pervasive sentimental romantic 'sickness' and is based more on pity for Tarchetti's poverty and early death than on a serious evaluation of his writing.[6] However, the historical position of these writers does not entirely account for the general paucity of critical attention afforded them. In these pages, I posit a psychoanalytically motivated assessment of this school and its critical fate and suggest that its Gothic and macabre sensibility, presented in so raw and naked a form, met with resistance precisely because of its untempered presentation of the grotesque. This dark sensibility found more success when it resurfaced in a subtler guise, clothed by more homely themes, in the poetry of Giovanni Pascoli.

A direct comparison between a poem by I.U. Tarchetti and Pascoli's well-known 'La tessitrice' from his *Canti del Castelvecchio* offers a concrete example of this kind of resurfacing. In 'Composition VI' of his collection *Disjecta*, Tarchetti dramatizes a midnight rendezvous between the speaker and his beloved:

M'avea dato convegno al cimitero
A mezzanotte – ed io ci sono andato:
Urlava il vento ed il tempo era nero
Biancheggiavan le croci del sagrato;
E alla smorta fanciulla ho dimandato:
– Perché darmi convegno al cimitero?

– Io son morta, rispose, e tu nol sai:
Vuoi nella tomba mia giacermi allato?
Molti anni or sono che viva ti amai,
Che mi serra l'avello inesorato ...
Fredda è la fossa o giovane adorato!
Io son morta, rispose, e tu nol sai.

[She made a date with me at the cemetery at midnight – and I went: the wind was howling and the weather was black, the crosses of the church-square were flashing white; and I asked the wan girl: – Why did you ask me to come to the cemetery? – I am dead, she answered, and you do not know it: do you want to lie next to me in my tomb? It has been many years now since, alive, I loved you, since the inexorable tomb has enclosed me ... The grave is cold, o my young beloved! I am dead, she answered, and you do not know it. (my translation)]

The romantic encounter, to the speaker's surprise, takes place amid the howling winds of a cemetery. When the speaker asks his beloved why she has chosen this place, she responds, 'I am dead, and you do not know it.' She goes on to explain that she has been dead for many years, locked in the cold grave, and asks the speaker to lie with her in the tomb. The beloved's chilling request, 'Vuoi nella tomba mia giacermi allato?' recalls the necrophilia evoked in Poe's famous 'Annabel Lee.'[7] However, it is the intellectually shocking and logically impossible assertion 'Io son morta, rispose, e tu nol sai' that provides the direct connection to Pascoli's composition. Here, too, the beloved addresses the speaker at the end of the poem and reveals what he 'does not know:' ' E piange, e piange; "Mio dolce amore, / Non t'hanno detto? non lo sai tu? / Io non son viva che nel tuo cuore"' [And she cries, and she cries: 'My sweet love, / didn't they tell you? Don't you know? / I am alive only in your heart'].

Here we encounter the first instance of what I have described as a 'borderline' literature. The ghost embodies the trangression of death into life. As Cixous has asserted, 'The direct figure of the uncanny is the Ghost ... What is intolerable is that the Ghost erases the limit which exists between two states, neither alive nor dead; passing through, the dead man returns in the manner of the Repressed.'[8] In both poems, the ghost appears in the dramatic scenario of an encounter, and engages in a dialogue. These encounters stress the crucial role of relationship and confrontation; specifically, the subject's relationship with (and repression of) death. 'Death will recognize us, but we shall not recognize it,' writes Cixous.⁹ The men in these poems are both inexplicably unaware of the death of their beloved. It is hard to imagine even the most neglectful of partners remaining ignorant of his lover's demise. This odd 'ignorance,' I believe, is the figure of repression, and the dramatic scenarios staged by the poems play out the subjects' confrontations with the repressed. In both scenarios, the dialogue takes place between a man and a beloved woman, underscoring death's simultaneous otherness and intimacy, unknowability and familiarity. Finally, we should note that Death has summoned the speaker to the cemetery; she has called him into being, as it were: the subject, Tarchetti implies, does not exist outside his ambivalent relationship to death.

Macabre, Gothic fright dominates in Tarchetti's representation of the ghost. The first six lines, spoken by the 'poet,' describe the cemetery at midnight with all the Gothic trappings: 'Urlava il vento ed il tempo era nero, / Biancheggiavan le croci del sagrato.' In the next and final six lines the dead beloved speaks. Her words 'Fredda è la fossa' elicit more fear than compassion, and her above-cited request, given the tone Tarchetti creates throughout, appears all the more as a horrifying threat for its resemblance to a seductive invitation. For Pascoli, the stark horror of death and the explicit eroticism give way to a predominant tone of compassion and sentimentality. He replaces the zombie-like image of the speaking undead with the reassuring notion of the beloved living on in her loved one's heart and memory. But the sentimentality is not trite. The poem retains a subtle sense of ghostliness through the uncanny device, imported from Tarchetti, of having the dead woman speak directly and announce her own death.¹⁰ And Pascoli indeed maintains a hint of Tarchetti's macabre sensibility in the brief yet chilling suggestion that the weaver is weaving her own shroud ('Se tesso, tesso / per te soltanto; ... in questa tela, sotto il cipresso, / accanto alfine ti dormirò' [If I weave, I weave only for you ... in this cloth, under the cypress, I will sleep beside you at last]). In short, the *scapigliati*'s 'demons' are repressed, but these repressed forces return in a more palatable form as the spectres that haunt the Pascolian opus.¹¹

The shift I am undertaking here from a psychoanalysis of the *scapigliatura* texts themselves to a psychoanalytically informed reading of a literary historical development should be understood within two paradigms. The first engages the reader on a ethical-social level, and, to put it most starkly, entails issues of 'otherness.' These poems and tales persistently confront the reader with the strange and bizarre, but very often do so, explicitly and implicitly, within the framework of social reality. Some examples of this kind of political agenda within the *Scapigliati*'s work have been pointed out and analysed by two recent American critics of Tarchetti. Lawrence Venuti argues in his introduction to the *Fantastic Tales* that 'The narrative form that Tarchetti recommended was less social realism than politicized fantasy, the evocation of a "marvelous world" of "man free" ... Tarchetti's was a peculiarly democratic vision, in which the "I" is discovered to be the many others it excludes in order to preserve its identity.'[12] In 'Osso di morto,' for example, the ghost of a laboratory worker whose body was dissected by a scientist for research purposes comes back to demand his kneecap from its more socially elevated owner, who now uses it as a paperweight. In this tale of the poor unskilled labourer who from beyond the grave can finally demand a sort of symbolic restitution from the professional class who exploited him, Venuti sees 'the disquieting return of the socially repressed.'[13] Similarly, David del Principe, in his study of Tarchetti's novel *Fosca* in the context of vampirism, suggests that we should see the deformed and marginalized Fosca, and indeed Gothic monsters and vampires in general, 'as a paradigm for any individual cast out of monolithic society.'[14]

By staging the issues of otherness in the exaggerated and horrifying realm of the Gothic and the fantastic, the writers are able not only to elicit a strong emotional response from the reader, but also to transpose the themes they explore onto a less historically circumscribed plane. Tarchetti's mystery story 'Lo spirito nel lampone' provides an example. A Calabrian baron eats from a raspberry bush that, unknown to him, grows from the buried corpse of his murdered female servant. After eating the berries, the baron takes on a dizzying and delirious double identity as both himself and the servant, 'Clara.' Finally, horrified by the spectacle of the raving baron-servant, Clara's frightened murderer reveals himself. The tale does not merely critique the complacency of the nineteenth-century southern aristocracy, but dramatizes questions relevant to readers of other historical and cultural moments, namely, the construction and tenuousness of gender and class identities. Arrigo Boito, too, takes up social and ethical questions, developing them in a Gothic mode. In two poems that I discuss below, 'Una mummia' and 'Lezione d'anatomia,' Boito engages, respectively, the problem of exoticizing the culturally 'other' and the limits of scientific enquiry when it begins to impinge upon the dignity of human life. One need only think of such areas of current debate as the Human Genome Project to see the continuing, indeed even urgent, relevance of these issues in contemporary American society.

The ability of this literature to transcend its particular historical moment in relation to the 'ethical' question of scandalizing otherness brings us to the second paradigm within which to read the repression of the *scapigliatura*: namely, as analogous to psychoanalysis itself, a hermeneutic often critiqued for erasing historical specificity in favour of essential structures of the human psyche. This quality that it has in common with psychoanalysis is not, of course, the quality for which it has been critically neglected. On the contrary, literature is valued for its ability to engage enduring transhistorical questions. What would it mean, then, to suggest a connection between this specific collection of poems and prose on the one hand and psychoanalysis on the other, and how would it enlighten, first, our understanding of this literature and, second, our understanding of what I am alleging as its repression?

One such connection is the gesture, common in *scapigliatura*, of what I would call the materialization of metaphors. A particularly grotesque and disquieting example can be found in Emilio Praga's 'A un feto.' As in Camillo Boito's 'Un corpo,' Arrigo Boito's 'Lezione d'anatomia,' and Tarchetti's 'Osso di morto,' we find ourselves once again among the anatomists. Here, the speaker explains that, between the torso of a gymnast and the hand of a consumptive girl, he saw 'a horrible thing.' He sees, in a glass jar, the fetus of a dead pair of twins joined at the chest:

> Questo, ironia satanica,
> due cuori ha chiusi in petto,
> e accanto a lui, crisalide
> di non terreno affetto,
> un corpicin di femmina, ...
> Guarda: son due putredini
> ed eran due gemelli,
> concetti insieme al gaudio
> di chiamarsi fratelli;
> guarda: un orrendo bacio
> nell'almo sen li strinse,
> e colla morte avvinse
> gli sventurati amor ...   (lines 137–52)

[This, satanic irony, has enclosed two hearts in one chest; and next to him, a chrysalis of unearthly affection, the tiny body of a girl, ... Look: they are two rotten [bodies] and they were two twins, conceived together for the joy of calling themselves siblings; look, a horrendous kiss clasped them in the nurturing breast, and bound with death the unfortunate loves ... (my translation)]

The choice of Siamese twins as a subject, an 'anomaly' of 'nature' that resists easy distinctions between self and non-self, as well as Praga's shifting use of singulars and plurals throughout the poem with which to refer to the fetus, powerfully illustrate the themes developed above of scandalizing otherness and the construction of identity and individuality. But while the actual existence of Siamese twins certainly throws into doubt notions such as the borders of the self, Praga's poetic representation of this existential phenomenon further unsettles the reader. We should notice in the above quoted description Praga's deployment of a love-lyric register: 'due cuori ha chiusi in petto,' 'non terreno affetto,' 'bacio,' 'almo sen li strinse,' 'amor.' More specifically, Praga seems to play with the topos of an unearthly, sublime love that can transcend the corporeal separation of the lovers and fuse them in a spiritual union (one may think, for example, of John Donne's 'The Ecstasy'). Hinting at this topos, Praga undercuts the metaphorization of the sublime union by starkly presenting its grotesque realization in the bodily union of the dead twins.

A further example of this materialization of metaphors can be found in Arrigo Boito's fabulous poem 'Re Orso.' The Cretan Bear King, so named for his ferocity, is tormented by voices telling him to beware of the 'bite of the worm.' He commands his jester and later his executioner to kill, one by one, all possible sources of this voice, until one night in a drunken frenzy he has his entire court executed. Years pass, and after the king's own death his coffin is invaded by a worm who has travelled over the oceans on the dead body of a cat, and who now begins chewing on Orso's mouth. The tale concludes with a warning to beware of the nightly roaming of the undead king and worm. The grotesque and even comic odyssey of the worm over the seas as he makes his way to Crete casts him as an unlikely hero in this tale, and indeed it is only he who is able to defeat the nearly omnipotent king.[15] As Finotti has pointed out, the tale echoes, or rather elaborates and dramatizes, the poem recited by the dying Ligeia in Edgar Allan Poe's eponymous tale. In the poem, man's life is described as a tragedy, and the 'hero' is the 'conqueror worm.' In this poem, as in many other literary works, the 'worm' is, of course, a metaphor, or, more precisely, a synecdoche representing the idea of death, which inevitably, Ligeia laments, overcomes or 'conquers' all life. Boito exploits the physical image used to represent the abstract idea of death, literalizing the poem from Poe's tale into a full-scale odyssey of the conqueror worm, forcing us to contemplate the physical decomposition of bodies while curtailing any possible escape into spiritual solace.

The figure of the vampire provides a final instance of the *scapigliati*'s typical materialization of figurative speech. Del Principe convincingly argues that Tarchetti's novel *Fosca*, as well as his short stories 'I fatali' and 'Le leggende del castello nero,' insert themselves within the vampire tradition, which received its most notable expression in Bram Stoker's *Dracula* and which was explicitly taken up again in Luigi Capuana's 1906 short story 'Un vampiro.'[16] He points out that the vampire is a kind of Antichrist. I would formulate this more precisely by characterizing the vampire as a literalized or desublimated Christ: Christ's invitation to 'drink my blood' is replaced by his demand to drink the victims' actual blood; Christ's promise of an eternal spiritual life in heaven is replaced by an eternal undead existence of the body on earth. Finally, by way of situating the discussion within the moral framework elaborated above, we can say that the vampire is the ethical inverse of Christ: where Christ sacrifices (in the senses both of 'giving up' and of 'making sacred') himself for others, the vampire incorporates (with a stress on the root of the word) others into himself – sucking their blood and condemning them to his fate.

The gestures I have been exploring all enact literalizations. In other words, concepts that other discourses refer to a higher realm of abstraction are here depicted as earthly and base. The immediate and desired effect of these gestures is horror: the *scapigliati* were motivated by the intent to shock the bourgeoisie, which had come to prominence in post-unification Italy and whose capitalistic self-interest and complacency disillusioned those who had other hopes for the new regime. But beyond the explicit agenda of shocking and horrifying, these writings have the effect of forcing us to rethink the figurative language they exploit: specifically, they suggest the possibility that the metaphors used to express the sublime (whether it be love, death, or eternal life) are at root sublimations – displacements to an abstract realm – of what is always a desire for and fear of a bodily reality. And it is here that we can locate a first strong connection with the program of psychoanalysis. In the introductory remarks to his *Civilization and Its Discontents* (1930), Freud considers the vague 'oceanic' feeling of brotherhood that some suggest as a basis for religious sentiment.[17] He evacuates any spirituality from this feeling and replaces the metaphoric 'ocean' with the literal amniotic fluid of the maternal womb, which remains as a desired memory in the human psyche. More fundamentally, in *The Ego and the Id* (1923), Freud asserts that '[t]he ego is first and foremost a bodily ego; it is not merely a surface entity, but is itself the projection of a surface.'[18] Freudian psychoanalysis and *scapigliatura* literature share the project of directing our attention to the body, and in locating there the roots of such psychological phenomena as desire, fear, and the self.

This is not to suggest that a 'classic' psychoanalytic methodology would necessarily bear the most interpretive fruit when approaching these texts. Indeed, the nearly naked way in which this literature seeks to shock by desublimation renders almost superfluous a psychoanalytic interpretation carried out along the lines of Freud's own interpretation of dreams. According to Freud, for the illicit latent content of the unconscious to be able to manifest itself, it must undergo various distortions in order to evade the censoring agents of the conscious mind. Through 'dreamwork' or in the guise of a harmless joke, the potentially scandalous content masks itself through 'displacements' and 'condensations' (which Lacan has aligned with metonymy and metaphor, respectively). If we consider the reader to be undertaking the role of the analyst in this kind of interpretation, then a literature that sets out to scandalize and therefore holds distortions to a minimum is probably not very rewarding as an interpretive challenge. In his study of the English Gothic novel, William Patrick Day comes to a similar conclusion. In his chapter entitled 'The Gothic in the Twentieth Century,' he writes,

> No discussion of the Gothic can avoid discussing Freud; one of the most obvious ways of thinking about the genre is to read it in terms of Freud's system. Its monsters become the id, the dynamics of sadomasochism the result of Oedipal anxieties, and the self-destructive impulses of the protagonists the expression of the death instinct.[19]

Day, instead, undertakes a comparison of the Gothic genre and Freudianism, seeing the two as 'cousins.' He suggests that the Gothic genre in a certain sense paved the way for psychoanalysis by shifting our conception of inner life from a spiritual notion of the soul to a more materialist notion of the psyche. Both discourses, he argues, are 'focused on the nature of human identity,' particularly in terms of sexual identity as it is forged in the structure of the family, and both 'unite fear and desire, fusing sexuality and violence.'[20] But where Gothic fiction explodes the contemporary norms of identity and thus critiques their inadequacy, Freud reassembles 'the pieces into wholeness,' constructing a new synthesizing system. In this way, Gothic literature can be seen as a kind of intermediary stage between traditional religion and psychoanalysis as a language of the unconscious. But, according to Day, the Gothic does not attempt to subsume the irrational forces it explores under a rationalizing master discourse, whether spiritual or materialist. My approach here resembles Day's in that I am comparing the *scapigliatura* movement to psychoanalysis, and many of the parallels he delineates between Freudianism and the English tradition obtain in the Italian context as well. However, I do not subscribe to the assessment of psychoanalysis as a controlling, synthetic system. Rather, I suggest that its status as an open, unstable, and destabilizing discourse provides the most substantial affinities with Gothic Italian literature.

The British Gothic novels of Anne Radcliffe, such as *A Sicilian Romance* (1790), *The Mysteries of Udolpho* (1794), and *The Italian* (1797) represented Italy as the culture most conducive to eliciting the effect of anxiety. Mirella Agorni has shown how Radcliffe's displacement of the British heroines onto Italian soil masks her implicit social criticism and simultaneously allows for a process of self-definition in terms of individual, sexual, and national identity.[21] I suggest that this perspective derives from Italy's position as neither entirely 'same' nor entirely 'other' vis-à-vis British culture. Rather, Italy occupied a porous, ambiguous boundary space between the domestic and the exotic. Italy was, like Britain, a Christian country, but its Catholicism marked it as different, more archaic. Geographically European, the peninsula is closer to African and Slavic countries than to Britain. Its inhabitants were neither black nor white, but a hybrid-like 'swarthy.' In the late nineteenth century, the *scapigliati* belatedly appropriated the language of the Gothic and spoke from this boundary space. Taking on the position of subject rather than object of this literary genre, they self-consciously maintained the tensions and undecidability of the border. Whereas Radcliffe's novels famously end with the dispelling of doubts and a comforting, rational explanation for all seemingly otherwordly phenomena, the texts of the *scapigliati* do not offer any such resolutions. Rather, the body of work produced by these writers (and the dead metaphor of 'body' comes back to life in their case) never allows the reader to come to rest in one or another explanation or perspective. Their body of writing instead negotiates between opposing discourses and becomes a space of encounters and confrontations: most markedly between the discourse of positivism (most often embodied in the characters of anatomists and other scientists) and the discourse of romanticism (articulated through the poet and artist figures). As I show in my readings of their texts, these encounters result in a mutual destabilization of each perspective rather than the eventual triumph of one over the other. Rather than positioning Freudian psychoanalysis as an example of either positivism or romanticism, I instead emphasize the correspondence between this body of Italian Gothic writing and the Freudian conception of the ego as a space of negotiation, and as inherently discursive and relational.

Further, both discourses give prominence to *illness* as a privileged phenomenon towards which to direct their attention. In clinical practice, illness is the raison d'être for psychoanalysis, the 'talking cure.' I want to emphasize here Freud's methodological use of illness: that is, the way in which he viewed the illness of some individuals as a window onto the universal psychic structures of all people. *Three Essays on the Theory of Sexuality* provides a clear example of this methodological approach. Here, Freud treats so-called perversions first, and only then, with the insights gleaned from this study, does he turn to 'infant and child sexuality.' As Freud states early in the text: 'The importance of these abnormalities lies in the unexpected fact that they facilitate our understanding of normal development.'[22] It is as though, to be able to define and analyse normality, one must first go through the abnormal. A parallel example can be found in Roman Jackobson's ground-breaking essay 'The Metaphoric and Metonymic Poles.'[23] Not himself a psychoanalytic critic but one whose work becomes a fundamental lens through which Lacan reads Freud, Jackobson develops his theory of metaphor and metonymy by means of studying the linguistic disorder of aphasia. Disorders and perversions are used not as essentially different or deviant modes but rather as exaggerations of the norm, and their hyperbole, as it were, allows us to see the structures typically obscured by familiarity. Shoshana Felman summarizes this gesture in her critique of Joseph Wood Krutch's 'approach of normative evaluation' undertaken in his analysis of Edgar Allan Poe: 'Krutch believes that his own work is opposed to Poe's as health is opposed to sickness, as "normality" is opposed to "abnormality," as truth is opposed to delusion. But this ideologically determined, clear-cut opposition between health and sickness is precisely one that Freud's discovery fundamentally unsettles, deconstructs.'[24] In other words, Freud posits not so much a boundary between healthy and ill but a continuum of behavioural manifestations of the same basic underlying structures.

Scapigliatura works in a similar fashion. The madness of Boito's 'Re

Orso' and the insanity of the protagonist in Tarchetti's 'La lettera U' bespeak an 'unhealthy' literature that privileges illness and 'deviations' from the norm. Two further examples that I will examine here are Tarchetti's novel *Fosca* (translated under the title *Passion*) and Arrigo Boito's short story 'L'alfier nero' ('The Black Bishop,' not, to my knowledge, translated into English).

Giorgio, an officer in the military and the narrator and protagonist of *Fosca*, recounts his two recent love affairs. His first, happy relationship with Clara is interrupted by a transfer to another city. Here Giorgio meets the sick relative of his superior officer, in whose home he resides. This second woman, Fosca, develops an obsessive attachment to him, which ultimately drains him of health to the point of his near death. The contrast drawn between the two female characters is seemingly thorough, Clara represented as emotionally, physically, and morally healthy, Fosca as ill in all these senses. Clara's name, further, evokes 'light,' while *fosca* is an adjective meaning 'dark' or 'gloomy.' Finally, Clara has succeeded as a wife and mother, whereas Fosca has been stripped of her wealth and abandoned by her husband, Ludovico, and has suffered a failed pregnancy with his child. At the same time, however, the text invites us to move beyond these overt contraries and to read Fosca not as Clara's opposite but as her shadow. As such, she provides the 'chiaroscuro' that allows us to see the 'truth' of Clara or, more precisely, the truth of the relationship of love that Giorgio thought he had with Clara. Fosca is not merely ill, she *is* illness, as the colonel makes clear, remarking to Giorgio, 'my cousin is illness personified, hysteria made woman.'[25] Her relationship with Giorgio, at once heart wrenching and almost silly in its hyperbole, does not, as Giorgio claims, contrast with his love for Clara, but repeats it in exaggerated form. We remember, for example, that Giorgio's first 'love note' to Clara was a plea for her pity, declaring to her, 'I am sick.' The romantic trappings of flowers and the secret cabin in the woods that marked his affair with Clara obscure the essentially vampiric nature of the relationship. The text makes clear that Clara, in her compassion for Giorgio, plays the role of a mother figure for him. As he remarks early in the novel, 'I later discovered the secret of the immediate fascination that she exercised upon me. She resembled my mother. My mother possessed her same beauty, and at just the age when I was born.'[26] Later, his reflections on the power of Clara's 'scent' prompt a memory related to his mother: '[Clara's] evening clothes, warmed by the sun, exhaled this electrifying fragrance ... Women, furthermore, carry their own scent ... I could never recall my mother, whom I lost as a boy, if I were not kissing a handkerchief of hers, which I kept, and which after so many years, is still suffused with the relic of her holy scent.'[27] More than being simply 'motherly' in her affection for Giorgio, then, Clara is strongly associated with Giorgio's real mother. By substituting Clara for his beatified ('relic of her holy scent') and 'lost' caregiver, Giorgio can place himself in the role of the demanding, narcissistic infant ('at just the age when I was born') in relation to her. The explicit casting of Clara as 'lost mother' is another way in which Giorgio's account seemingly sweetens and yet unwittingly reveals the essentially vampiric nature of his relationship to Clara. Furthermore, the disturbing meditations that make up the third chapter (a chapter that seems unnecessary to the narrative) put the category of motherhood itself into flux, stripping it of its univocally positive connotations. Here, Giorgio speaks of his 'paese natale,' asserting that he has a deep love for the earth, which he describes as 'questa gran madre, questa gran patria commune' (13). There is one exception to his feelings of unity and affection for the land: the one hated point is the 'angolo freddo e uggioso dove son nato' ['the cold, wearisome corner where I was born'].[28] He would love to dig up the ashes of family in order to break his only bond with his 'patria,' and the chapter ends with his obsession that he will surely be crushed if buried in that land: 'Fui torturato lungo tempo da un'idea insistente e malinconica: mi pareva che quelle relique adorate non potessero aver pace là sotto, perchè io stesso, io sento che le mie ossa fremerebbero se sepolte sotto quelle zolle aborrite' (14) ['For ages I was tortured by an insistent, melancholy idea: I believed that their beloved relics could never find peace there, because I myself – I feel my bones would shatter if they were buried beneath those abhorrent clods'].[29] The move from birth to death in this short chapter is immediate. The category of origins (including motherhood, and thus, by implication, Clara) is associated with resentment and with fears of being buried and crushed. Significantly, this culminating image links Giorgio directly with Fosca herself, who confesses an identical fear later in the novel. Explaining to Giorgio why she had fainted at the sight of the funeral procession, she explains that she does not fear death itself, but rather its trappings: 'quel vedersi chiusi tra quattro tavole, quel sentirsi buttare la terra adosso, quel disfarsi' (47) ['seeing yourself sealed within four planks, feeling the earth thrown onto you, decomposing'].[30]

The shift in subject positions in the second affair, with Giorgio taking over the role of Clara as victim and Fosca now as an exaggerated spectre of Giorgio, permits us to find the parallels in the first affair and forces us to acknowledge that the two were not 'black and white' opposites but rather more or less exaggerated gradations along the same scale. Tarchetti's novel has, in fact, been the subject of an insightful psychoanalytic reading undertaken by Elio Gioanola.[31] Gioanola regards Clara as the embodiment of Eros, and Fosca as that of Thanatos. He insists that the events and obstacles that separate Giorgio from the first 'desired' woman and drive him towards the second are not, as Giorgio consciously believes, forces of 'fate' or 'destiny' or 'chance' but rather the results of his own unconscious wishes. Because of Clara's maternal characteristics, Giorgio unconsciously registers his desire for her as incestuous. He is then unconsciously driven to punish himself for the breaking of this fundamental taboo by fleeing from her and embracing Fosca/Thanatos. The essay clearly reduces the characters of Fosca and Clara to personifications of Freud's two hypothetical drives and thus polarizes the characters in a way that the text invites – even tempts – us to do. But the text also complicates this dichotomy by revealing the (albeit subtle) vampiric and narcissistic elements of Giorgio's relationship to Clara and the sympathetic and even erotic attributes of Fosca. The story of Fosca's exploitation by her husband, Ludovico – an element of the text disregarded by Gioanola – elicits the reader's sympathy, and Giorgio himself insists several times on the exceptional beauty of Fosca's long dark hair.

Of course, every reading must subordinate certain elements in order to emphasize others, and Gioanola's insights are, I believe, convincing. However, his emphasis on Tarchetti's biography neglects crucial aspects of the text. Early in the essay, Gioanola examines Tarchetti's personal letters, and underscores the autobiographical status of the novel *Fosca*. The essay insists upon not only Giorgio's but Tarchetti's 'neurotic guilt complex' and his unconscious drive for self-punishment elicited by his desire for Carlotta (the 'real life' Clara). The critic here, in short, adopts the stance criticized by Felman: that of the 'healthy' reader who can analyse the deviant, neurotic, unconscious life of the (dead) author, in this case I.U. Tarchetti. Indeed, Gioanola distances himself even further from the object of his analysis by disavowing any belief in the universal applicability of Freudian psychoanalysis. He explains that he is deploying this methodology here because it had not yet been undertaken and because in this particular case it seems especially fruitful. Thus Gioanola seeks to polarize himself from Tarchetti in the same way he polarizes Clara from Fosca. It is this kind of polarization that both *Fosca* and Freud resist.

The reading of Giorgio as a transparent figure for the author overlooks the heavily critical mode in which Tarchetti textualizes his personal experiences. Giorgio's first note to Clara, in which he laments 'io sono infelice, io sono malato, io soffro' (17) ['I am unhappy, I am sick, I suffer'],[32] reveals through its grammatically unnecessary triple repetition of the first-person subject pronoun Giorgio's profound self-absorption. Furthermore, Tarchetti positions Giorgio within a *relational* structure, as the counterpart to the medical doctor. The reader of Foscolo and passionate lover plays off the calm rationality of the scientist. Both perspectives, however, are brought up short when confronted by Fosca. Chapter 26, in particular, stages a dialogue between the two characters in which each attempts to unravel the truth behind the dark unknowable 'myth' of Fosca. Yet throughout, Fosca frustrates and refutes any attempts to assimilate her, to cure her, to know her. Through her, both the materialist world view of the doctor and Giorgio's romanticism are revealed as ultimately narcissistic interpretive lenses.

Another instance of illness, this time psychological rather than physical, is presented by Arrigo Bioto in his short story 'L'alfier nero.' In this tale, Boito describes an all-night chess match played in a hotel lobby in Switzerland. The opponents are an American who has recently fought in the Civil War on the side of the North yet who believes 'from experience' that all blacks are savages, and 'Tom,' an African and former slave who has become a 'gentleman,' and whose brother has recently led a slave uprising. The opening scene presents us with the sharply defined and exaggerated 'dualism' typical of Boito: Tom dressed entirely in black and playing the black pieces, his opponent dressed entirely in white to match his skin colour and game pieces. The white player, a world chess champion, remains calm and almost aloof as he deploys his rational, carefully planned strategy, and looks with some condescension upon the seemingly erratic, illogical confusion with which Tom positions his pieces. After many hours of play, the American realizes that Tom has staked his entire strategy on the piece of the black 'bishop.' Before the match, this piece had fallen, and the head, having cracked off, had been glued back on with red adhesive. The red, 'bleeding' neck of the black bishop is the only point that disrupts the perfect symmetry between black and white. The figure's ability to disrupt this order with its oozing red glue, and Tom's irrational identification with it, mark it as the supremely *uncanny* figure in the story.

The American's discovery of his opponent's strategy comes too late; and when Tom puts him in checkmate, the American shoots and kills him. We learn that he later confesses and is acquitted of the murder, but that he loses everything and goes mad, hopping about the streets as if he were a living chess piece. The surprise ending, like the dualism, is a hallmark of Boito's style: here the calm, 'civilized' American reacts savagely to the victory of his opponent, who throughout the game has been sweating and almost manic. And where Tom, throughout the game, has forged a seemingly irrational identification with the black bishop, it is the American who fulfils such identification as a symptom of his subsequent madness.[33]

Boito's choice of setting neutralizes the playing field: a hotel lobby in Switzerland, a foreign and public space where neither opponent is at home, equalizes the match. The chess game, their point of contact, is a metaphor for language: the infinite possible positions (signified by the numeral 8, the flipped sign of infinity, indicated by the chessboard's layout of eight squares by eight) parallel the infinite lexicon, while the fixed rules of positioning parallel the order of syntax. Each player, having left the familiar space of home, confronts the other within and through this regulated 'symbolic order,' yet each speaks his own language, incomprehensible to the other. Weber's analysis of Saussure's analogy is particularly helpful here. As Saussure notes, 'But of all comparisons that might be imagined, the most fruitful is the one that might be drawn between the play of language [*langue*] and chess. In both instances we are confronted with a system of values and with their modifications. A game of chess is like an artificial realization of what language offers us in natural form.' Samuel Weber examines this passage as a segue into his analysis of Lacan's 'return to Freud.' He insists that it destabilizes, rather than illustrates, Saussure's distinction between *langue* and *parole*. There are two types of rules, Weber points out: the formal rules of the game, and the less fixed rules of strategy. Because there are always two players, 'the subject of this system, far from being unitary [as the individual whose actual speech constitutes "parole"] ... is split, agonistically.'[34] The result of this confrontation reveals Tom as the shadow and truth of the American. The American's savage attempt to exorcise this spectre through murder only manifests the truth of his own repressed 'darkness,' as, in his madness, he acts out in exaggerated form the irrationality he scorned in his opponent. In both *Fosca* and 'L'alfier nero,' stories otherwise unalike, the figures of darkness, madness, and 'illness,' exteriorized and demonized, prove to be disturbingly present within the very subjects who wish to alienate them. In this sense the tales, like Freud (to use Felman's above-cited terminology), 'deconstruct' the boundaries between health and illness.

Both psychoanalysis and *scapigliatura* propose to disclose, uncover, reveal what is unpleasant, impolite, and even threatening behind the illusory veil of the healthy and normal. The gesture of revelation is powerfully described in Tarchetti's poem 'Memento' of 1867, where the speaker visualizes his 'dear girl's' skeleton, 'hidden' by her 'shapely body.'

> Quando bacio il tuo labbro profumato,
> Cara fanciulla, non posso obbliare
> Che un bianco teschio vi è sotto celato.
> Quando a me stringo il tuo corpo vezzoso,
> Obbliar non poss'io, cara fanciulla,
> Che vi è sotto uno scheletro nascoso.
> E nell'orrenda visione assorto,
> Dovunque o tocchi o baci, o le man posi,
> Sento sorger le fredde ossa di un morto. [35]   (*Tutte le opere*, 2:459)

[When I kiss your perfumed lip/dear girl, I cannot forget/that a white skull is concealed underneath./When I clasp your charming body to me/I cannot forget, dear girl/that hidden underneath there is a skeleton./And engrossed by the horrendous vision/Wherever I may touch, or kiss, or place my hands/I feel bursting forth the cold bones of death. (my translation)]

The afflicted speaker cannot but confront the 'horrendous vision' that looms 'hidden' and 'veiled' 'underneath' the beautiful skin, and his sense of trapped helplessness is underscored by the 'o ... o ... o ...' and triple subjunctive of the penultimate line: 'wherever I may touch, or kiss, or place my hands.' The hideous skeletal vision described contrasts jarringly with the register of seduction conveyed by the phrases 'perfumed lips' and 'shapely body.' Even more jarring is the repetition of the endearment, 'cara fanciulla,' which, in this context, takes on a bitterly ironic and even sinister and sadistic tone. In addition to its themes (revelation and madness) and tone (trapped helplessness and sinister irony), the poem displays several extremely interesting formal features that call for attention.

The first such feature is an elaborate structure of chiasmi: between lines two and five we encounter the chiasmus 'cara fanciulla – obbliar // obbliar – cara fanciulla.' Within the middle term is embedded another chiasmus: 'non posso – obbliar // obbliar – non poss'io.' We see a looser chiasmus between lines three and six: 'bianco teschio – vi è sotto // vi è sotto – scheletro nascoso,' with again a second embedded chiasmus, this time between the outside terms and less obvious because primarily grammatical and not lexical: 'bianco – teschio // scheletro – nascoso' (adjective – noun // noun – adjective). Tarchetti links these inside terms not only grammatically (as nouns) but also semantically (as 'bones').

Thus Tarchetti erects a network of crosses that evoke a burial ground, culminating in the last phrase, 'ossa di un morto!' The speaker is mentally killing the beloved, crossing her out, as it were, by visualizing her death and decomposition. Indeed, given the form of direct address *to* the beloved, he seems almost to threaten her with this deadly vision.

Finally, we should notice the appearance, grammatically unnecessary, of the pronoun 'io' at the 'dead' centre of the poem – the middle word (sixth and seventh syllables) of the middle line (fifth out of nine). The speaker's own subjectivity, then, is at the heart, the focal point of the poem, and while it is clearly the speaker's own perception that strips the beloved of her body (she is not 'really' decomposing before him), the centrality of the 'io' suggests something more: that the speaker's identity is somehow at stake in this murderous fantasy. Yet while the 'io' is inscribed at the centre of the poem, it is simultaneously undercut by the repetition of 'non posso,' the insistence, as noted earlier, that the perceiving and speaking subject is subjected to (not in control of) this fantasy.

Interestingly, Tarchetti repeats his presentation of this uncontrollable and hideous vision three other times in his writings, although as prose passages rather than poetry. Indeed, one critic has called the female skeleton a 'thematic obsession' for Tarchetti.[36] In his *Pensieri*, he writes, 'Se una donna mi bacia, io non sento che freddo; se mi sorride, vedo i suoi denti a muoversi senza gengive, minacciando di uscirle di bocca; se mi abbraccia, non ho che la sensazione di un corpo stringente e pesante come la creta. All'oscuro una fanciulla amante mi sembrerebbe un cadavere che sorge per effetto magnetico come la rana di Galvani, destinato a cadere subito dopo sotto l'esanime peso' (*Opere*, 2: 492) [If a woman kisses me, I feel nothing but cold; if she smiles at me, I see her teeth moving without gums, threatening to come out of her mouth; if she embraces me, I have the sensation only of a pressing and heavy body like clay. In the dark, a loving girl would seem to me a cadaver that rises by means of magnetism, like Galvani's frog, destined to fall right afterwards under its dead weight (my translation)]. We find the image again in his short story 'Le leggende del castello nero,' where it appears as dream linked to memories of a previous life. Embracing a woman of angelic beauty, the protagonist is transported by an ecstasy of joy. But suddenly, during the intoxicating embrace:

> sentii compiersi in lui un'orrible trasformazione. Le sue forme piene e delicate che sentiva fremere sotto la mia mano, si appianarono, rientrarono in sè, sparirono; e sotto le mie dita incespicate tra le pieghe che s'erano formate a un tratto nel suo abito, sentii sporgere qua e là l'ossatura di uno scheletro ... Alzai gli occhi rabbrividendo e vidi il suo volto impallidire, affilarsi, scarnarsi, curvarsi sopra la mia bocca; e colla bocca priva di labbra imprimervi un bacio disperato, secco, lungo, terribile. (*Opere*, 2: 51)

> [I felt a horrible transformation take place. Her full, delicate form, which I felt trembling under my hand, smoothed out, returned into itself, and disappeared. Under my stumbling fingers, among the folds that had suddenly formed in her clothes, I felt jutting out here and there the bones of a skeleton ... I raised my shuddering eyes and saw her face turn pale, thin out, lose its flesh, and lean over my mouth; and with her mouth deprived of lips she pressed upon me a desperate, dry, long, terrible kiss. (my translation)]

The specific image appears yet again, briefly, in the novel *Fosca*, and in addition to this particular moment in the text we should see Fosca herself, consistently described as emaciated and pale, as a living skeleton. Though these second two instances occur within the context of a story and therefore should each be considered within that diegetic role, the fact that the same image occurs four times, including in the non-diegetic form of a poem, allows us also to consider the image in isolation.

We see that all the manifestations of this image describe (hetero)sexually charged moments involving physical contact between the male speaker/protagonist and a female lover. Roberto Tessari has vividly compared the threat of death coupled with sexuality to the female mantis, who kills her mate after copulating with him.[37] David del Principe, focusing on the scene from *Fosca*, has argued that the protruding bones felt by Giorgio are a metaphoric substitution for the absent phallus. He goes on to suggest a bone-fang-phallus line of association, concluding that the scene is penetrated by both vampiric and homoerotic energy. I propose a different reading of the image, based upon Freud's interpretation of the head of the Medusa.[38] Freud underscores precisely the dynamic at work within the (male) subject that Tarchetti implies in his 'Memento': that the viewing subject creates the very image that in turn subjects or victimizes him. Specifically, by defleshing the woman, by stripping her down to the bare bones, the narrator/protagonist succeeds in degendering her. He erases the threatening difference between her and himself by finding the lowest common denominator that they share beneath the flesh: a human skeleton. Ironically, then (as in Freud's evaluation of the Medusa's snakes as penis substitutions), what appears to be the creation of an image that evokes fear through its affinities with death and bodily decomposition may at the same time be an image created to console – that is, to deflect fear by cancelling the unbearable difference perceived and brought to the fore during a sexually charged encounter. Hence the centrality of the 'io' in Tarchetti's poem: for it is to maintain this centrality of the self that the otherness of the lover is stripped away. The double function of this 'crossing' out of sexual difference, as both frightening and consoling, accounts for the seemingly incompatible tones of helplessness and sadism, and for the double position of the speaker as both victim and perpetrator of the fantasy.

Elio Gioanola has insightfully suggested that the poem 'Memento' encapsulates the dynamic of the two female characters from Tarchetti's novel. Reading Giorgio's first lover, the 'robust' and beautiful Clara, as 'Eros,' and the sickeningly thin Fosca as 'Thanatos,' Gioanola notes how here Fosca's skeletal form uncontrollably erupts from Clara's voluptuous body.[39] This reading, I believe, suggests that it is not only the recognition of sexual difference that threatens the centrality of the 'io' but also the transports of erotic ecstasy itself. Tarchetti poses this most directly in his short story, cited above. The description of the erotic embrace compares it to a voluptuous intoxication, to being transported outside of oneself. Thus the ecstasy that accompanies the most intense experiences of love also entails moments of losing oneself, moments of the dissolution of the imaginary boundaries that stabilize our sense of being an individual. At this moment, the poem elicits but immediately short-circuits the possibilities of both a 'romantic' sublime of mastery and a 'pre-Oedipal' sublime of nearness.[40] Instead we witness a kind of anti-sublime of fear: the subject neither possesses nor respects the other, but rather becomes overwhelmed and threatened by it. For the *scapigliati* and for Tarchetti, such uncanny moments (in the Freudian sense of an infantile regression) are grotesque rather than sublime. Partaking of the materialist world view of their time, embodied repeatedly throughout their texts in the numerous depictions of the anatomist and the embalmer, the *scapigliati* were focused squarely and unrelentingly on the physicality of the body. As such, any 'dissolution of the self' could only be experienced as a 'decomposition of the flesh,' in all its horror and sordidness. The transports of Eros, again and again in Tarchetti's Gothic imagination, inevitably give way to the threatening spectre of Thanatos.

I would like to make further use of this poem by suggesting it as an emblem of the very interpretive process I have just undertaken. The speaker's reduction of his lover to a skeleton, as we have seen, is a double-valued gesture (frightening and consoling). In this way, I find that it serves as a vivid illustration of the psychoanalytic methodology. This process, too, tends to focus on what underlies and motivates various utterances, allowing us to articulate clearly the effect they have on us as readers and to pinpoint what is historically transcendent in them. At the same time, by stripping away the 'manifest' content and getting beyond the historically specific details in its analyses, this process runs the risk of reducing or even eliminating the differences between texts, cancelling the uniqueness of literary creations and offering instead a collection of so many well-defined and clearly articulated skeletons.

The emblem of the skeleton obtains in a double sense. We can see psychoanalysis, and *scapigliatura* literature, as engaged in the task of taking the skeletons out of the closet, excavating and bringing to light buried and repressed dark secrets. At the same time, psychoanalysis seeks to articulate the essential structuring principles of the mind – the universal framework, or skeleton, that defines the development of the human psyche. In a literary context, we might think of the work of Peter Brooks, who identifies the dialectic developed by Freud in *Beyond the Pleasure Principle* as the basic structuring formula around which all narrative is built. The struggle between Eros and Thanatos becomes the 'master-plot,' the blueprint or, indeed, the skeleton, which is then fleshed out in infinite variatious and permutations by novelists.[41] This duplicity within the emblem of the skeleton points to a potential split within 'the' psychoanalytic methodology, specifically in relation to its applicability to literary texts. On the one hand, one may describe and evaluate the precise nature of the 'repressed,' decoding the distortions of censorship to arrive at the true content, thus undertaking, in short, a thematic criticism. A classic and elegant example of this approach is Marie Bonaparte's 'Life and Works of Edgar Allan Poe.' In the essay, she succinctly articulates the theoretical assumption that justifies this approach: 'it must not be forgotten that though, on the surface, a literary work relates a manifestly coherent story, intertwined with it and simultaneously, another and secret story is being told which, in fact, is the basic theme.'[42] However, Bonaparte herself comments, with some wit, on the inevitably 'skeletal' reductions of this kind of analysis:

> To the reader, our analyses may at times have seemed overmuch to stress these symbolic devices which, monotonously, bring everything in the universe back to the same human prototypes – father, mother, child, our members and organs, and, in particular, the genitals. The fault, however, is not ours. We cannot help it that the unconscious monotonously reiterates certain themes, governed as it is by our most primitive memories and our most archaic instincts.[43]

Conversely, one may analyse the way in which the economy of drives or the developmental phases elaborated by Freud parallel structuring principles of literature, thus making use of psychoanalysis in a more formal vein (here the work of Brooks is an example).

The two methodologies converge on the point of the *uncanny*,[44] which I will present as the thematic and formal paradigm for Pascoli's work. *Scapigliatura*'s Gothic and macabre sensibility can be seen as one aspect of the repressed that returns in the imagery of Pascoli's opus.[45] The playful, transrational thought of *Il fanciullino*, akin to Kristeva's 'semiotic chora,' is his poetry's mode of expression.[46] Indeed Pascoli is considered the main exponent of symbolism in the Italian tradition, and it is upon the symbolist texts of Mallarmé that Kristeva bases her analysis of modern poetry in her *Revolution in Poetic Language*. The transgressive nature of this predominantly phonic poetics allows us to experience it, too, as a 'return of the repressed,' as both foreign (to our everyday use of language) and familiar (undulating with the memory of rhythmic, semiotic motility). In reactivating the 'maternal chora' both thematically (in his ambivalent evocations of maternal figures) and formally (in his pre-grammatical, ana-logical *linguaggio*), Pascoli's poetry talks about uncanny things in an uncanny way.

But before turning to Pascoli's work with this paradigm in mind, in the remaining pages I explore further connections between the *scapigliatura* and psychoanalysis, though now focusing specifically on the Freudian uncanny. My agenda thus far has been not so much to psychoanalyse the literature of the *scapigliatura* as to put the two discourses side by side and locate certain connections. Once again, the notion of the uncanny emerges as the hinge, assembling together the various links (the scandalizing effect on dominant culture, the gesture of exposing the sordid, the focus on illness and perversity) between the two. One could say, simply, that the uncanny is what they have in common. In this vein, and having re-evaluated Todorov's seminal work on the fantastic through a Lacanian perspective, Mladen Dolar concludes her essay on the uncanny with the following suggestion:

> Todorov deals with a well-circumscribed corpus of texts, a clearly cut realm of the fantastic. Its beginning coincides roughly with the advent of moder nity and its scientific background; its closure, somewhat surprisingly, coincides with the advent of psychoanalysis: 'Psychoanalysis has replaced (and thereby made superfluous) the fantastic literature.' What appeared indirectly through the fantastic can be dealt with directly by psychoanalysis. So psychoanalysis appears to be the most fantastic of all fantastic tales – the ultimate horror story.[47]

Given this assessment, discussing the Gothic literature of *scapigliatura* in terms of the uncanny seems potentially redundant. However, putting the two approaches to this phenomenon side by side will allow each to shed light on the other and help us to be more precise about the issues at stake in this literature and, later, about the ways in which Pascoli develops these issues in his poetry.

In line with such an approach, I find the parallels in the following two passages particularly striking and illuminating. The first is a vignette excerpted from Freud's essay on the uncanny, and is one of several autobiographically narrative moments in the text, in which Freud relates, in a markedly literary way, experiences from his own life to support and illustrate his scientific theories.[48] He writes,

> As I was walking, one hot summer afternoon, through the deserted streets of a provincial town in Italy which was unknown to me, I found myself in a quarter of whose character I could not remain long in doubt. Nothing but painted women could be seen at the windows of the small houses, and I hastened to leave the narrow street at the next turning. But after having wandered about for a time without enquiring my way, I suddenly found myself back in the same street, where my presence was now beginning to excite attention. I hurried away once more, only to arrive by another detour at the same place yet a third time. Now, however, a feeling overcame me which I can only describe as uncanny, and I was glad enough to find myself back in the piazza ... Other situations which have in common with my adventure an unintended recurrence of the same situation, but which differ

radically from it in other respects, also result in the same feeling of helplessness and uncanniness. (*Standard Edition*, 17: 237)

The second passage appears as the opening scene from Tarchetti's short story 'The Lake of the Three Lampreys,' set in an enchanted forest. In the tale, which Tarchetti claims to have based on a popular tradition, a woman explains to the narrator that he has been put under the spell of a magic herb. She then relates to him the story of the three monks who, in a time of drought, did not share their water with the community and who were therefore punished by being turned into fish. The woman enables the narrator to free himself from the spell, but before he is made aware of the enchantment, he experiences the inexplicable repetition compulsion with the same sense of 'uncanniness' as that described by Freud. The narrator recounts:

M'inoltrai una volta per questa foresta, e senza avvedermi d'aver percorso un tratto lunghissimo di cammino mi trovai molto addentrato fra quegli alberi, e il sole stava per tramontare. Me ne avvidi dagli ultimi raggi, che colorivano obbliquamente le grandi foglie degli ontani e delle quercie. A malincuore mi accinsi a ritornare; pure temendo della notte e dell'inesperienza del luogo, avevo già fatti molti passi verso l'aperto; il sentiero mi pareva ed era certamente lo stesso; io mi lusingava d'essere già quasi arrivato nei vicini campi di cotone, allorquando arrestatomi per raccogliere certo fiore che aveva colpito la mia attenzione, mi accorsi di trovarmi tuttora nello stesso luogo dal quale era poc'anzi partito! Dolente, e più? ancora meravigliato di questo avvenimento, rifaccio per la seconda volta la strada medesima – mi impauriva l'idea di essere sorpreso dalla notte in quella foresta – cammino con passi accelerati, mi pare che gli alberi si diradino, io rido meco stesso del mio scoraggiamento e mi fermo ad osservare quanto cammino mi rimane ancora a percorrere. Ma ... ohimè! Chi lo crederebbe? Io non mi ero mosso ancora d'un solo passo, e mi trovavo precisamente in quel primo luogo, donde aveva deliberato il mio ritorno.
   'Questa è senza dubbio una fatalità incomprensibile,' io dissi a me stesso. (Tarchetti, *Opere*, 2: 107–8)

[On one occasion, I entered this forest, and without realizing that I was traveling a very long distance, I found that I had penetrated deeply among the trees, and the sun was about to set. I became aware of the time from the last rays of sunlight, which obliquely colored the broad leaves of the alder and oak trees. Reluctantly, I prepared to return; anxious about the night and my unfamiliarity with the place, I had, moreover, already taken many steps toward the clearing. The path appeared to me and certainly was the same. I flattered myself with the thought that I had nearly reached the neighboring cotton fields, when having stopped to pick a certain flower that caught my eye, I noticed that I was still in the very place I had just left! Worried – no, astonished at this development, I retraced the same path for the second time; the thought of being overtaken by nightfall in that forest was frightening me – I walked with precipitate steps, it looked as if the trees were thinning out, I had a private laugh at my dismay and stopped to see how much distance remained to be traversed. But ... oh, no! Who would believe it? I had still not moved a single step. I found myself precisely in the original place where I had resolved to turn back.

'This is without a doubt an incomprehensible fate,' I said to myself.][49]

Both passages thematize a loss of self. On the narrative level this loss has a literal sense: both speakers are lost, either in a foreign city or in a strange wood, and unable to find their way out of these unknown places. But, more fundamentally, each speaker suffers from a loss of his own agency, his own power of decision. Both speakers have been overtaken by a mysterious force that undermines and overrides their own will. The shame of being noticed repeatedly among prostitutes and the frightful prospect of spending a night alone in a dark wood do not in themselves account for the clear sense of fear conveyed in these excerpts. Both speakers are 'perturbati' by the paradoxical experience of doing something, over and over, that they have consciously decided *not* to do (return to the same spot), as if their feet were acting on their own, carrying them off in a direction they did not want to go. This apparent inefficacy of will obviously has important ethical and moral consequences, which I will discuss in my final chapter.[50] For now, I want only to underscore how the 'loss of self,' or the dissolution of one's sense of independent subjectivity, evokes the effect of the uncanny for both Freud and the *scapigliati*.

Though focusing specifically on castration anxiety, Freud indicates a more general basis for the 'infantile fears' that are elicited by the uncanny. He notes that all types or classes of the uncanny effect a 'regression to a time when the ego had not marked itself off sharply from the external world and other people.' Beyond the specific fear of castration upon which Freud insists, then, the uncanny taps into a more general moment of fluidity between self and other, an infantile stage of pre-difference. In the essay, Freud does not submit the image of the maternal body to the kind of rigorous analysis he undertakes with other themes, such as the double or repetition compulsions. He does cite it as the repressed signified of the common terrifying fantasy of being buried alive. Tarchetti succinctly describes just such a fantasy in his poem 'Sognai,' all the more chilling for its brevity:

> Sognai. L'orrido sogno ho in mente impresso
> In un avel calati eram per gioco ...
> Scende il coperchio immane a poco a poco,
> Ci chiude. Eternità sovr'esso. (*Opere*, 2: 455)

[I dreamt. I have the horrible dream etched in my mind. We were lowered into a tomb as a prank ... little by little the huge cover descends, encloses us. Eternity over it. (my translation)]

The shift in the tense of the verbs before and after the ellipsis, and ultimately the absence of any verb in the last phrase, enacts an eruption of the past dream into present reality. The verbs 'sognai,' 'ho impresso,' and 'eram [eravamo] calati' are all in past tenses. These give way to the present tense in 'scende' and 'chiude,' as if the speaker, transported by the memory of the dream, has forgotten that it was a vision and is experiencing it as a present reality. The verbs also reveal a shift in agency: the speaker is the active subject of the first two verbs, but, along with the addressee, becomes only the passive subject of the third. Finally, both speaker and addressee become the object ('ci') of the final verbs, as the subject position is ceded to the 'huge cover' of the tomb. The grammatical structure, then, helps create the sense of helplessness and powerlessness over the inevitable and eternal closing of the lid, which lowers 'little by little.'[51] The detail that the event described took place as part of a 'prank' ('per gioco') heightens the horror of the vision and anticipates Freud's similar detail: 'To some people being buried alive *by mistake* is the most uncanny thing of all' (244, my emphasis). The German word translated in the *Standard Edition* as 'by mistake' is 'scheintot,' which more literally means 'seemingly dead' (*Gesammelte Schriften*, 10: 397). The mistake, then, is the misreading of a live body as a dead one. Both Tarchetti and Freud here offer rational explanations for the occurrence of a highly unlikely scenario. Such explanations seem unnecessary and insignificant in the discussion of the profound fear attached to this fantasy. The 'mistake' and the 'prank,' however, imply that the subject who is buried alive is himself insignificant. To be the object of a joke is not to be taken seriously; to be assumed dead while still alive is to be forgotten – in other words, to have one's narcissism dealt a deadly blow.

In his analysis, Freud asserts that this most horrifying and uncanny of visions is a transmutation of the universal fantasy of 'intra-uterine existence,' a fantasy, he claims, 'which had originally nothing terrifying about it at all' (244). The return of this originally 'lascivious' fantasy after its repression elicits the terror of losing oneself, akin to the terror felt by Tarchetti's narrator in the woods and by Freud himself among the Italian prostitutes. The fluidity of the womb, for Freud the source of the vague religious feeling of universal brotherhood, triggers also the fear of the death of one's own individuality.[52] The maternal body encapsulates the same ambivalence or bifurcation as does the word 'heimlich': it represents our original 'home,' the oceanic wholeness of pre-difference to which we long to return, and at the same time threatens with its ability to destabilize our notion of the self. In a careful analysis of all the instances in which Freud returns to the image of the maternal body in this essay, Robin Lydenberg, who refers to the maternal body as 'the most uncanny thing of all,' argues that Freud 'avoids the more disturbing specter of the pre-oedipal, phallic mother, who threatens castration, and of the mother as envied source of plenitude and procreation.'[53] This ambivalently charged maternal figure is elicited by Boito in his shocking 'Lezione d'anatomia,' and, as I explore in the following chapter, is the figure that haunts much of Pascoli's opus.

Arrigo Boito's 'Lezione d'anatomia,' from his *Libro di versi*, is one of three poems that treat a similar theme: in each of the three, a narrator offers a sentimental lament as the rational forces of nineteenth-century progress and positivism invade and demystify objects held by the narrator to be in some sense sacred. In 'Case nuove,' the old Milanese homes and their imagined 'lares' are razed to prepare the way for urbanization; in 'Una mummia,' the cadaver of an Egyptian, so painstakingly enshrouded by loved ones centuries ago, is put in a glass case and gawked at by tourists as the museum guide mangles the pronunciation of his name. Finally in 'Lezione,' the cold-hearted, dispassionate anatomist, spouting Latin phraseology, cuts open the cadaver of a young consumptive woman.[54] These poems stage a 'dualism' (to use the title of Boito's programmatic poem) that reflects contemporary philosophic and aesthetic debates: as critics have pointed out, the rationalist current would lead to an aesthetic of 'verismo,' while the co-present sacralizing idealism would develop into symbolism and decadentism. Boito here dramatizes the tension of this debate, exploring both the aesthetic and the ethical stakes. On a microcosmic level, we might note that the woman in 'Lezione,' like the woman in Praga's 'A un feto,' is 'consumptive' and, as such, a topos of late romantic aesthetic taste; but both women are specifically called 'etica,' meaning 'consumptive' but also evoking 'ethical.' He problematizes his own presentation of the issue by the surprise ending of 'Lezione': the sentimentalizing fantasies of the narrator, who bemoans the treatment of the pure young virgin, are overturned as a month-old fetus is discovered in the girl's womb: 'E mentre suscito / Nel mio segreto / Quei sogni adorni / In quel cadavere / Si scopre un feto / Di trenta giorni' [And while I conjure up, secretly, those adorned dreams, in that cadaver a thirty-day-old fetus is discovered]. The jarring ending has created a challenge for interpretation: Mazzoni, who focuses on the poem's conclusion, asserts that Boito is mocking hyperbolic romantic idealism and, as a demystifying *scapigliato*, that he is taking sides with the scientist. Del Principe, focusing on the main body of the poem, argues that the romantic narrator is the mouthpiece of Boito, a proto-aesthete who critiques non-aesthetic positivism. Still others (Lavagetto and Gioanola) argue that Boito remains dispassionately aloof from the debate, which he uses primarily as an occasion to exercise his formal virtuosity in parallelisms, antitheses, and metrics.[55] Finotti, surveying Boito's opus in general, suggests that his is a poetics of melancholic irony: desiring to achieve the sublime, absolute beauty that would obviate form, Boito is painfully aware of its impossibility and instead turns to the grotesque and to a hyperconstrictive form.[56] This turn results in an ironic dualism of comic and tragic modes. Unable to soar to one extreme, he delves into the other, always shunning the mediocre and mundane.

Finotti's argument underscores, on the aesthetic level, the parallelism in the two extremes. I would agree with his assessment, and suggest that Boito uses this parallelism thematically to balance one extreme against the other, using each to criticize and be the foil of the other. Indeed, Mazzoni, undertaking a feminist-historical analysis, concludes with a similar equation on the ethical level: both the artist and the scientist, seemingly in opposite camps, essentialize the female corpse and use it to discover their 'truth.' In both cases, the integrity of the nameless woman is erased as, with either pen or scalpel, the men in search of abstract truth use her to construct their systems.[57] Interestingly, del Principe, who begins from the opposite premise, reaches the same conclusion. We can notice how, on a linguistic level, the poem makes this parallelism clear: 'Ed era giovane, Ed era bionda, Ed era bella,' passionately exclaims the narrator. 'Ecco le *valvole*, Ecco le *celle*, Ecco l'*aorta*' coldly notes the scientist. And while the scientist's narcissism is the ostensible theme of the poem as a whole, the narrator's narcissism is revealed in his own references to his fantasy constructions: 'Ed io, travolto, Ritorno a leggere / Le *mie* visioni / Sul bianco volto,' and finally, 'E mentre suscito / Nel *mio* segreto / Quei sogni adorni ...' (my emphases) ['And I, crushed, return to read my visions on the white visage'; 'And while I arouse in my secrecy those ornate dreams ...']. The pronouns emphasize the solipsistic nature of the visions and dreams he spawns. The image of the maternal body and the ghastly appearance of the dead fetus undercut the discourses of both the scientist and the artist.[58]

The consumptive woman in 'Lezione d'anatomia' holds the place held by the mummy and by the Milanese homes in the other poems by Boito noted earlier: all three subjects are violated and desacralized. The comparison is telling, as the woman is both 'other' – strange as the exotic mummy brought in from a faraway place and time; and 'same' – as familiar as the home. The comparison with the home goes still farther: both are laid bare by pitiless forces that shamelessly open up to sight what should be covered. In 'Case nuove,' Boito writes,

> E la casa s'è fatta invereconda,
> Gli straziati lari
> Mostrano al sole l'alcova e la fogna
> Senza pietà di vel che li ripari.   (*Opere*, 8, lines 28–31)

[And the house is made shameless, the tormented household gods reveal the alcove and the sewer to the sun, without the courtesy of a veil which might screen them. (my translation)]

Similarly in 'Lezione' we read 'quella vergine' was made to lie 'senza sudario,' without the dignity of a shroud, and that the 'sanctuary' of her heart was opened up and 'revealed' by the clinician. The homeliness and sacredness of both are revealed, when opened by the demystifying agents, to be already within themselves profane: the alcoves and sewers – the dark, dirty recesses of the home – were not put there by urbanization but revealed by it, just as the fetus, the secret sign of the girl's lost virginity, is revealed by the anatomist. Once again, as in Tarchetti's 'Memento,' the literature of the *scapigliatura* seeks to expose the unpleasant. The discovery of the dead fetus in the womb of the mother, clearly the dominant and most gripping image in the poem, does more than deflate the hypersentimentalized fantasies of the narrator about the virginal purity of the girl on the table. The fetus is dead, conflating the two end points of life, birth and death, and introducing the element of fear into the most homely of spaces: the protected environment of the maternal womb. Thus the revision enacted by the discovery of the fetus is not only that this particular alleged virgin was actually pregnant but that the 'familiar' figure of the mother is invested with the frightening: that she is, in short, unhomely, *unheimlich*, uncanny.

Indeed, the figure of the uncanny mother serves as a synecdoche of *scapigliatura* in general. As inassimilable and abject, this figure evades and defies the master discourses that try to lay claim to it. This evasion and defiance hold true both for the idealizations of religion and romanticism (though *scapigliatura* may be seen as an exponent of late romanticism) and for the rationalizations of science (which *scapigliatura* imports but cannot be reduced to). The persistent undercurrent of this regressive and transgressive sensibility returns in and fuels Pascoli's uncanny poetry.

As a final direct illustration of the legacy of the *scapigliati* in Pascoli's work, before leaving them and turning in the next chapter to an examination of Pascoli's *Poemi conviviali*, I conclude with a comparison of two poems. I began this chapter with a brief reference to the canonical, even monumental, Italian poet Giacomo Leopardi. Pascoli himself published critical essays on Leopardi, and many critics have noted the philosophical affinities between the poets. A very clear, local point of continuity appears in Pascoli's short poem 'Il passero solitario,'[59] from his first collection, *Myricae*, which evokes and in many respects echoes a poem of the same name from Leopardi's *Canti*. A comparison of the two poems reveals how the influence of the Gothic *scapigliatura* inserts itself in the genealogical line from Leopardi to Pascoli.

Leopardi's longer and more discursive composition specifies and elaborates several points of comparison between the bird of the title and the poet himself: both retreat from communing with their peers, and rather than participate in the joyful merrymaking of the other groups of youths/animals, the bird passes the spring, as the poet passes his youth, singing and alone. The comparisons culminate in a final contrast: the bird will never regret having lived as he does, because nature formed him for such a life. However, the poet fears that, when he comes to the emptiness of old age, he will lament his solitary life and look back with sadness.

Pascoli's composition evokes Leopardi's in several concrete ways. In addition to the shared title, both poets apostrophize the bird, addressing it with the 'tu,' or familiar 'you.' Both poems open with an image of the bird on an old tower – for Pascoli the 'torre avita,' for Leopardi the 'torre antica.' Finally, both poems are structured around a central, sustained metaphor or conceit: in Leopardi's, the comparison of the bird with the poet himself, in Pascoli's, the comparison between the bird and a cloistered nun. But Pascoli's composition departs from his predecessor's in several important ways, ways that reflect the influence of the intervening Gothic writers:

> Tu nella torre avita,
> > passero solitario
> > tenti la tua tasteria
> > come nel santuario
> > monaca prigioniera
> > l'organo, a fior di dita;
>
> che pallida, fugace,
> > stupì tre note, chiuse
> > nell'organo, tre sole,
> > in un instante effuse
> > tre come tre parole
> > ch'ella ha sepolto, in pace.
>
> Da un ermo santuario
> > che sa di morto incenso,
> > nelle grandi archi vuote,
> > di tra un silenzio immenso
> > mandi le tue tre note,
> > spirito solitario.   (*Opere*, 1: 152–3)

[You in the ancestral tower, / Blue Rock-Thrush, / test your keyboard, / as in the sanctuary / an imprisoned nun / does the organ, grazing it with her fingers; / a nun who pale, fleeting, / sounded three notes, and marvelled at them, notes closed / within the organ, just three, poured out in an instant, / three like three words / which she has buried in peace. / From a lonesome sanctuary / which smells of dead incense, / in the great empty arches, / from among an immense silence / you send forth your three notes, / oh solitary spirit. (my translation)]

Pascoli's depiction of the lonely nun sounding the organ in the secluded, silent, immense convent seems to encapsulate the sad condition of Verga's protagonist Maria, from his epistolary novel *Storia di una capinera* (1871). (It is interesting that Verga, too, compares the nun to a bird: in this case to a caged blackcap who, like the unfortunate Maria, dies of heartbreak.) The tone of the poem, however, is not primarily sadness. Where Leopardi's composition creates a strong tone of melancholy and loneliness, Pascoli's poem engenders a vague but insistent sense of fear and anxiety, coupled with a profound sense of awe in the face of the silent and sublime grandeur of the setting. The three stanzas parallel the three notes sung by the bird and the three keys struck by the nun, which in turn allude to the three vows that committed the woman to the convent. These three notes are far different from the song Leopardi's bird sends out over the countryside. Rather, in light of the vocabulary deployed ('sepolto,' 'morto') these notes ring out as a death toll echoing hollowly in the enormous halls. The 'pale, fleeting' woman and the small bird seem overwhelmed by the huge and ancient architecture. Indeed much of the imagery – the pale nun imprisoned in the immense silence of the secluded sanctuary and amid the scent of dead incense – evokes a haunted and strongly Gothic atmosphere. At the same time, the depiction particularly of the architecture ('torre avita,' 'grandi arche vuote,' and of the 'silenzio immenso') conveys a tone of sublimity and awe. Pascoli's brevity of description departs from Leopardi's longer, more discursive lines. This economy of language culminates in the final line, where the vocative 'solitary spirit' may refer to both the bird and the nun. This compact, more evocative style (as opposed to the more thoroughly articulated and, in a sense, intellectual comparisons and contrasts of Leopardi) allows the poem to suggest subtly, if not actually describe, the sense of being buried alive, a situation we saw depicted more explicitly in I.U. Tarchetti's 'Sognai.' The contrasts with Leopardi's earlier text demonstrate, then, Pascoli's absorption and subtle reworking of the uncanny sensibility of his Gothic forerunners.

2 Returning: The *Poemi conviviali* and the Uncanny

'Siamo sette'

Vidi una cara contadinella,
ch'aveva ott'anni, come mi disse
bionda, ricciuta, bella, assai bella
con le due grandi pupille fisse.

Presso il cancello stava. Ed io; 'Figlia,
quanti tra bimbi, siete, e bimbette?'
chiesi. Con atto di meraviglia,
ella rispose: 'Quanti, noi? Sette.'

'E dove sono? dì, se ti pare'
le dissi, ed ella mi disse: 'Ma ...
noi siamo sette: due sono in mare;
altri due sono nella città;

altri due sono nel camposanto,
il fratellino, la sorellina:
in quella casa che c'è daccanto
io sto, con mamma, loro vicina.'

(*Opere* 2: 34)

[I met a little cottage girl,
She was eight years old, she said;
Her hair was thick with many a curl
That clustered round her head.

'Sisters and brothers, little maid,
How many may you be?'
'How many? Seven in all,' she said,
And wondering looked at me.

'And where are they, I pray you tell?'
She answered, 'Seven are we,
And two of us at Conway dwell,
And two are gone to sea.

Two of us in the church-yard lie,
My sister and my brother,
And in the church-yard cottage, I
Dwell near them with my mother.'][1]

In addition to his nine volumes of Italian poetry, his prize-winning Latin poetry, and his critical essays, most notably on Dante and Leopardi, Pascoli also translated much poetry, both from the classics (such as passages from *The Iliad* and *The Odyssey*) and from modern poets such as Tennyson, Shelley, and Hugo. The Italian rendering of 'We Are Seven,' the beginning of which is reproduced above, is the only translation from William Wordsworth's poetry that Pascoli undertook. Pascoli's choice of this particular poem to translate seems motivated not by the fact that it was Wordsworth's best-known piece but by its strong resonance with Pascoli's own life experiences and poetic philosophy.

The eight-year-old girl who speaks in the poem has suffered the deaths of two siblings. The biographical connections to Pascoli are clear. The fourth of ten children, he too suffered the deaths of several family members. Two sisters died in early childhood. His father, Ruggero Pascoli, was killed on 10 August 1867, when Giovanni was only eleven, and his mother, Caterina Allocatelli Vincenzi, died in December of the following year. Within the space of a few years, Giovanni also lost his older sister, Margherita, to typhus, his brother Luigi to cerebral meningitis in 1871, and finally his oldest brother, Giacomo, who had assumed the paternal role in the family, in 1876.[2] These tragic losses pervade and indeed motivate a great part of Pascoli's Italian poetry. He dedicated his first collection, *Myricae*, to the memory of his father, and his later *Canti di Castelvecchio* to his mother, and explicitly based several of his best-known poems (such as 'X agosto,' 'La cavalla storna,' and 'La voce') on these deaths. Even the poems that do not speak explicitly about the various lost family members are infused or haunted with the idea of unjust, premature death. We can think of 'Orfano' and 'In ritardo' to name just two. The haunting of Pascoli's poetry by the ghosts of his family members reveals that the poems are not an exercise in 'working through' their deaths.[3] On the contrary, the poems are neither the symptoms nor the staging of an effective mourning but rather a resistance to mourning. Wordsworth's 'contadinella,' who resists the speaker's logical conclusion that there are only five in her family, personifies this active refusal to mourn and to work through the deaths of family members. She, like Pascoli, creates a psychic space for the living on of these undead loved ones.

The young girl's insistence that 'we are seven,' in spite of the fact, admitted by herself, that two of her siblings are dead and buried in the 'camposanto,' demonstrates a seeming failure of reason: the correct response, of course, would be 'we *were* seven' or, as the grown-up and rational interlocutor explains, 'se que' due sono in cimitero, / cara bambina, cinque voi siete.' It becomes clear through the course of the poem that the two protagonists are speaking at, rather than with, each other: despite a shared language, they are operating with two incompatible conceptualizations of the world. As readers, we are brought into sympathy with the transrational thought of the child, who continues to bring her dinner to the cemetery to eat with her two siblings that 'sleep' together a mere ten paces from the home. The poem refigures her inability to see the truth as an ability to see more, and represents the reasonableness of the adult interlocutor as unsympathetic obtuseness. In this respect, the girl embodies the essential principles of Pascoli's 'fanciullino,' the 'little child' ('little boy') who looks with wonder ('meraviglia') on the world and thus represents the soul of poetry.[4] Indeed, twice in his translation Pascoli uses the word *meraviglia* to describe the emotional stance of the child (line 7, 'con atto di meraviglia,' and line 56, 'meravigliando tutta nel viso'). It is precisely this sense of 'meraviglia' that, for Pascoli, defines the perspective of the inner child: 'Tu sei il fanciullino eterno, che vede tutto con maraviglia [sic], tutto come per la prima volta'(*Fanciullino*, 35) ['You are the Eternal Child, who sees everything with a sense of wonder, everything as if for the first time'].[5]

However, to equate the perspective of the child with that of Pascoli would be to oversimplify matters. The perspective offered to the readers to adopt as their own is one that incorporates and transcends both points of view presented in the dialogic encounter. That is, we as readers are assumed to 'know' and acknowledge (as the adult speaker does and the child cannot) that really there are only five children. At the same time we are asked to appreciate and indeed believe in the deeper, marvellous truth (that the child sees and the adult cannot) that really there 'are seven.' This double perspective obtains in one of Pascoli's own compositions, in which once again we witness an encounter between a rational speaker and an 'interlocutor' of sorts who defies that rationality. The first-person speaker of 'In ritardo' sees, on a stormy autumn day, a pair of swallows belatedly tending to their nest.[6] He 'reminds' the birds that the rest of their flock have by now migrated to Africa and won't be back until spring. However, because the first nest of this pair of swallows had met with misfortune, they had started over with a new one late in the season and hence had failed to migrate south with the others. Through a series of semantically and phonetically strong verbs – 'scrosciare' (to pelt), 'rugliare' (to roar), and 'sferzare' (to whip, lash) – Pascoli conveys the harsh and relentless nature of the storm, against which the speaker must close his window for protection. At the same time, he emphasizes the helplessness of the brood, 'sei rondinini non ancor pennuti' [six little swallows not yet feathered], thus underscoring the poignancy of the scene and eliciting our sympathies. In this encounter, we see a permutation of the same conflict we saw in 'Siamo sette.' The human speaker is the voice of reason and logic, underscored by his ability to talk in very specific terms of time (San Benedetto's feast day as the exact time of the birds' spring return) and place ('Baghirmi' and 'Bornù,' and not merely 'south' as the destination of the migrations). The concreteness of this information or knowledge of the speaker contrasts with the evocative, impressionistic description of the appearance of the swallows: 'mi parve di vedere un nereggiar di piume' [I seemed to see a blackening of feathers]. His rationality, however, is defied by the instinctual love of the swallows and their irrational attempt to reconstruct a family 'in ritardo.' Indeed, as in Wordsworth's poem, the clash in perspectives centres not merely on a way of seeing the world but specifically on the refusal to mourn. The birds, like the child, will not accept the finality of death. They resist death's ability to obliterate their family, and thus appear foolish under the gaze of the rational observer. But, as in 'Siamo sette,' we are invited to look at the question not from just one or the other point of view but from a double perspective. The last line of the poem, while presumably enunciated by the speaker who has narrated the entire composition, seems to transcend a merely 'logical' criticism of the birds and to embody instead an understanding of both their desire and its impossibility: 'e quello ch'era non sarà mai più' [and what once was will never be again]. This closing statement explicitly symbolizes the plight of the little family of swallows and raises it to universal significance.[7] As such, it echoes verses from Wordsworth, this time not from the translated 'We Are Seven' but from his better-known ode on 'Intimations of Immortality,' where he writes, 'it is not now as it has been of yore ... The things which I have seen I now can see no more.'[8] The invitation to the reader to adopt a double or transcendent perspective, an understanding that encompasses both 'truths,' creates yet another level of pathos.

By conveying the poignancy, and not merely the foolishness, of the 'contadinella' and the 'rondini,' the poems suggest that this particular point of view itself is to be counted among the dead who are being mourned or, more precisely, to be counted among the 'loved ones' whose death is to be resisted. The ability to see in this transrational way has died in the dramatized speakers who confront it in the poems, and the poetry itself attempts to resuscitate it for the readers. Indeed, this perspective is valued partly because it is always in the process of being lost. As 'law' creates 'desire' by establishing lacks and prohibitions, so too the 'wonder' of the *fanciullino* becomes precious only in the light of its having been replaced, or indeed prohibited, by grown-up rationality.

Pascoli's desire to resist mourning, to revive the past and the dead, reveals itself not only thematically in the poems that dramatize aspects of his biography but in his choice to revive a 'dead' language and write extensively in Latin.[9] Pascoli discusses explicitly the nostalgia for the dying past and the nobility of actively working to preserve it in his homage to Diego Vitrioli given in 1898 in Sicily, published as 'Un poeta di lingua morta.'[10] He apostrophizes Vitrioli and asks why he chooses to write in Latin (and Greek), noting that such a choice may be construed as elitism. He then imagines the poet's response and, in a kind of prosopopoeia, 'quotes' his explanation.[11] Pascoli (speaking as Vitrioli) reasons that, by using Latin and Greek, he broadens rather than narrows his potential audience:

> la natura va dal semplice al composto, dall'omogenio all'eterogenio, e non viceversa; e le lingue e i dialetti moltiplicheranno sempre d'anno in anno e di secolo in secolo. Per questa parte, ospite, tant'è che io usi il latino e il greco, quanto qualunque lingua parlata; anzi, se si computa bene, devo credere di esser per avere più intenditori, in tutto il mondo, del mio latino che, nella sola Italia, del mio italiano. (*Opere*, 2: 476)

[nature moves from the simple to the complex, from the homogeneous to the heterogeneous, and not the other way. Languages and dialects always multiply from year to year and from century to century. For this reason, friend, I use Latin and Greek as much as any spoken language; indeed, if one calculates carefully, I am led to believe that there are more readers [understanders] of my Latin throughout the world than there are of my Italian in Italy alone. (my translation)]

In responding for his fellow Latinist, Pascoli also, clearly, provides us with his own motivations for writing extensively in Latin. In the reply, he values Latin for embodying an original unity. With the passage of time, he argues with an almost apocalyptic tone, the diversity of languages multiplies, moving farther and farther away from the universalism, the unity, of the past and towards an ever-increasing fragmentation. Recuperating Latin, then, means reaching back and trying to salvage some of that unity, resisting the inevitable disintegration of time. It is important to note that Pascoli speaks not of potential 'readers' ('lettori') of poetry but of 'understanders' ('intenditori'). This implies something beyond an intellectual capacity and connotes a kind of sympathetic union. This connotation, I believe, allows us to see a connection with one of Pascoli's arguments in his famous *Il fanciullino*, discussed above. Here, he values the voice (and the vision) of the child precisely because it (like Latin) is more 'universal': we all cried in the same 'language' before learning to speak our various and disparate 'native' languages:

> l'uomo impara a parlare tanto diverso o tanto meglio, di anno in anno, di secolo in secolo, di millennio in millennio; ma comincia con far gli stessi vagiti e guaiti in tutti i tempi e luoghi. La sostanza psichica è uguale nei fanciullini di tutti i popoli. Un fanciullino è fanciullino allo stesso modo da per tutto. (53)

> [man learns to speak so differently and so much better, from year to year, from century to century, from millennium to millennium; but in all times and places he begins with the same whining and whimpering. The psychic make-up is the same in the children of all peoples. A child is a child in the same way everywhere.][12]

By evoking this lowest common denominator of humanity, Pascoli argues, the poet-as-child can elicit a sympathetic union by reminding us of our essential sameness. The gestures of retrieving both Latin and the *linguaggio* of the *fanciullino,* then, are attempts to reach back into the past (whether phylogenic or ontogenetic) to recuperate a vanishing unity in order to promote 'understanding.'

The turn to Latin, then, reveals an agenda quite opposite to that of an alienating elitism. Linked to the retrieval of infancy, it is, paradoxically, another version of pre-grammaticality. However, the poet who resuscitates a dead language in an attempt to speak more fully runs the risk of killing his own poetic voice, of falling into the silence of unintelligibility. The *Poemi conviviali*'s 'L'ultimo viaggio,' to be discussed below, offers the character of Ulysses as a figure for Pascoli himself in this regard. Ulysses' plunge into the sea again dramatizes Pascoli's dive into the dead language; both have the intention of living more fully, and both risk death as they attempt the impossible return to origins.[13] Pascoli's linguistic use of Latin and thematic turn to the classics become, then, not an exercise in erudition but ways in which he effects a turn backwards. Like the privileging of children and even of birds and insects, these gestures allow Pascoli to delve into the 'prehistory of consciousness.'[14]

This chapter examines Pascoli's 1904 collection, the *Poemi conviviali,* within the multivalenced gesture of 'turning backwards' and with a poststructuralist understanding of psychoanalysis. Specifically, I argue that this collection resonates with, and indeed figures poetically, Freud's essay 'Das Unheimliche'(1919).[15] Freud's introductory foray into dictionary definitions of *heimlich* demonstrates that this word potentially coincides in meaning with its opposite, *unheimlich.* As he notes, 'What interests us most in this long extract is to find that among its different shades of meaning the word "*heimlich*" exhibits one which is identical with its opposite, "*unheimlich*" ... on the one hand it means what is familiar and agreeable, and on the other, what is concealed and kept out of sight' (224–5). This insight provides the first intersection with Pascoli's poetic enterprise, namely, the gesture of locating the eerie, frightening, and uncanny not in foreign objects but nestled deep within the most familiar and intimate aspects of the self. In the *Poemi conviviali,* figures that represent the home, particularly Calypso, Helen, Myrrhine, and the image of the nest, embody this ambivalent, strange familiarity.

Freud then moves to analyses of both literary and experiential examples of the uncanny in an attempt to define the origins and 'common core' of this particular class of the frightening. His strategy, like Pascoli's, entails turning back to infantile thought processes, thought processes marked by ambivalence and the coexistence of logical contradictions. Freud posits initially that 'the uncanny is that class of the frightening which leads back to what is known of old and long familiar' (220), and later in the essay, more specifically, that 'an uncanny experience occurs either when infantile complexes which have been repressed are once more revived by some impression, or when primitive beliefs which have been surmounted seem once more to be confirmed,' qualifying this definition with the caveat that 'the distinction is often a hazy one' (249). The inescapable haziness that emerges in the search for the 'core' of the uncanny motivates the movement of Freud's essay. While the piece is punctuated (at least six times) by tentative definitions of the uncanny (such as the two cited above), none of these formulations remains adequate as the definitive definition. The essay moves from one example to the next, each one in some way not quite hitting the mark dead on, each one generating yet another example in a series of detours. The discussion ends rather abruptly, not coming to rest in any summation or conclusion, but rather referring the reader 'elsewhere.'[16] Freud's suggestive essay, then, demonstrates that the evocation of the uncanny is linked to the impossibility of locating definitively its source or origin.[17]

The first and most obvious occasion of turning back in Pascoli's collection emerges thematically as the decision to base all the poems on ancient texts (Homer, Plato, Hesiod, Apuleius, and other Greek and Roman writers). Although this retrieval of classical authors often entails a revival of their heroic characters (Achilles and Ulysses both appear in the poems, as does Alexander the Great), such illustrious figures appear not in their grand, heroic, conquering guise but in a humbled, even fragile state. While almost all of the poems in the collection illustrate this point, I here mention only the remarkable depiction of Achilles in 'La cetra d'Achille.' The poem is set the night before the hero's destined death, and he sits alone, while his comrades sleep, awaiting the dawn. The poem's emphasis on the sleep of all the comrades and on Achilles' knowledge of his own inevitable death recalls Christ's anguished night in the garden of Gethsemene and underscores the solitude of the protagonist. Achilles attempts to console himself through song, but even that 'intoxication' is denied him on this lonely eve, as a Theban bard arrives to take back his zither and reminds the hero that he himself has chosen this destiny. The poem ends with Achilles embracing the slave girl Briseis and lying down to await the morning. In the closing stanza, having relinquished the zither, Achilles stands and listens to his horses, and 'più lontano il pianto / delle Nereidi, e dentro i lor singhiozzi / sentì più trista, sì ma più sommessa, / la voce della sua cerulea madre' (lines 152–5) [to the more distant weeping / of the Nereides. Amid their sobbings

/ he heard, sadder, yes, but softer, / the voice of his cerulean mother].[18] The dominant tone of the poem is, precisely, 'triste' and 'sommesso.' The Homeric hero appears not in his militant, virile role as warrior but as sad, alone, almost Christlike in his expectation of death.

Also striking, along with the fragility and vulnerability of the ancient figures, is the number of *mothers* that appear in the poems. We encounter the mother of Memnon, who complains that Achilles has killed her son; Olympia, the mother of Alexandros, who daydreams about her absent son; Livia, the mother of Tiberius, who appears nursing the future emperor; the mother of Narcissus, who consoles her son over his deceased twin sister; Myrrhine, the courtesan, cast as a radically failed mother; the infinitely self-sacrificing mother of 'La madre'; and finally, in the closing poem of the collection, the Virgin Mother seen with the Christ child at his nativity. Thus, the turn back to classical antiquity carries with it a turn back to infancy as well.

We find this gesture and the ambiguities inherent in it forcefully dramatized in one of Pascoli's longest Italian lyric compositions, 'L'ultimo viaggio.'[19] This poem owes much thematic material to Homer's *Odyssey*, and belongs to the group of '*Odyssey* sequels' that includes Dante's *Inferno* XXVI, Tennyson's 'Ulysses,' and Arturo Graf's 'L'ultimo viaggio di Ulisse.' Graf, a contemporary of Pascoli, develops the story model found in Dante, especially in Ulysses' rallying speech to the men. Graf emphasizes the desire for novelty and greatness, as the hero sets out to discover 'un *altro* mondo / Assai *maggior* di questo nostro, e dove / Sono *incogniti* regni e genti *nuove*, / E *d'inaudite* cose e peregrine / Indicibil dovizia' (my emphases) [another world much greater than ours, and where there are unknown realms and strange peoples, and the unspeakable wealth of rare and unheard-of things]. Similarly, Tennyson's Ulysses assures his comrades ' 'Tis not too late to seek a newer world' (line 57). However, Pascoli's piece is closer in spirit to Wordsworth's above-mentioned immortality ode than to any of these fellow sequels. Whereas these other poems depict, whether with praise or blame, the desire of an older Ulysses to strike out on a new adventure, to push farther into the unknown and prove himself once again a hero, in Pascoli's piece Ulysses desires to leave Ithaca and *turn back*. He returns to the sea in order to go back over his past epic voyage and, through refinding Circe, the Cyclops, the Sirens, and Calypso, recapture his youth and rediscover himself. The image of the sea as an idealized point of origin and of visionary capability; the progressive and inevitable loss of that capability through time, represented spatially as travel inland away from the sea; and the desire to turn back to it are major points of contact between the Pascoli's epic and Wordsworth's ode. Wordsworth figures the above notions discursively, discussing the power of the imagination to bring back to us some remnants of our 'glorious' youth:

> Hence in a season of calm weather
>   Though inland far we be,
> Our Souls have sight of that immortal sea
>   Which brought us hither,
>   Can in a moment travel thither,
> And see the Children sport upon the shore,
> And hear the mighty waters rolling evermore. (lines 163–9)

Pascoli instead dramatizes these same themes in his account of Ulysses' final and fatal adventure at sea. Because of the poem's length and complexity, a brief descriptive summary will be useful before we turn to an analysis of it.

The *poema* is divided into twenty-four brief cantos, and as such structurally imitates the Homeric epic that it continues. The opening canto harks back to the eleventh book of the *Odyssey* and shows Ulysses fulfilling the prophecy given him by Tiresias in Hades. There, the prophet explains that he will not find peace until, having returned home and disposed of Penelope's suitors, he travels inland so far that he encounters a man who mistakes his oar for a shovel. When he encounters such a man, Tiresias directs, he must plant the oar and sacrifice to Poseidon. Pascoli depicts Ulysses on Ithaca carrying out the directives of the prophet, and indeed peace is subsequently established. We learn that the hero spends nine years in tranquility with his faithful wife, while Ithaca prospers.

Despite the peace and security of home and family, the hero feels himself essentially displaced. Pascoli creatively links the inaugural act of the poem – the planting of the ship's oar in the earth – with the hero himself, emphasizing his fundamental 'out of placeness' within his own home:

> E il Laertiade ora vivea solingo
> fuori del mare, come un vecchio remo
> scabro di salsa gromma, che piantato
> ungi avea delle salse aure nel suolo,
> e strettolo, ala, tra le glebe gravi. (V: lines 35–9)

[And the son of Laertes now lived,
lonely, outside the sea, like an old oar
scabrous with crusts of salt, which the hero
planted in the ground, far from the salt winds
of the sea, a wing buried in the earth. (1: 82)]

Like a fish – or 'oar' – out of water, Ulysses can never be fully 'at home,' and therefore, though surrounded by the comfort of his wife and the warm fire, his mind wanders in dreamlike states to his past life in the sea. The sparks that flicker up from the hearth become the constellations he would observe from his deck, and the crackling of the fire becomes the wave-tossed raft in the tempest.

Finally, Ulysses makes his move, sneaking out of his own home to the shore. He first encounters Femio, the bard, who sits listening to the sea in a shell. The hero argues for the merits of deeds over contemplation, and Femio accompanies him to the ship. The two find the ship prepared and the companions waiting on the shore. The party boards, singing songs of youth, and they set out. Significantly, the men insist upon their youth not in the register of 'men in their prime' but explicitly in the register of 'children': '"Apri, chè non siam vecchi ma fanciulli!" – Cantavano; e il lor canto era fanciullo, dei tempi andati' [' "Open! For we are not old men but youths!" They sang; and their song partook of childhood, of time gone by' (1: 110)]. Even more striking is the poignant and lengthy comparison Pascoli draws between Femio's zither, found on the ship, and a dead swallow. The men, in tending to the old instrument with loving care, behave as does the little child who attempts to heal the bird, and then both hopes and fears that it will fly away – hardly the image one might expect of burly, experience-hardened sailors:

> ed era a tutti, l'aurea cetra, a cuore,
> come a bambino infante un rondinotto
> morto, che così morto egli carezza
> lieve con dita inabili e gli parla,
> e teme e spera che gli prenda il volo.　　　　　(XIII: lines 34–8)

[and they cared for the golden zither
as a child cares for a small dead swallow:
though dead he pets it lightly with clumsy
fingers and he speaks to it fearing
and hoping that it will fly off. (1: 108)]

The touching metaphor of the 'rondinotto' recalls explicitly humbler poems from the earlier collections, poems such as 'X agosto' and 'In ritardo,' and in so doing distinguishes Pascoli's *poema* from the grandly heroic works of Tennyson and Graf. More importantly, the comparison elicits once again the Pascolian notion of the 'fanciullino,' and establishes the voyage as an attempt to recapture the 'fanciullino's' vision.

The second part of the poem, which recounts the voyage itself, is divided into three main quests. The companions land first on the island of Circe, where Ulysses pursues his 'dream of Love.' Next, they rediscover the land of Polyphemus, the Cyclops, where the hero attempts to recapture his 'dream of Glory.' Canto XXII rapidly narrates the ship's passing of many other places significant in the Homeric epic: the land of the lotus eaters, the giants, and Scylla and Charybdis, after which Ulysses guides the ship towards the Sirens, in his final quest in search of the 'Truth.' In each case, however, more is lost than found. The bard Femio dies on the island of Circe, after he and Ulysses fail to find the enchantress. The poem's comic figure, Iro, the beggar-turned-steward, decides to stay behind as a family servant in the cave of the Cyclops, now inhabited by a kindly shepherd family. Ultimately, in response to his desperate demand to know 'Who am I? Who was I?' Ulysses receives from the Sirens not an answer but death, as his ship crashes into the reefs. The poem concludes with the depiction of the hero's body washing up on the shores of the island of Calypso, who laments the death of her beloved.

The voyage reveals that what has been lost is a visionary, or more generally a psychical, capability rather than a physical one. The poem does not imply that the sailors' bodies are too old and weak to perform the feats of daring they once did, but rather that Ulysses can no longer see his surroundings as he once did. The characters who had figured so large in his past he discovers now to be merely figures, believed-in metaphors, similar to the way in which the hordes of 'Gog and Magog' believed that the sounds of the wind were Alexander's army (see the discussion of 'Gog and Magog' later in this chapter). To his dismay, Ulysses discovers that the roaring of the lions that guard Circe's home is nothing but the wind rustling through the leaves. The giant Cyclops who hurled the enormous stone at the escaping ship appears now as merely a volcano that sometimes rains rocks into the sea, and the seductive Sirens, this time maddeningly silent and aloof, are revealed to be two 'scogli' – reefs upon which the ship crashes. In short, the second voyage discloses the mundane natural phenomena that the young hero had perceived as personified, grand, and marvellous. The disillusionment of adult rationality strips these phenomena of their mythical qualities, just as the interlocutor of 'Siamo sette' cannot see the living siblings of the 'contadinella.'

Only Calypso, in the final canto, actually reappears. The sudden and moving appearance of this mythical character, following the loss of all the other figures, retrieves then, at the last moment, the marvellous vision of the hero. The naturalization of the mythical landscape that goes on in the previous cantos makes this sudden reappearance of a fantastic figure unexpected. Freud suggests that 'an uncanny experience occurs ... when primitive beliefs which have been surmounted seem once more to be confirmed' (249), and indeed the appearance of Calypso strikes the reader as uncanny – as a disquieting, and at the same time reassuring, return of an animistic world. The fact that the marvellous vision can return only at the moment of death suggests that the hero's death should be read not only as his punishment (as we clearly must read it in Dante) but also as a fulfilment, as the ultimate attainment of the quest.

As the logical fulfilment of his desire, Ulysses' death and the uncanny appearance of Calypso that accompanies it reveal the essential bifurcation of his desire: his yearning for the infinite, shown by his intrinsic dissatisfaction with the cosy security of the home, reveals itself ultimately as a yearning for the destruction of the self. Psychically realized as an infant, 'a time when the ego had not yet marked itself off sharply from the external world and from other people' ('The "Uncanny,"' 236), such a desire can now be fully reachieved only through death.

The poem prefigures this disintegration on a linguistic level: the proper names of the authors 'omero' and 'pascoli' each appear in the poem as common nouns, meaning 'shoulder' and 'fields.' This gesture suggests the dissolution from unique individuality into undifferentiated commonness. Indeed, this fading into commonality reverses the process of distillation described by Tennyson's Ulysses, who laments 'I am become a Name.' The unusual copulative here, which replaces the expected auxiliary 'have,' as well as the capitalization of the common noun 'name,' both forcefully assert the theme of a stable identity. Tennyson's Ulysses no longer does, creates, or acts but rather is trapped and defined by the immobility and abstraction of his name and reputation, a singular and fixed identity. Pascoli, instead, weaves his own name and that of his source text's author into the textual fabric of the poem, uncoupling these signifiers from their stable and singular designations. In so doing, he alerts the reader to the hero's desire to detach himself from his own Name. Pascoli, furthermore, permeates the poem with childlike metaphoric displacements among the words 'ala,' 'pala,' and 'remo' (wing, shovel, and oar), and calls our attention to these words by using them as canto titles. Such shifting occurs, for example, when we are told that the birds 'andavano, e coi remi battean l'aria' ['flew on, their wings, like oars, beat the air' (1: 76)]; and again when Ulysses, holding his oar at his shoulders, replies to the land-bound man who mistook it for a shovel, exclaiming, 'Uomo terrestre ala! non pala!' ['Land-bound man, this is a winged oar, not a swingle!' (1: 70)]. The poem carries these displacements of discrete signifiers further by presenting imaginative metaphoric exchanges among the activities they imply: sailing, ploughing, and flying. Again, the interchangeability, here ranging from the microcosmic (the tools used) to the macrocosmic (the elements of air, earth, and water they imply), bespeaks a disintegration of clear-cut distinctions, the very distinctions necessary to construct identities.

The specific metaphors evoke Dante's Ulysses, who announces to the pilgrim, describing his last voyage, 'de' remi facemmo ali al folle volo' (*Inferno* XXVI: 125) ['of our / oars we made wings for the mad flight' (trans. Durling, 405)]. Figuratively turning their oars into 'wings,' then, the sailors set out on a mad flight. Repeating the Dantean metaphors, Pascoli reminds us of the folly of this quest. Indeed, Ulysses' death can be seen, as in Dante, as a kind of punishment, though not as a punishment for the hubristic search for too much knowledge or for his having misled his companions through a perverted use of rhetoric. In Pascoli's rendition, the transgressive nature of the turn backward is implied by the necessity for the hero to 'slip away' to the ship, sneaking out of his own home and lying twice to conceal his intentions. A comparison with the parallel scene from Graf's poem underscores the illicit nature of the Pascolian departure. Graf depicts a ceremonious leave-taking in which Ulysses officially confers authority on his son, Telemachus, and reassures the faithful Penelope that his great deeds will once again bring her honour. For Graf, Ulysses remains, even in departure, kingly, 'Maestro, Duce, *Padre*' (my emphasis), as his men hail him, a lawgiver and embodiment of authority. Pascoli, instead, emphasizes Ulysses as lawbreaker, as embodiment of desire. In his quest for self-dissolution and complete abdication of paternal responsibilities, he seeks to enact a return of the maternal. Pascoli presents the hero's regressive journey as simultaneously sympathetic and illicit, as both admirable and suspect. In this way, the poem functions according to the structure of the Freudian 'compromise formation.'[20]

In this sense, the sea figures as an archetypal image of the womb, and the voyage becomes a true return home.[21] Such a reading is linguistically supported by the double use of the word 'poppa,' which appears both as a reference to the part of the ship in which Ulysses undertakes his 'backward' voyage and as a reference to the breast of the shepherd's wife who is nursing her baby in the cave of the 'Cyclops.' Furthermore, the poem is structured around units of time that appear in groups of nine. Ulysses remains in Ithaca with Penelope for nine years before setting out to sea again. The ship sails in calm weather for nine days before a storm rises up, then continues sailing for another nine days before landing at Circe's shores. Finally, the sea carries the hero's dead body for yet another nine days before delivering it onto Calypso's island. If Pascoli's poem were dramatizing a Christian theme, the 'nines' could be read in a Trinitarian mode (as one sees in Dante's treatment of Beatrice), where nine is regarded as the perfect number, being three times three and thus a triple evocation of the Holy Trinity. However, nothing else in this work suggests an interpretation along these lines. Looking more closely we see that not only is the number itself repeated, it is, in fact, part of a repeated structure: a time period of stasis measured in nine units (days, years) followed by a radical change of condition. The structure as a whole evokes the nine months of gestation in the womb that precede the cataclysm of birth. Thus, Ulysses' initial setting out from Ithaca can, I believe, be seen as a kind of 'rebirth' or, more precisely, a birth in reverse, a turning back to the oceanic wholeness of the womb. But this illicit voyage is truly a reversal of birth and thus can deliver only death, culminating in the uncanny appearance of Calypso as the desired and dreaded end.

Pascoli develops this theme in 'Antìclo,' where Helen figures, as Calypso does in 'L'ultimo viaggio,' as the uncanny marker of the ambivalent desire for home.[22] His source for the poem is found in book four of the *Odyssey*, where Menelaus, in the presence of Telemachus, recounts a scene from the final moments of the war to Helen. The soldiers were inside the 'hollow horse,' he explains,

> when all of a sudden, you came by – I dare say
> drawn by some superhuman
> power that planned an exploit for the Trojans;
>
> Three times you walked around it, patting it everywhere,

> and called by name the flower of our fighters,
> making your voice sound like their wives, calling.
> Diomedes and I crouched in the center
> along with Odysseus; we could hear you plainly;
> and listening, we two were swept
> by waves of longing – to reply, or go.
> Odysseus fought us down, despite our craving,
> and all the Akhaians kept their lips shut tight,
> all but Antiklos. Desire moved his throat
> to hail you, but Odysseus' great hands clamped
> over his jaws, and held. So he saved us all,
> till Pallas Athena led you away at last. (61)

Pascoli opens his poem with the image that closes the Homeric account, that of Odysseus' hand preventing Antìclo's reply to Helen. In Pascoli's version, the image is far more violent: Odysseus does not merely cover his comrade's 'jaws' with his hands, but thrusts his fist into Antìclo's mouth:

> E con un urlo rispondeva Antìclo,
> dentro il cavallo, a quell'aerea voce;
> se a lui la bocca non empìa col pugno
> Odisseo, pronto, gli altri eroi salvando; (lines 1–4)

> [In the horse would have cried out Anticlus
> responding to that aerial voice,
> had not Odysseus, promptly, stopped his mouth
> with a fist, saving the other heroes; (1: 46)]

This powerful mouth imagery with which the poem opens resurfaces at the poem's conclusion, where Antìclo, less violently than Odysseus but with equal emotional 'punch' for the reader, silences Helen's 'rosea bocca.' In the seven strophes between the silencing of mouths that begins and ends the poem, Pascoli details the battle in Troy, during which Antìclo, who cannot forget the siren-like voice, is mortally wounded. The poem, particularly in the third strophe, contrasts the peacefulness, fecundity, and wholeness of home (Greece for Antìclo) with the divisiveness and violence of the war in a foreign land (Troy). Throughout, voice is the sign of presence: Antìclo's voice, had it been heard responding to

Helen, would have betrayed the Greeks' presence in the horse. Helen's voice restores the presence of the distant wives, 'la sua donna lontana,' as Pascoli so vividly describes. But in Pascoli's re-elaboration of the myth, we see a revision of the notion of the voice just at the jolting punch line of the poem. We are not surprised when the dying warrior asks to hear his wife's voice through Helen's mouth. But when she actually appears, what he demands is silence. Here, the silence is not absence but a higher presence – the presence of the absolute that overrides the desire for the particular manifestation of love and beauty with which each warrior is familiar in his earthly exile. The refrain, which repeats three times in the course of the poem, preceding the appearance of Helen to the dying Antìclo, refers to the unique power the voice of each love has over the hearts of the soldiers: 'parli la voce dolce più che niuna / come ad ognuno suona al cuor sol una'(lines 1●●–1) ['as only the sweetest voice can speak, as only one voice answers another's heart' (1: 52)]. The refrain underscores the intimate unity between a husband and wife, and the heavy assonance of the lines, made up almost entirely of 'o's and 'u's,' reinforces the idea of a harmony between the couples. However, the 'sol una' of these undulating lines is replaced, finally, by the 'te sola' with which Antìclo indicates his ultimate desire for Helen alone. Pascoli figures a kind of reversal in which the one woman who seemed to be mimicking the real voices of the various wives turns out to be the prototype of which the others are merely simulacra.

However, this ideal of love and beauty is revealed in its full presence to Antìclo only at the moment of his death. Indeed, as Odysseus warns, Helen *is* death: 'Helena! Helena! è la Morte, infante!' (line 41) he desperately exclaims, thus succinctly juxtaposing the two endpoints of life – death and infancy – both of which are marked by a lack of speech, much as the poem itself is born and dies, opens and concludes, in acts of silencing. But both moments are indeed a fullness, rather than a lack, of what is desired by speech, which, through the supplanted voices of the wives, is itself revealed to be a simulacrum. The double figure of Helen, as feared spectre or harbinger of death and at the same time as angelic incarnation of absolute love and beauty, bespeaks yet again the bifurcation at the heart of the homely: the uncanny, (un)homely voice tempts with the promise of oceanic wholeness and simultaneously threatens the dissolution of the self.[23]

The ambivalent role of Calypso and Helen is played by the courtesan Myrrhine in 'L'etèra,' a poem that clearly displays strong influences from the *scapigliatura*, and particularly from Boito's 'Lezione d'anatomia.'[24] Here, Pascoli powerfully dramatizes the association between the life-giving mother and the infant's destruction.

'L'etèra' appears as one of three poems dedicated to the theme of justice in the *Poemi conviviali*. In it, Pascoli dramatizes certain passages from Plato's *Phaedo* in which Socrates, awaiting his own death, describes the fate of souls in the afterworld. Socrates explains that, upon the body's death, each soul is led by a guardian spirit to the appropriate place, but that 'the soul that is passionately attached to the body ... hovers around it and the visible world for a long time.' When such a soul finally arrives in the afterworld, it is shunned by others and 'wanders alone completely at a loss ... until forcibly led to its proper dwelling place' (147). Such is the fate of Myrrhine: the poem opens with the announcement of her death. But, as others come to visit her final resting place, we learn that her spirit has resisted the guide who was to lead her, for she is unwilling to leave her beloved body. When she finally does progress to the beyond, no one will show her the proper path among the many crossroads, and indeed even her own former lover, now dead himself and coming face to face with her, does not recognize her.

Pascoli departs from the philosophic model by including an uncanny scene that lends his poem particular force:

Vide lì, tra gli asfodeli e i narcissi
starsene, informi tra la vita e il nulla
ombre ancor più dell'ombre esili, i figli
suoi, che non volle. E nelle mani esangui
aveano i fiori delle ree cicute,
avean dell'empia segala le spighe
per lor trastullo. E tra la morte ancora
erano, e il nulla, presso il limitare.
E venne a loro Myrrhine; e gl'infanti
lattei, rugosi, lei vedendo, un grido
diedero, smorto e gracile, e gettando
i tristi fiori, corsero coi guizzi,
via, delle gambe e delle lunghe braccia
pendule e flosce; come nella strada
molle di pioggia, al risonar d'un passo
fuggono ranchi ranchi i piccolini
di qualche bodda ...   (lines 138–54)

[She saw, standing there among the asphodels
and the narcissi, the unborn children
she had refused, shadows more thin than shade,
formless, 'twixt life and nought. Their bloodless hands
held the flowers of the baleful hemlocks,
held the spikes of the poisonous rye:
these were their toys. And they were still
'twixt death and nought, there, on the threshold.
To them came Myrrhine. On seeing her
the infants, milk-pale and wrinkled, let out
a dull, languid scream, threw away
the gloomy flowers and off they ran,
hopping on their legs, their long arms,
drooping and limp. As when, at the sound
of footfalls on a rain soaked way,
hobble and wobble off the little ones
of a toad. (2: 35, 37)]

The effectiveness of these verses derives not only from Pascoli's skilful description; specifically, his choice of adjectives, the enjambement between 'figli' and 'suoi,' and the powerful metaphor of the frog on the muddy road. Its strength, I submit, primarily derives from its evocation of the seemingly paradoxical repressed fear of the mother, specifically the memory of the 'infant' state: the pre-linguistic moment when the self, like the alienated children of the courtesan, was 'unformed.' The references to various liquids – blood, milk, and mud – underscore the fluidity of the infants' liminal status, three times expressed as 'between life and nothingness,' 'between death and nothingness,' and 'near the threshold.' The morbidity of the scene is unexpected and shocking. Its strangeness, however, proves to be at the same time essentially familiar, in two senses of the term: that is, it dramatizes a family relationship, and it evokes something repressed and therefore already known.

This strange familiarity elicited by Pascoli helps to bring home the poem's moral lesson. For Plato, the 'sin' that is punished in this way is one of materialism: of clinging too closely to the things of the earth rather than adopting a philosophical outlook. In the poem based on the dialogue, Myrrhine's sin is more specifically one of narcissism: she is overly infatuated with her own 'bel fiore di corpo,' overly enamoured not just of the material world in general but of her own body. To emphasize this, the narcissus flower itself is named in these lines as an infernal toy of the children. Further, Pascoli evokes Ovid's Narcissus in his depiction of the courtesan's spirit looming silently behind her lover, Eveno.[25] As he opens her coffin to admire her beauty one last time, Myrrhine peers over his shoulder to gaze upon her own body.

This same image provides an instance of the kind of doubling analysed by Freud in 'The "Uncanny."' Drawing on the earlier analyses of Otto Rank, Freud includes among examples of the double 'the belief in the soul,' and argues that 'the "double" was originally an insurance against the destruction of the ego ... Such ideas, however, have sprung from the soil of unbounded self-love, from the primary narcissism which dominates the mind of the child and of primitive man. But when this stage has been surmounted, the "double" reverses its aspect. From having been an assurance of immortality, it becomes the uncanny harbinger of death' (235). For Freud, the construction of the double seeks to guarantee stability and presence. However, the necessity of this defence strategy reveals the subject's instability and self-difference. Pascoli's poem dramatizes the subject's failed strategies to preserve a pristine identity, and as such the poem may be read as a mythical rendering of Freud's essay. The uncanny fruits of Myrrhine's narcissicism return to haunt her.

Her 'unbounded self-love' leads Myrrhine to 'refuse' her children: to deny the existence of an other. From the perspective of the mother, the aborted, 'spurned' ('i cacciati / prima d'uscire a domandar pietà' ['children ... spurned ere coming forth to implore for love' (2: 37)]) children are 'abject' in the sense developed by Kristeva. While the filth, mud, and other repulsive elements of the description offered by Pascoli contribute to the sense of the infants' abjection, it is in their having been expelled, 'cacciati,' in order that the courtesan might maintain her stable sense of self that the aborted children are truly 'ab-ject.' Kristeva writes, 'It is ... not the lack of cleanliness or health that causes abjection but what disturbs identity, system, order. What does not respect borders, positions, rules' (*Powers* 4). The fluid and liminal qualities of the infants pointed out above underscore their abject role. As Kristeva continues, 'abjection ... is a precondition of narcissism ... The more or less beautiful image in which I behold or recognize myself rests upon an abjection that sunders it as soon as repression, the constant watchman, is relaxed' (13). Kristeva's words recall precisely the image of Myrrhine's spirit gazing upon her 'beautiful flower of a body,' a body whose beauty she preserved by refusing her pregnancy.

Pascoli, then, brilliantly and shockingly stages a confrontation between subject and abject, imagining this confrontation as an otherworldly punishment for that subject's narcissism. Her self-centredness leads to a decentring of the self, seen first in her uncanny doubling, and finally in her punishment of placelessness. In his account of the courtesan's punishment, Pascoli departs from the Platonic dialogue: where Plato's Socrates asserts that the recalcitrant soul will eventually be brought to its proper place, Pascoli gives no indication that Myrrhine will ever cease wandering.

The home surfaces as the last image of the poem: the children she refused in life flee from her to the protection of a house guarded by barking dogs. Myrrhine is locked out of the house, and this 'unhomely' mother is condemned to roam homelessly in the 'immense obscurity.' Thus the poem exorcises the spectre of the threatening mother – as though the terror of the self's intrauterine dissolution were transferred onto the mother herself and made a product of her agency.

The monstrosity of the mother appears in a more cosmic if also more metaphorical guise in the striking and apocalyptic 'Gog and Magog.' The penultimate poem of the collection, though one of the earliest to be composed, depicts 'motherhood' in the metaphorical sense of creativity and the 'mother tongue.' It is not surprising that the recurrent image of the nest makes its most singular and, I think, most uncanny appearance here, where sources of creativity are most overtly implicated with forces of destruction.

Pascoli drew the inspiration for this poem from the philological study of his colleague Arturo Graf, who traced the origins and diffusion of the legend and published his findings as the appendix to his study *Roma nella memoria e nelle immaginazioni del medio evo*. Various elements of the story derive from the Bible, particularly from Genesis, Numbers, Deuteronomy, Ezekiel, and Revelation. In Ezekiel, Gog (an individual) is the King of Magog (the people) and a threat to Israel, while in Revelation, it is prophesied that the peoples of Gog and Magog will attack the city of the saints but will be conquered and cast into the pool of fire. The Koran speaks of Gog and Magog as doing corruption in the earth, and thus Dhool Karnain builds a rampart to separate them from the righteous. Other representations appear in the *Romances of Alexander* and in Giovanni Villani's *Chronicles* of 1308.

According to Graf, the figures of Gog and Magog, though taking on various characteristics in different permutations of the legend, have always been portrayed as a serious threat to 'civilized' humanity, and their feared escape has been apocalyptic in tenor. (In Pascoli's version, the use of Dantesque *terza rima* in some passages contributes to the apocalyptic tone.) In one account recorded by Graf, we read that 'Gog e Magog sono use cibarsi di topi, di serpenti, e di altri animali immondi, di feti abortive, o non ancora formati nell'alvo materno, e non sepelliscono i morti, ma li divorano' (771–2). ['Gog and Magog are accustomed to eating mice, snakes, and other filthy animals, as well as aborted fetuses or those not yet formed in the maternal womb, and they do not bury their dead but eat them instead (my translation)]. This description codes the threat to humanity not merely in military terms – the horde as a conquering army – but in the more fundamental terms of self-representation: the hordes break the basic taboos upon which civilization depends and around which humanity defines itself. They not only fail to marginalize and expunge what Kristeva designates as the 'abject,' but indeed consume and incorporate it.

Monstrous and threatening, closed in and controlled by the heroic efforts of civilizing forces, the peoples of Gog and Magog may stand for transgressive sexual desires that would threaten the stability of civilization were they to be released and given free rein. However, I do not see any evidence in the poem to link them exclusively with a specifically sexual form of 'monstrosity.' Gog and Magog may just as easily represent any repressed social group (a feared and exploited foreign culture, a proletarian class, women in patriarchal cultures) that comes to realize its oppression and mobilizes itself for retribution. Rather than attempting to isolate in a deterministic way a single allegorical significance, I would instead observe that the persistence and proliferation of the legend through time and space bespeak its ability to accommodate multiple interpretations. The longevity and adaptability of the legend suggest that it articulates fundamental fears and desires. The specific contents can be (and were) filled in by the culture choosing to interpret it. Graf points out that the hordes were often identified with different foreign races at different times: St Jerome, for example, associated them with the Huns. But the form – the story of the return of the repressed – had a lasting hold on the imaginations of many peoples. It is telling to note that the English translators of Pascoli's version use the word 'repressed' (line 7) to describe the hordes, though that particular word does not appear in the Italian original (*Conviviali*, 2: 133).

In Pascoli's version, the two peoples of Gog and Magog have been enclosed within a valley of the Caucasus behind an enormous door constructed by Alexander the Great. Although generations have passed, Alexander still apparently keeps watch over the door and at times is even heard festively dining with his men. Eventually, however, the stratagem is discovered: there is no army standing guard but merely bell-like constructions through which the wind blows to simulate the sounds of the conquerors. Undeceived at last, the hordes break down the bronze door and prepare to emerge from their long captivity. The giants with black tongues and the dwarfs with moving ears (and we should note the childlike, fabulistic quality in these descriptions) gaze hungrily on the world that is now 'their bread.'

Pascoli maintains the dichotomies established by many of the source texts, which distinguish clearly between good and evil, chosen people and enemy, God and Satan. The topology of the poem, for example, suggests a clear hierarchy: Alexander is 'lassù' (up on the mountaintop), while the horde is 'laggiù' (down in the valley). Furthermore, Alexander is depicted as eternal and unchanging. In stanza VII, for example, Alexander's feast, the 'convito,' is made to rhyme with 'infinito.' More explicitly, the third stanza underscores that he has remained on the mountain while generations of Gog and Magog have come and gone:

V'era il Bicorne ... E gli ultimi che, infanti,
aveano udito il gran maglio cadere
su le chiavarde, erano grigi vecchi;

e non partiva ... E i figli lor, gigantic
dagli occhi fiammei, dalle lingue nere,
o nanni irsuti dai mobili orecchi,

erano morti; e d'ognun d'essi, i mille
erano nati, quante le faville
da un tizzo: ma il Bicore era lassù.

[There, was the Two-horned ... The last ones to hear
when infants, the huge maul fall upon
the bolts, were now grey old people;

nor was He leaving ... And their children,
giants with flaming eyes and with black tongues,
or hirsute dwarfs with moving ears,

were dead; and from each of them a thousand
were born, as many as the sparks
from a brand: but the Two-horned remained there. (2: 112–5)]

Pascoli's fantastic image of each female bearing a thousand offspring derives from Graf's citation of a source text: 'Ciascuna femmina partorisce mille figliuoli' (779–80) [each female gives birth to a thousand little children (my translation)] and provides an image of uncontrollable fertility and exponential growth. The horde is thus associated with multiplicity and mutability, while Alexander signifies stability and singularity. (This fear of uncontrollable fecundity resonates with the image of the multiplicity of modern languages spawning from Latin, the single, stable, mother language, articulated in the essay on Vitrioli.) Finally, the poem associates Alexander with cultured refinement while the hordes embody subhuman barbarism. The winds carry the sounds of the elegant banquet and sophisticated musical instruments enjoyed by Alexander and his men, while the hordes are repeatedly compared to or associated with animals such as donkeys, hyenas, dogs, and bison. Significantly, Pascoli uses the word 'convito,' a term that not only carries the weighty philosophical connotations of Plato's *Symposium* and Dante's *Convivio*, but more immediately pays homage to the journal – *Il Convito* – in which the first version of this poem appeared in 1895. The mission of this literary periodical, to which d'Annunzio was a regular contributor, was to promote high culture in fin-de-siècle Italy. The association thus reinforces Alexander's role in the poem as representing Western culture and implicates Pascoli's own literary context within the economy of the poem.

Pascoli, however, does not simply import and maintain these distinctions – high versus low, eternal versus transient, culture versus barbarism – but rather complicates and undermines them. The opening stanza immediately elicits the reader's sympathy for the hordes by depicting them as exploited beasts of burden, who come and go pulling their carts in vain with only the mountains to witness their cries of pain. The chiasmus of line two along with the imperfect tense of the verbs underscore the futile, repetitive nature of their lives: 'in vano andava e ritornava in vano.' More generally, Pascoli's overall narrative strategy marks a radical departure from the tradition of the source texts: the tale is told from the monsters' point of view. The races of Gog and Magog are described in detail, both their physical characteristics and their daily activities. They are even 'quoted' directly when individuals speak, describing their own perception of their situation. This strategy humanizes Gog and Magog and at the same time casts Alexander as the shadowy figure, as the unknown object of speculation, fear, wonder, and dim memory-become-legend.

Most powerfully, Gog and Magog emerge, I believe, as the poet-figures in the text. (It is not a random choice on Pascoli's part, I think, to emphasize the tongues and ears of the monsters – the organs of speaking and hearing.) In the final stanza, the monsters, and the readers, discover that all the while it has been Gog and Magog's own imagination that has constructed the figure of Alexander. In fact, all the rich detail we as readers have been offered about Alexander in the course of the poem, including the story of the fountain of youth that explains his longevity, the list of specific instruments at the banquet, and even the account of the particular kinds of leaves (ivy and acanthus) that wreathe his head, have been woven from the monsters' creativity with the raw material of only a few echoing sounds carried by the wind. This ability to construct fantastic figures from simple natural phenomena recalls the young Ulysses from 'L'ultimo viaggio.' Ulysses' visionary capacity, which embodied the ability of the *fanciullino*-poet to see the everyday world with wonder, reappears in the capacity demonstrated by Gog and Magog in their imaginative construction of the wonderful and powerful Alexander. Ultimately, then, the poem suggests an association between the threatening, monstrous forces personified by Gog and Magog and the visionary, childlike nature of poetry.

This association of the poetic and primitive with the threatening and abject questions the notion of a simple desired regression to the safety of infancy. In fact, the image of the nest appears at the most crucial point of this poem. After three years of silence from the mountain, the horde becomes convinced that the armies have left. Mustering the courage to investigate, they discover the bell-like constructions built to deceive them. Inside one, blocking the wind, they find a filthy owl's nest: 'un nido immondo riempiva il vuoto.' Here, the nest is hardly the safe, protective home, or the desired point of origin and fulfilment. Rather, it is a stand-in, which imperfectly fills up the void of what was thought to be the omnipotent seat of authority. Earlier in the poem, a dwarf had proclaimed of Zul-Karnaien (Alexander), 'è sempre ciò che fu' ['he is always what he was'], an almost religious declaration of the eternal, self-identical nature of the godlike figure. The appearance of the nest in his place marks the absence of this guarantor of order and stability. At this moment of discovery, Gog and Magog break down the door and dramatize a threatening return of the repressed.

The linguistic nature of the poem dramatizes this as well: the untranslated Arabic names, the heavy use of onomatopoeia, and the emphasis on evocative and often animalistic sounds (*squillo, grido, urlo, nitrir, tintinno*, etc.) perforate the logical narrative composed in Italian and structured by the poem's metre and rhymes. The space within the mountains and the space of the poem itself become an echo chamber of vibrating and vibrant sounds that do not conform to the dominant linguistic code but that are nevertheless structured and interpreted by that code. The strength of this daring poem lies in its shift from an external, physical fear to the anxiety attendant upon the destabilization of identity. Redeploying the dichotomy dramatized in 'We Are Seven,' Pascoli discloses the nature of poetry as a precarious compromise formation between the rational, repressive powers of the civilized adult and the creative, transgressive capacities symbolized by the 'child.'

The universality of the infant's cry, which cannot be meaningfully articulated, the turn to the singularity and stability of Latin at the risk of unintelligibility and silence, Ulysses' heroic return voyage that ends in shipwreck, the privileging of a childlike vision that verges on the irrational and bestial, and the deployment of maternal imagery that offers both comfort and death all strive to recuperate the fluid and fleeting moment before, as Freud writes, the 'ego was clearly demarcated' from its surroundings. At the same time, each of these poetic gestures movingly announces its impossibility. As a dramatization of the retrieval of an imaginary, lost wholeness, the *Poemi conviviali*, like 'Das Unheimliche,' stages a (necessarily) failed yet fertile recuperation of this ambivalent and hazy point of origin.

3 Positioning Pascoli in the Fin de Siècle: The Case of Infanticide

Difficilmente il cuore di una madre è cattivo; è la solo maternità che ha divinizzato la donna. [With great difficulty is a mother's heart evil; it is only motherhood that has made woman divine.]

I.U. Tarchetti, *Paolina*, 149

La maternità è – quasi diremmo – essa stessa un vaccino morale contro il delitto e il male. [Motherhood is – we could almost say – itself a moral vaccine against crime and evil.]

Lombroso, *La donna*, 499

In the first chapter, I explored the ways in which the *scapigliatura* writers often bring two divergent epistemological perspectives into direct confrontation with each other. Typically, these writers deploy an uncanny image (the bleeding neck of the black bishop), moment (the discovery of the fetus in the cadaver's womb), or character (Fosca) as an expression of the 'real' that uncouples both competing perspectives and escapes comprehension by either mode of discourse. The positivism of anatomists and other scientists and the heightened romanticism of artists and poets were inscribed in the literature of the *scapigliati*, given voice through their central characters, and critiqued in their confrontation with each other and with the uncanny phenomena they attempted to unmask.

A similar dynamic can be located in the larger cultural discourse of fin-de-siècle Italy. This chapter explores the historical phenomenon of infanticide and examines a range of Italian texts that sought to describe, understand, or exploit it. In the writings I discuss in this chapter, the figure of the infanticide – particularly of the mother who kills her own child – becomes an uncanny apparition, a kind of unthinkable, incomprehensible spectre that encompasses within herself seemingly mutually exclusive categories: life-giving and murderous, protective and threatening, angelic and fiendish. The image of the mother-infanticide, in short, occupied the position of the uncanny and elicited uneasy attempts by different epistemologies to describe and explain it. Pascoli's narration, I will show, is unique in its treatment of this topic. Rather than striving to close the issue, Pascoli's story sets in motion the uncanniness of this figure and, in so doing, questions the stability and purity of origins.

Europe in the late nineteenth century did, in fact, see an appallingly high rate of infanticide, the economic and social factors of which have been studied by recent historians whose analyses I briefly summarize below. This acutely disruptive phenomenon clearly put into question the culturally diffuse and deeply ingrained notion of the sanctity of motherhood – an ideal personified by the Virgin, called a 'sacro titolo' by Silvio Pellico, and expressed in the epigrams to this chapter.[1] Invernizio registers the crisis of reason engendered by infanticides with the terms 'madre snaturata' and 'enigma veramente inesplicabile.'[2] The translation of infanticide, and infanticides, into written, public discourse took several forms, repeating the dichotomies fictionalized by the *scapigliati*. Specifically, practitioners of both positivism and late romanticism engaged the figure of the infanticide in their writings.[3]

The positivist school of criminal anthropology sought to understand and account for this deviant behaviour through the studies of its founding figure, Cesare Lombroso. By measuring cranial capacity and other physiological features, Lombroso sought to define the type of woman who could become a criminal. Infanticide was among the offences committed by the subjects observed. His monumental 1893 study, *La donna delinquente, la prostituta, e la donna normale*, presented the fruits of his research, grounded in anthropometry and the identification of physical anomalies. The influence of Lombroso's methodology and theories was not limited to the scientific community. Both popular fiction and belles-lettres engaged Lombroso's ideas in creative and provocative ways. For example, the Sicilian writer Luigi Capuana dedicated a 'little volume' of two short stories to Lombroso in 1906, prefacing the book with a letter to his 'illustrious friend.' One of the stories, 'Un vampiro,' stages once again the typical confrontation of sensitive artist and rational scientist as they attempt to come to terms with the ghost that is slowly killing the artist's newborn baby.

The popular fiction of Carolina Invernizio also shows an engagement with Lombrosian concerns. In the tale 'Razza maledetta' ('Cursed Race'), for example, the protagonist's monstrous physical deformities seem to correlate with his act of murder.[4] The story both suggests and questions a causal link between physical deformity and moral depravity. The colourful fiction of Invernizio – in *rosa* (romantic stories), *giallo* (detective stories), and *nero* (tales of Gothic horror) – reached a large readership, mostly via the form of the *romanzo d'appendice*. The popular Invernizio took up the theme of infanticide twice, penning both an Italian and a Piemontese version of the story of a poor seamstress who kills her newborn. *Ij delit d'na bela fia* (the crimes of a beautiful young woman: in instalments from September 1889 to February 1890), written in Piemontese, and *Storia d'una sartina* (story of a little seamstress: 1892), in Italian, offer the infanticide as protagonist in emotionally charged, decadent tales of betrayal, jealousy, and horror.[5]

In the arena of belles-lettres, the theme of infanticide found expression in the work of Gabriele d'Annunzio, Italy's most celebrated and internationally recognized writer of the day. In d'Annunzio's novel *L'innocente* (1892, later rendered in film by Luchino Visconti), the protagonist and decadent hero, Tullio, exposes his wife's baby ('the innocent' of the title) to the elements to precipitate his death. In this tale, presented as a confessional in the first person, the murderer is not the biological mother but rather the man whose family name and reputation are threatened by the fruit of his wife's infidelity. D'Annunzio's contribution registers and explores the anxiety concerning paternal origins attached to the theme of infanticide.

Although they suffer from some critical neglect in comparison with his poetry, the short stories of Giovanni Pascoli hold particular interest in articulating his literary intervention within the larger cultural discourses I am describing. His 'Il ceppo' ('The Yule Log': 1 January 1897) recounts the murder of the infant, Cecchino, on the night of his birth by his mother, Marietta. Rather than attempt to explain and rationalize this crime, or to sensationalize it for heightened emotional effect and entertainment, Pascoli opens up the figure of the infanticide precisely in its uncanniness, dramatizing its irreducible contradictions. He translates this figure, one that had such weighty cultural relevance, into an exploration of originary moments. The infanticide for Pascoli does not embody a freakish anomaly to be either rationalized or voyeuristically enjoyed; rather, it becomes a powerful deconstruction of the myth of pure origins.

The constellation of literature surrounding the theme of infanticide reveals preoccupations with origins. Specifically, we can witness the desire to assert and maintain the 'purity' of origins in various guises. For example, Mary Gibson discusses Lombroso's efforts to portray the methods of criminal anthropology as his own original contribution to the field. She notes that '[a]ccording to Lombroso, the central idea for his life work in criminology came to him in 1871 in a literal flash of light while doing an autopsy on the body of Giuseppe Villella, a notorious brigand ... Despite Lombroso's perpetuation of the myth that criminal anthropology sprang fully formed from the skull of Villella, he owed debts to both earlier and contemporary thinkers.'[6] In short, Lombroso sought to assert the purity of his metaphorical paternity in regard to this intellectual creation. In a similar way, d'Annunzio's protagonist Tullio suffers tormenting anxieties over the paternal origins of his wife's illegitimate child, Raimondo. Though Giuliana never reveals the name of her adulterous lover, Tullio remains convinced that the culprit is the dandyish author Filippo Arborio, whose surname suggests the role of natural roots and family trees. The child contaminates not only his blood line but the purity of his redemptive reunification with the idealized Giuliana as well, and thus must be eliminated.

The popular Invernizio exploits the conventions of Gothic literature in her treatment of this theme. The author lingers over the account of the murder, writing 'I lineamenti di Giselda si contrassero con un'espressione infernale ... Con una mano aferrò attraverso il corpo la sua creaturina, coll'altra la cinse per il collo ... La sua creatura aveva mandato un altro lievissimo gemito, un lamento indefinabile, ed ella continuava a stringerla per il collo. La sciagurata stava dunque per compiere uno dei delitti più orribile, che abbiano spaventato l'umanità. Uccideva la sua creatura, il sangue suo!' (14–15) [Giselda's features contracted with an infernal expression ... With one hand she grasped her child around its body, with the other she clutched its neck. Her child had managed another fragile whimper, an indefinable lament, and she continued to squeeze its neck. The wicked woman was, then, about to commit one of the most horrible crimes that have ever shocked humanity. She was killing her child, blood of her blood!]. The following morning, she awakes to find the baby's ice-cold, bloody corpse, and her own hands covered in blood. She wraps the body in a towel and leaves it in her bedroom drawer all day, waiting for the opportunity to dispose of it. At midnight, during a storm, she sneaks out of the house and throws the bundle into the Arno, where she is terrified by a man's shadow. Initially, the reader is left free to assume that Giselda's guilt-induced paranoia has imagined this shadowy figure, who pursues her (as Poe's protagonist in 'The Tell-Tale Heart' is convinced that he hears the beating heart of his victim). However, we later learn that indeed there was a witness, and Giselda is ultimately convicted and sentenced to three years in prison.

Here, as in d'Annunzio's novel, the crime of infanticide enacts a kind of purgation. The seamstress Giselda strangles her own 'creaturina' immediately after her birth in part to purify herself of the stain of her lover. Confronting Gerardo years after the crime, she exclaims, 'vostra figlia doveva avere del sangue vostro nelle vene, e l'uccisi' (111) [your daughter had your blood in her veins, and I killed her]. The tale implies that Giselda's crime was motivated at least partially by a desire for revenge against the man who had seduced and abandoned her (though this malicious agenda is not revealed until the end of the novel, after we have been won over to sympathy for the protagonist). More substantially, the novel dramatizes the complete destruction wrought by the transgression of class boundaries: when Count Gerardo made love to the poor Florentine seamstress, the two engendered the doomed child whose blood illicitly fused that of the aristocracy and the working class, and who therefore had to be destroyed. The novel implies that this class contamination was so threatening as to require even greater expiation: by the end of the story, all the characters involved – Giselda, Gerardo, Gerardo's innocent fiancée, Amalia, and both Giselda's parents – are dead by murder, suicide, or grief.

The most fascinating aspect of this novel is how Invernizio stages the dramatic clash of aristocracy and proletariat for the enjoyment of a bourgeois audience. The trial scene becomes an explicit and telling moment of this kind of staging. Invernizio writes,

> Una folla avida, ansiosa, empiva fino dalle prime ore del mattino le adiacenze del tribunale. Ed in mezzo a quella folla si distinguevano tutte le vicine di Giselda, le sue antiche compagne e amiche. (51)

> [An eager, avid crowd began filling the vicinity of the tribunal from the early morning hours. And in the midst of that crowd one could see all Giselda's neighbours, her old peers and friends.]

And shortly after,

> Pareva di dover assistere alla prima rappresentazione di un dramma, di un celebre autore. E qual dramma più vero, più orribile di quello, in cui era protagonista la Giselda? (52)

> [It seemed as if one were attending the opening night of a play by a famous author. And what drama could be more real, more horrible, than the one in which Giselda was the protagonist?]

The courtroom becomes a theatre in which an avid audience gathers for the spectacle of the trial, with its enticing protagonist, the infanticide Giselda. The narrator criticizes the avidity of the crowd, and particularly that of the women in the crowd who want voyeuristically to enjoy the tragedy of this crime. The narrator points her critique specifically at women, announcing, 'io non posso comprendere come una donna, quest'essere gentile, e per natura timido e debole, creato pei miti sentimenti, per le aspirazioni delicate, possa godere di simili spettacoli morbosi, possa prendervi parte' (52) [I cannot understand how a woman, this gentle being, shy and weak by nature, created for sweet sentiments and delicate aspirations, could possibly enjoy such a morbid spectacle, could possibly take part in it]. Invernizio here seems to play with the reader's expectations: her invocation of women's shy, mild, delicate, and weak nature seems to be leading to a criticism of the act of infanticide, a shocked and appalled rhetorical 'How could a woman do such a thing?' Instead, it is the women in the courtroom as spectators who seem to be defying the nature of their sex by their desire to watch and enjoy the trial. Such criticism of the perverse desire to revel in another's misfortune is still heard today, particularly concerning the circus-like atmosphere created around high-profile court cases. Indeed it is likely that Invernizio is here registering her criticism of contemporary social mores.

A closer examination of these passages reveals that Invernizio, perhaps unwittingly, inscribes her own project into the narration. In other words, she herself becomes the 'celebre autore' whose melodramatic works are avidly consumed by a largely female reading public. In fact, the dramatic defence speech by Giselda's lawyer reads like a plot summary of a typical Invernizio novel. The lawyer constructs a defence narrative about Giselda's having been seduced and abandoned by an uncaring *cavaliere*. Not only does his account turn out to be in fact the 'truth' of Giselda's situation (and thus a summary of *Sartina*), but it reproduces the elements of other Invernizio tales, in particular 'La fine di un Don Giovanni.' In a telling detail, the lawyer insists that 'Ella deve essere stata colta da un momento di pazzia, che la rese irresponsabile dei suoi atti' (65) [She must have been seized by a moment of insanity, which absolves her from responsibility for her acts]. His claim repeats verbatim the words of the narrator earlier in the text, at the moment in which Giselda was strangling the infant: 'Bisognava credere che Giselda fosse stata colta da un momento di pazzia!' (15) [It was necessary to believe that Giselda had been seized by a moment of insanity!]. The lawyer, in short, offers a public performance of Invernizio's own fiction for the delectation of the bourgeois women who can consume the spectacle from the safety of their homes. Invernizio's popularity (note the many editions of *Sartina*) makes it unlikely that many readers saw themselves as the oblique object of the narrator's social criticism in the trial scene.

The narrator of *Sartina* wonders aloud, with rhetorical flourish, at the seeming oxymoron of the mother-infanticide: 'È forse possibile che scientemente, freddamente, potesse commettere un così mostruoso delitto!?'(15) [Is it perhaps possible that knowingly, coldly, she could have committed such a monstrous crime!?]. The scientific community of the day sought to account for this scandal of reason by focusing not on woman's fragility and delicacy but on her developmental stage in human evolution. Replete with charts, photographs, and diagrams, Lombroso and Ferrero's massive study attempts to define an anatomical type of female deviant. Among the various groups of criminals examined are infanticides. We are told, for example, that the average cranial capacity of the infanticide is 1,280 cubic centimetres, somewhat lower than that of the 'normal' female. After tabulating and analysing a whole array of physical measurements, the authors are frustrated in their attempt to delineate a solid 'type.' They conclude that the infanticides, whom they describe as 'quasi-normal,'[7] must be classed among the 'occasional' and not the 'born' criminals. It should be noted that the infanticides are not unique in their resistance to anatomical classification: Lombroso admits that a 'type' of female delinquent does not seem to exist for any category of crime. The study then moves from an attempt to define anatomical anomalies to a marshalling of socially and historically contingent factors in order to account for incidences of various crimes. In the chapter on 'Ree d'occasione' (occasional criminals), the authors note that 'la vita sociale nei diversi paesi offre diverse occasioni ai reati' [different social conditions in each country offer opportunities for different sorts of crime].[8] As an example, they identify a specific economic explanation for the particularly high rate of infanticide in Sweden. In the United States, on the other hand, the female crime of choice is abortion, motivated by advanced capitalism and the entrance of women into professions and business.[9]

Criminal anthropology insisted on atavism as an indicator of criminal potential: those individuals who are closer to humanity's origins, as evidenced in an array of possible physical 'anomalies,' are therefore less developed, less cultured, and thus more inclined to deviant behaviour, 'il crimine è sopratutto un rigermoglio dell'uomo primitivo' [the criminal being only a reversion to the primitive type of his species].[10] Confronting sexual difference in general, Lombroso asserts that, 'essa è più indietro nello stadio atavistico' [atavistically [the female] is nearer to her origin than the male],[11] women being essentially 'big children.'[12] Her latent 'evil tendencies'[13] tied to her atavism, are held in check by the surrounding culture and by the call of motherhood.[14] In this schema, the phylogenic origins embodied in women threaten the progress and stability of civilization, while simultaneously, of course, women's physiology enables humanity's continued existence.

In his dedicatory letter to Lombroso, Capuana offers his stories as a gift in honour of the scientist's 'jubilee.'[15] He mentions that the subject of his novellas 'avendo qualche relazione coi suoi ultimi spassionatissimi studi intorno ai fenomeni psichici, dei quali abbiamo ragionato in Roma ogni volta che ho avuto il piacere di riverderla' [bears some relation to your latest dispassionate studies concerning psychic phenomena, about which we have spoken in Rome every time I have had the pleasure of seeing you].[16] Capuana's use of 'spassionatissimi' and 'ragionare' mirror the empirical ideals of emotional disengagement and rationality espoused by Lombroso's science (and by Capuana's *verismo*). The evocation of the author's encounters with Lombroso in Rome, by depicting a dialogic scene between artist and scientist, seems to anticipate the setting of 'Un vampiro,' which opens with just such a conversation. Though referring to his own 'fioca voce di novelliere' with rhetorical humility, Capuana in this prefatory letter does not represent his artist's voice as being at odds with Lombroso's scientific epistemology. Rather, the two seem harmonized in their shared interest. The short stories, offered in homage, treat a subject that 'evitava all'omaggio il difetto di una troppo grave stonatura' [spared the homage the defect of an overly grave false note].[17] The desire to avoid a 'stonatura' underscores the image of the harmonized voices of *verista* and *positivista*. However, what the gift-story offers is precisely a *stonatura*, 'ciò che non s'accorda con l'insieme di cui è parte, cosa inopportuna' [that which does not harmonize with the whole of which it is a part, something inappropriate], namely, the vampire.[18] Far from being in accord with the family in whose home he appears ('l'insieme di cui è parte'), this figure disrupts and threatens their familial harmony. Further, and more significantly, the vampire disrupts the belief systems both of the poet in whose home he appears and of the scientist who is enlisted to explain the phenomenon. The vampire is profoundly 'inopportune,' breaking into the home and the epistemologies of the protagonists.

The opening lines of the story are, precisely, a breaking into – an interruption of a conversation in progress: '"No, non ridere!" esclamò Lelio Giorgi, interrompendosi' ['No, don't laugh!' exclaimed Lelio Giorgi, breaking off].[19] Giorgi is speaking with Mongeri, a scientist whose rational explanation of the vampire allows him to assert 'Siamo in piena fisiologia' [We are fully in physiology], and who thus evokes the methodology of Lombroso himself. Giorgi seeks the aid of his friend in understanding the supernatural, vampiric reappearance of his wife's first (and deceased) husband. This ghost is nightly sucking the blood of the poet's newborn baby. Referencing (as does *L'innocente*) the contemporary notion of telegony, Mongeri remarks, 'qualcosa permane sempre del marito morto, a dispetto di tutto, nella vedova' [in spite of everything, something always remains of the husband in the widow] and adds, 'non sposerei una vedova per tutto l'oro del mondo' [I wouldn't marry a widow for all the gold in the world].[20] In other words, the very flesh of the widow bears the continuing mark of her first possessor (and later in the story Luisa will be 'possessed' by her first husband, who uses her body to speak while she enters a kind of trance). She is permanently branded, and, from the point of view of prospective future husbands, contaminated by the first. The vampire-husband, similarly, seeks to purify his wife's contamination by Lelio (who has broken into the upper class from his position of poverty) by destroying the child they have produced. The first husband's body is eventually cremated to exorcise his lingering influence and to save the couple's baby from his murderous revenge.

As Lelio and his double, the vampire, struggle to lay claim to the body of Luisa, Mongeri engages in a similar dynamic in his struggles with 'female irrationality,' ways of knowing that seem to lie outside his own, a more advanced epistemology. In discussing the efficacy of herbal remedies employed by women, he notes, 'quei rimedi empirici, tradizionali siano i resti, i frammenti della segreta scienza antica, e anche, più probabilmente, di quell'istinto che noi possiamo verificare nelle bestie. L'uomo, da principio, quando era molto vicino alle bestie più che ora non sia, divinava anche lui il valore terapeutico di certe erbe ... Le donnicciuole, che sono più tenacemente attaccate ad essa [cioè: 'questa virtù primitiva'], ci han conservato alcuni di quei suggerimenti della natura mediatrice' [those empirical, traditional remedies are the remains, the fragments of secret, ancient science, and also, most likely, of that instinct that we can verify in animals. Man, in the beginning, when he was much closer to the animals than he is now, understood the therapeutic value of certain herbs. Silly women, who are more firmly connected to [this primitive virtue], have saved for us a few of those hints of nature's remedies].[21] For Mongeri, as for Lombroso, women (like criminals), are closer to humanity's primitive, bestial, precultural origins. In the schema of linear, progressive development, women conserve within themselves the attributes, both constructive and destructive, of those origins: instincts, intuitions of herbal remedies, traditions, violence, and irrationality. And like Lombroso, Mongeri resorts to appropriating these feminine, primitive belief systems to support his own 'rational' enterprise: Lombroso quotes adages and proverbs to substantiate his claims, while Mongeri studies popular superstitions and seeks to incorporate them into his scientific purview. He seeks to diffuse the threat of difference by revealing it as really more of the same.[22]

The range of texts circulating around the image of infanticide, then, reveals a desire to identify a clear, pure point of origin from which to trace a sequential, logical line of development and progress – for individuals, families, sexes, races, and even social class. Further, I would argue that the spectre of the contaminated woman that haunts many of these stories represents a more generalized anxiety. The threat of contamination posed by the lower-class woman, the unfaithful woman, or the widowed woman signals the fantasy of dispensing with women altogether, and of a re-creation that would be a pristine doubling of the self. (We recall that Lombroso, ultimately, can locate no significant difference between the 'donna normale' and her deviant sisters, the prostitute and the criminal.) It is within this general cultural discourse, this 'narcissistic narrative of origins,'[23] that Pascoli's work intervenes.

In introducing her analysis of Lombroso's work, Gibson provides a demographic overview of the situation of women in Italy in the late nineteenth century, taking into account childbearing, crime, employment, migration, the role of the church, marriage, and changes in legal and political standing.[24] Of interest for the present study is the account of the marked increase in births, illegitimacy, and abandonment during this period. Gibson notes that '[i]n contrast to the small families of early modern Italy, married women during the first decade of unification after 1861 raised nearly five children on the average ... The first six decades after unification, from 1861-1921, constituted a unique demographic period in Italian history, one in which married women bore, cared for and helped to support extraordinary numbers of children ... Single women were not exempt from the cares of childbearing as illegitimacy rates peaked in the late nineteenth century. The two decades between 1871 and 1891 saw the highest rates of illegitimacy, with over 7 percent of all babies being born outside of marriage.'[25] As the author goes on to note, 'the desperation faced by both single and married mothers unable to care for their children is reflected in the sharp increase of admissions to foundling homes.'[26]

In her essay 'Charity and Welfare,' Rachel G. Fuchs offers a study of the structures of private, public, and religious forms of assistance to the poor in Europe throughout the nineteenth century.[27] She examines in particular the notion of the 'deserving' poor; economic and religious motivations for offering relief to the poor; the attempts to control morality and sexuality, particularly among poor women, by those providing assistance; and concepts of gender roles, the family, and marriage. Among the structures examined are Europe's foundling hospitals. The kind of care these institutions were able to provide resulted in the death of 'more than half, and sometimes as many as three-quarters of abandoned babies,' statistics that prompt Fuchs to describe this form of poverty relief as 'tantamount to culturally sanctioned infanticide.'[28] Fuchs's account of the typical scenarios that could drive a woman to commit infanticide is of particular interest for the present study, because, as we will we see, it documents the historical typicality of Pascoli's fictional narrative and protagonist. Fuchs writes that

> Those who committed infanticide were generally young, single domestic servants, in the cities or in the countryside, alone and lacking family support, filled with shame, afraid to dishonor themselves and their families, and abandoned by their lovers. Infanticide often functioned as a form of delayed abortion, a back-up measure of family limitation and a desperate strategy among destitute and isolated women ... From the mid 1860s, regulations regarding abandonment became restrictive, making anonymity virtually impossible. Such regulations no doubt deterred many women, but others may have thought that killing the newborn was more merciful than subjecting the child to a lifetime under the sometimes cruel tutelage of public assistance. Infanticide may also not have been a conscious strategy, but an act of temporary insanity as the women sometimes claimed. Isabelle

Caze's situation was emblematic. At her trial for infanticide she cried that 'I would rather see him dead than placed in the [foundling home where he would] suffer a miserable existence.' In her tearful response to interrogation she added 'if the blood did not mount to my head, all this would not have happened.'[29]

In addition to providing a concrete social context for the literature I am exploring in this chapter, Fuchs's piece is of methodological interest as well. Her focus is almost entirely on the economic, social, and political factors that motivated infanticide and abandonment: 'Most single mothers could not work and care for a baby themselves. In Paris, at least a third of the single women who gave up their babies were unmarried domestic servants who could not keep both their babies and their jobs. Survival dictated that they keep their job ... Economic exigencies more than a lack of maternal love led women to abandon their babies.'[30] As such, we can contrast her approach with Lombroso's method, which sought to identify physiological markers located in the body of the criminal as an explanatory method. The recent surge in scholarly interest in Lombroso's work may reflect a growing shift back from cultural and economic modes of accounting for 'deviant' behaviour to an emphasis on locating and intervening in biological determinants.

Fuchs's account of the type of woman who might be driven to commit infanticide in the late nineteenth century could well be a portrait of the protagonist of Pascoli's story 'Il ceppo.' Here, a domestic servant named Marietta, working for a couple in the Romagnolo countryside, gives birth on Christmas Eve. Pascoli's tale has many aspects in common with Invernizio's earlier novel – the poverty of the protagonist, the hidden pregnancy, and the narration of a courtroom scene, for example. However, these shared elements most likely derive from a common historical context (that described by Fuchs) rather than from any indebtedness of Pascoli to Invernizio. This story, published on New Year's Day, embodies many of Pascoli's dominant themes, images, and stylistic innovations. In fact, the tale weaves together and re-elaborates specific images found in a group of poems entitled 'Creature' from the volume *Myricae*. The fourth edition of *Myricae* contains a section of five brief, evocative poems, all centred on a child or baby figure. 'Fides' ('Faith,' in Italian with a Latin title) is the first of the group. In this eight-line composition, a child, at his mother's suggestion, dreams of paradise as a golden garden, while the real cypress outside is blown by storm winds. The third poem, 'Morto' ('The Dead Boy'), offers a brief image of a deceased child whose tiny hand seems to clutch some unknown precious object. 'Orfano' ('Orphan') enchantingly portrays an old woman who sings an infant to sleep, her song evoking images of a beautiful garden, while outside the snow slowly falls.[31] 'Abbandonato' ('The Abandoned Child'), in eight couplets, recounts the last moments of a child without bread, blanket, or the comfort of his mother, and whose death is attended only by 'the saint,' 'the angel,' and the 'Virgin.' The poem 'Ceppo' shares its title with the short story mentioned above.

The introductory note to this section in the 1994 edition of *Myricae*, edited by Franco Melotti, reads, 'Sono immagini di bambini sofferenti o ignari della loro sorte di dolore. Emerge in questa raccolta uno dei temi fondamentali della poesia pascoliana, quella del "nido" familiare come difesa da una realtà ostile'[32] [They are images of suffering children, or of children ignorant of their destiny of grief. In this collection emerges one of the fundamental themes of Pascoli's poetry, that of the familial 'nest' as a defence against hostile reality]. This note summarizes key points of the dominant critical understanding not only of Pascoli's poetry but even of his life: namely, a regression to the safety of the family as a reaction to a fear of the outside world. However, while expansive, outdoor spaces (the country landscape during a snowfall or storm, the wind carrying the sound of church bells) often contrast with enclosed, protected indoor spaces (the crib, the fireplace), the contrasting terms usually do not carry univocal values, as we have already seen in the poems examined in the previous chapter. For example, in the poem 'Ceppo,' the most powerful, albeit veiled, allusion to death is found at the very heart – indeed, the very 'hearth' – of the home.

'Ceppo' takes its title and setting from the tradition of the yule log. In pagan times, families would gather and burn a log on the winter solstice, the shortest day of the year, to mark the rebirth of the sun. In his study of Italian folklore, Paolo Toschi comments that 'nell'accensione del ceppo che deve durare fino a Capodanno vengono a fondersi due elementi propiziatori: il valore profillatico e purificatorio e vitale del fuoco, e l'idea che insieme col grosso tronco che brucia, si consuma il vecchio anno, con tutto ciò che di male e di inerte si era accumulato' [in the lighting of the yule log that must last until New Year, two propitiatory elements fuse together: the protective, purifying, and vital value of the fire, and the idea that together with the huge log that burns, the old year itself, with its accumulation of evil and idle things, was burning away, too].[33] Christianity inherited and transformed the custom, requiring that the log be big enough to burn in the family hearth from Christmas

Eve to the Epiphany. In some regions of Italy, there arose the popular legend that, at midnight on Christmas Eve, the Madonna would go from house to house looking for a hearth at which to warm the Christ child. Thus, the log was kept burning, and swaddling clothes hung from the fireplace, to accommodate the anticipated holy visitors: 'la pia leggenda ... immagina la Vergine Maria entrare a mezzanotte nelle umili case a scaldare il figlioletto pur mo' nato al fuoco grande del ceppo; l'ampia cucina è vuota, perchè la famiglia è in chiesa per la messa di mezzanotte: si deve dunque lasciare il fuoco acceso perchè se capita il Bambin Gesù vi si possa riscaldare!' [the holy legend ... imagines that, at midnight, the Virgin Mary enters humble homes in order to warm her little newborn son at the great fire in the hearth. The large kitchen is empty, because the family is at church for midnight Mass. One must therefore leave the fire lit, so that if Baby Jesus comes he can warm himself].[34]

CEPPO

È mezzanotte. Nevica. Alla pieve   1
Suonano a doppio; suonano l'entrata.
Va la Madonna bianca tra la neve:
Spinge una porta; l'apre: era accostata.
Entra nella capanna; la cucina   5
È piena d'un sentor di medicina.
Un bricco al fuoco s'ode borbottare:
Piccolo il ceppo brucia al focolare.

Un gran silenzio. Sono a messa? Bene.
Gesù trema; Maria si accosta al fuoco.   10
Ma ecco un suono, un rantolo che viene
Di su, sempre più fievole e più roco.
Il bricco versa e sfrigge: la campana,
Col vento, or s'avvicina, or s'allontana
La Madonna, con una mano al cuore,   15
Geme: Una mamma, figlio mio, che muore!

E piano piano, col suo bimbo fiso
Nel ceppo, torna all'uscio, apre, s'avvia.
Il ceppo sbracia e crepita improvviso,
Il bricco versa e sfrigola via via: 20
Quell rantolo ... è finito! O Maria stanca!

Bianca tu passi tra la neve bianca.
Suona d'intorno il doppio dell'entrata:
Voce velata, malata, sognata.[35]

[It is midnight. It is snowing. At the parish church
They are ringing twice; they are announcing the Mass.
The white Madonna goes through the snow:
She pushes a door, opens it; it was ajar.
She enters the cabin: the kitchen
Is full of the smell of medicine.
A jug at the fire is heard bubbling:
The little yule log burns in the hearth.

A great silence. Are they at Mass? Good.
Jesus trembles; Mary approaches the fire.
But hark, a noise, a wheeze that comes
from above, growing ever weaker and hoarser.
The jug spills and sizzles: the bell,
With the wind, now comes near, now goes far.
The Madonna, with a hand to her heart,
Cries, A mother, my son, who is dying!

And very softly, with her child intent
On the yule log, she turns to the exit, opens, and departs.
The yule log suddenly crumbles and crackles,
The jug spills and hisses
That wheezing ... is over. O tired Mary!
White you pass through the white snow.
The church bells echo around you.
A voice veiled, sick, dreamt. (my translation)]

The poem's simple plot can be briefly paraphrased: the Madonna, carrying the baby Jesus, enters a cabin at midnight on a snowy Christmas Eve to warm the child at the fireplace. She hears a death rattle coming from upstairs, and her maternal heart aches for the dying mother. She leaves the house to continue her nightly journey, and the woman dies. The auditory accompaniments to these events include the melodious church bells from outside the cabin and the crackling of the fire in the hearth. A footnote in the Goffis edition adds deep poignancy to the brief composition: 'la madre del Pascoli sarebbe morta la notte di Natale.'

The simplicity of the story is reflected in the poem's syntactic simplicity. All verbs are in the present tense, creating a sense both of immediacy and timelessness. Most sentences consist of only subject and verb, with very few adjectives, adverbs, or prepositional phrases. This simplicity suggests that the story is being told from a child's perspective. However, the work's lexical richness and precision (evidenced, for example, by the variety of words – *sfrigolare, sfriggere, crepitare* – used to express the hissing, crackling sound of moisture in the fire), coupled with sophisticated rhetorical strategies (examples of metonymy, zeugma, and chiasmus will be explored below), imply, simultaneously, a second, adult perspective.

The preponderance of colons and semi-colons separating brief, staccato phrases creates the sense of a hesitant movement forward by fits and starts. The verbs that actually denote motion, however, imply more fluidity. Mary *si accosta* and then *s'avvia*, just as the sound of the bells *s'avvicina* and *s'allontana*. Both pairs of verbs denote a movement of approaching and withdrawing, a kind of swaying or floating that overlies and contrasts with the harsh, sudden movement of the staccato sentence structure. Similarly, the floating melody of the bells contrasts with the crackling of the fireplace and the hoarseness of the dying voice. 'Ceppo,' then, provides another example of Pascoli's poetic practice of combining sharp, discrete images with impressionistic fluidity.

Despite the seemingly straightforward nature of the plot, the poem at crucial points conveys a sense of disruption, eliciting disturbing uncertainties and ambiguities through a range of rhetorical devices and repetitions. The bell itself clearly does not approach and depart, as a strict grammatical reading of the verses would indicate, but the sound it makes seems to do so as it is carried on the wind. Similarly, the jug in lines 13 and 20, though the subject of 'versa,' 'sfrigge,' and 'sfrigola,' does not spill and hiss; rather, its contents do. These local, and easily resolved, misattributions of source signal an ambiguity of agency that emerges most powerfully at the end of the poem. The designation 'malata' implies that the *voce* of the final line is that of the dying mother. By the end of the poem this woman has 'ceased' her cries, and thus her voice remains only as a memory or echo. The agent of 'sognata,' however, like the source of the voice who speaks to Mary in the familiar 'tu,' remains uncertain. The voice, floating on the wind, as it were, seems to merge with the sound of the bells, the phrase's more immediate antecedent. The repeated echoing of this voice with which the poem ends (but does not conclude – note that the penultimate line brings us back to the poem's opening) both defies death by living on and at the same time announces death through its 'veiled, sick' nature.

The legend of the wandering Madonna provides the central, overt narrative source for the poem. We are invited, then, to take seriously the popular, transrational mode of thinking expressed in such legends. The poem, further, embeds within the Christian legend an oblique reference to Ovidian myth. This gesture boldly combines Christian and pagan, popular and erudite, oral and written legends, disclosing their shared, transrational, non-positivist modes of understanding death. In the poem, the yule log itself seems to mirror the woman's life, hissing as she hisses and then 'suddenly' disintegrating ('sbracia e crepita improvviso') at the moment of her death. This direct mirroring suggests primitive, 'childlike' superstitions that a human life can be harboured in a natural object, a kind of voodoo that goes deeper than pathetic fallacy. More specifically, the image recalls the myth of Meleager, whose life was bound up in the log that his mother, Althaea, kept protected (Ovid, *Metamorphoses*, VIII). Meleager's mother, having heard the decrees of the Fates at her son's birth, protected the log that would determine her child's lifespan. However, after Meleager kills his uncles, Althaea seeks revenge for the murder of her brothers. She casts the fated log into the fire, avenging her brothers by killing her son. Pascoli's description of the simultaneous extinction of the burning log and the suffering woman echoes Ovid's lines: 'Crescent ignisque dolorque, / languescuntque iterum: simul est extinctus uterque, / inque leves abiit paulatium spiritus auras / paulatim cana prunam valante favilla'[36] ['Fire and pain flared up, then both turned chill and gray, / And as red embers fell to smoldering ashes, / Slowly his spirit wandered into air'].[37] The Ovidian mother-son narrative evoked by the yule log casts a dark shadow on the nurturing Madonna and child of the manifest narrative, complicating the seeming simplicity of the tale and certainly destabilizing the 'safety within the home' theme ascribed to the poems.

The poem's depiction of the Blessed Mother displays several notable features that further develop these issues. In a kind of zeugma, the white of line three refers to both Mary and the snow, a double application spelled out in line twenty-two, which repeats line three, this time addressed in the familiar form to the Madonna by the speaker/observer, who remains unidentified. The whiteness may refer literally to the pallid hue of her complexion, or to her being snow-covered. Symbolically it refers, of course, to her purity. In line twenty-two, the doubled adjective is used in a chiasmus: 'Bianca tu / neve bianca.' This cross structure appears in relation to the Madonna and child, and thus cannot but evoke the image of the literal cross destined to be borne by the baby now held and protected by his loving mother. Pascoli here rhymes 'bianca' with 'stanca,' creating an unusual and touchingly human image of the Virgin Mother, and emphasizing her paleness and fatigue. These images, coupled with her hand at her heart in line fifteen, point to the pain Mary will undergo at the crucifixion of her son (Luke 2: 35). Thus Pascoli telescopes the end of Christ's life into the night of his birth, infusing death into the Nativity.

The juxtaposition of birth and death, and particularly the symbolic localization of death within not just the home but the hearth, the uncertainty of agency elicited by the use of metonymy and zeugma, the dramatization of transrational, 'primitive' legends like that of the wandering Madonna and the life-holding log, and the absence of the source of the central auditory components (we see neither the bells nor the dying woman, nor can we clearly identify the voice that generates the apostrophe 'O Maria stanca'), all contribute to the uncanniness of 'Ceppo.' While, as the footnote suggests, the poem commemorates the death of Pascoli's mother, the commemoration takes the form of a resistance to mourning: the Madonna comes in and goes out, she 'passes' through death and continues on. The present tense of the verbs, the annual repetition of the celebration of the Nativity, the repetition with differences of lines that reverberate and inflect each other (lines 2 and 23, 3 and 22, 13 and 20), the interpenetration of the 'great silence' and the sound of bells carried on the wind, and the survival of the dreamt voice beyond the woman's death, all elicit an intermixture of life and death, an intermixture that defies linear temporality or clear designations of original or terminal points.

Like the note to the poem 'Ceppo' that references the death of Pascoli's own mother, the prefatory discussion of Pascoli's recently published collected short stories also insists on a biographically grounded interpretive matrix for the fiction. Indeed Giovanni Capecchi suggests that every one of Pascoli's prose pieces corresponds to, and translates, specific emotionally charged moments in the author's life: 'Nella storia del Pascoli narratore, ogni racconto scritto o progettato appare legato ad una fase ben precisa della biografa del poeta' [In the history of Pascoli-as-narrator, every story he wrote or planned appears tied to a very precise moment in the poet's biography].[38] In this reading, the twin 'traumas' of Pascoli's broken engagement to his cousin and the marriage of his beloved sister Ida form the latent content of the narrative. A neat set of equations (in which poet equals Pascoli, Ines equals Ida, and Marietta equals Maria, forming the core of this reading) insists on a direct translation of personal desires into fictional narrative. The story,

Capecchi suggests, represents a fantasy of fecundity generated by the frustrated, sterile author, and masks his 'unconfessable' incestuous desires. 'In questa che può essere definita la novella dell'uomo sterile, dell'albero che non lega e non dà frutto, ma che pure sogna la fecondità, il nucleo famigliare appare perfettamente ricomposto: al fianco di Ines-Ida, che riprende il ruolo di reginella domestica, Pascoli pone se stesso e, confessando l'inconfessabile, toglie l'anello matrimoniale al possidente di Santa Giustina di Rimini, Salvatore Berti, legittimo marito di Ida, per metterlo al proprio ditto' [The tale can be defined as the novella of the sterile man, of the tree that leaves no legacy and bears no fruit, and yet dreams of fertility. The nuclear family appears here perfectly reconstructed: at the side of Ines-Ida, who takes on the role of the little queen of the home, Pascoli places himself. Confessing the unconfessable, he takes the wedding ring from the owner of Santa Giustina of Rimini, Salvatore Berti, Ida's legitimate husband, to place it on his own finger].[39] This biographical reading, while seductive for its coherence, elegance, and, indeed, voyeurism, does a disservice to the complexity of the tale and even diverts our attention from the central narrative event: the infanticide itself. The analysis captures the disquieting, destabilizing, uncanny elements of the narrative and neutralizes them by containment within Pascoli's biography. This gesture of containment effectively performs a kind of exorcism, allowing us to remove the uncomfortable elements of the text back to their origin: within the unique, deviant, and perverse person of the author.

A close reading of this prose piece reveals further issues at stake, issues that transcend the particular tragic events of Pascoli's life. As if gathering together luminous tesserae to form a mosaic, this short story assembles the images and themes of the various brief poems discussed above and presents a tale that, like a mosaic, is coherent yet disjointed. A reading of this narrative helps articulate the complexity of the seemingly childlike and simplistic verses, and complicates the dichotomy suggested by much of the criticism.

In Pascoli's tale, a servant girl named Marietta has succeeded in hiding her presumably illegitimate pregnancy from her employers. On Christmas Eve, the couple for whom Marietta works go out to a friend's home, and then to Mass, to celebrate the holiday and also the long-awaited pregnancy of the Signora, named Ines. Ines and her husband leave the house with instructions to Marietta to keep the yule log burning, in accordance with the tradition. As soon as the *padroni* are a safe distance away, Marietta struggles to the bedroom to deliver her child. She then proceeds to take the newborn to the riverside and secretly bury him. She returns to the house, cleans up the evidence of the birth, and sits by the fire. However, the sight of the Madonna, who comes into the house and lovingly caresses and warms the Christ child at the hearth, sends Marietta into a fit of remorse: she rushes from the house and begins a frantic search for her newborn child. Marietta is found the following morning completely covered with snow, hovering over a hole in the ground that contains the corpse of her child. Two months later, Marietta sits through an interrogation where she learns for the first time that her child was a boy. At the word 'bimbo,' she slips into a reverie and, no longer aware of the judge's questions, she internally names her son 'Cecchino.' The reader is led through Marietta's stream of consciousness, in which she imagines herself caring for Cecchino, suddenly remembers he is dead, and grapples with her guilt and justifications. We are then jolted out of this reverie and back into the courtroom, where a spectator ends the narrative with a prayer: 'Dio, – dice suor Anna – voi siete buono: fatela morire! Povera madre che *ha dovuto* uccidere la sua creatura!' ['God,' says Sister Anna, 'you are good. Let her die, poor mother who *was forced* to kill her child!'].[40]

On one level, the story can be understood as an act of social criticism, one whose message, sadly, is as pertinent today as it was a century ago. The well-to-do *padroni* are, after two years of marriage, expecting their first child, and eagerly await the birth with joyful anticipation. The joy with which this financially secure couple welcome their child into the world contrasts sharply with the predicament of the disenfranchised servant girl. Indeed, the couple are so wrapped up in their own good fortune that they fail even to notice Marietta's condition or her pain. On this night, we are told, her suffering is so apparent that a blind person would have seen it, yet the *padroni* remain ignorant: 'Ma quella notte pativa proprio; l'avrebbe visto un cieco. Ma quella notte i suoi padroni non videro nulla. Avevano altro a pensare' [But that night she was really suffering; a blind person would have seen it. But that night her employers didn't see anything. They had other things to think about].[41] This contrast may be read as a criticism of tragic social and economic injustice – a criticism encapsulated, perhaps with too heavy a hand, in the prayer that concludes the story.

The strategies, merits, and in some senses the short-comings of this disturbing tale can be put into even sharper focus by comparing it with a contemporary treatment of the same topic. Pascoli's literary portrait of this 'disgraziata' contrasts with the aloof, positivistic studies of Lombroso.

Pascoli employs a humanistic, literary discourse to grapple with the phenomenon that Lombroso approaches using an empirical register. The more crucial difference lies in the stance of the authors vis-à-vis the subject and in the position constructed for the reader with respect to the protagonist. Lombroso, as Barbara Spackman has pointed out, seeks differences, and specifically differences that can be measured, calculated, analysed, and arranged hierarchically.[42] His studies presuppose and aim to account for differences between the criminal and the normal woman, between the deviant and the healthy, and so forth. In short, the author stands outside of and gazes critically upon the subject under analysis, inviting the readers to do likewise.

Pascoli, I think, does not deploy this kind of polarizing rift. While he by no means mitigates the horror of the situation (as we shall see), he does not portray Marietta as a deviant 'other.' Rather, he brings us into the intimate recesses of the house – the bedroom, the hearth – where the tragic events unfold, and invites us to a compassionate understanding. At least four times in the tale, Pascoli does indeed refer to Marietta as a 'bestia,' and depicts her on her hands and knees in the forest. 'Ricadde in ginocchio, ma si rizzò puntellandosi con tutt'e due le mani su quella terra e su quelle foglie. Pareva una bestia in quelle tenebre' [She fell on her knees, but straightened up supporting herself with both hands on that ground and on those leaves. She looked like an animal in that darkness].[43] However, I do not read this association as a distancing, critical gesture: that is, I do not think that the depiction of Marietta as 'bestia' implies that her crime has reduced her to a vicious animal to be judged by civilized human readers. Rather, perhaps paradoxically, I think this depiction universalizes Marietta's plight by means of a strategy of regression. That is, by evoking the image of the animal Pascoli attempts to indicate the primitive, primordial, and thus common nature of the tragedy. The depiction of Marietta as animal suggests that Pascoli is positioning his inquiry prior to cultural, economic, or linguistic differentiations. By regressing to point of common origin, Pascoli attempts to universalize rather than distance or differentiate Marietta's situation.

Where Lombroso's study adopts a detached, critical stance towards its subjects, Pascoli's story may be criticized for playing too heavily on the reader's emotions and sympathies. For example, the preponderance of diminutives – *bimbettino, pianticella, calduccio* – go perhaps too far in emphasizing the small, precious helplessness of the mother and child. In addition, the narrator's parenthetical intervention at precisely the crucial moment of the child's burial seems infelicitous: 'fece una buca. Vi depose qualche cosa (qualche cosa!) e poi vi rimise su la terra' [she made a hole. She dropped something (something!) into it and then replaced the dirt on top of it].[44] The intervention disrupts the litotes that would have allowed the gravity of the moment to speak for itself. At the same time, however, the intrusive remark reveals that the moment cannot 'speak' for itself, that some voice is narrating the scene. But, to quote Hoffmann's Nathaniel, 'Whose voice is this?' The question of course remains open. Weber's analysis of the *style indirect libre* in his discussion of 'The Sandman,' I think, pertains to this moment as well:

> the *style indirect libre* blurs boundaries between authoritative third-person and engaged first-person narratives. It is not just the authority of the 'third-person,' but also the position of the *reader* as *spectator* that is called into question. Indeed, the *theatricality* of the uncanny consists precisely in inscribing every *perspective* into a scenario that can therefore no longer be taken in simply as spectacle. This is also what distinguishes such theatricality from 'theory' in the traditional sense: there is no longer the possibility of a stable separation from what is under consideration ... All we are left with, as readers, is the power of that exclamation point, which punctuates without forming a period ... For it confounds prediction, judgment, and lets a certain form of 'constative' discourse reveal itself as always already 'performative.'[45]

The position of the narrator (and, by implication, the reader) at this crucial moment, the very heart of the narrative, reveals itself as ambiguous – split: both inside and outside, a player and a spectator at the scene of the crime.

The strange poetic digression by the Signore (who, we later learn, is a professional poet) as he speaks to his wife during their stroll to their friend's home adds further nuance to the narrative. The passage meditates on the germination and growth of plant seeds, which beneath the blanket of snow await the spring to bloom. His pregnant wife responds with only a smile to his evocation of the little growing plants, and the conceit soon becomes apparent: his meditation refers as much to his 'own seed' as to the dormant vegetation.

Pascoli often transposes human dramas onto the natural world – typically employing birds and flowers as central metaphors. We recall, for example, that 'X agosto' ('10 August') figures the assassination of Ruggero Pascoli as the death of a swallow who leaves behind a nest of orphaned 'rondinini.' In a similar way, the epithalamium (wedding poem)

'Gelsomino notturno' ('Jasmine at Midnight') depicts a marriage's consummation as the nighttime opening of the jasmine flower, which releases its gentle perfume and closes again in the morning. This poetic strategy not only testifies to Pascoli's profound love of and respect for the humble beauty of the Romagnolo and Tuscan countryside but also reveals a complex preoccupation with origins. Pascoli's interest in and staging of primitive forms of natural life, his privileging of young children, his use of the Latin language, his evocation of pagan roots of Christian customs, all bespeak a reaching back to origins, sources, beginnings: whether ontogenetically, phylogenetically, or linguistically. The same strategy is at work, I believe, in the portayal of Marietta as a 'bestia.' The task then becomes to articulate what is at stake in this regression.

Indeed the overt thematic burden of the passage on the germination of plants is precisely the origins of life itself, and particularly of a life becoming conscious of itself. The soliloquy-like meditation emphasizes the role of pain in eliciting consciousness. 'La pianta è, ma non sa nulla. Questa notte comincia a sapere. E come? Il dolore rivela lei a lei, un dolore acuto e dolce ...' [The plant is, but does not know anything. Tonight it begins to know. And how? Pain reveals the plant to itself, a pain acute and sweet].[46] Pascoli, in short, locates pain at the very roots of life.

More than once in the story, Pascoli strikingly juxtaposes birth and death. First and foremost, of course, is the central, tragic paradox that the selfsame mother who brings forth a life immediately and violently snatches it away. Further, Pascoli chooses to set the story on Christmas Eve and to highlight the originally pagan tradition that accompanies it. He thus evokes the birth of Christ and of the Christian era, yet at the same time colours that birth with the tomblike darkness of the winter solstice and emphasizes the dead, frozen landscape buried under the wintry snows. Finally, the agonized description of Marietta's torturous labour, reinforced by Pascoli's hallmark onomatopoeia, reads almost as a graphic murder scene: 'lo sgretolìo dei denti e lo scricchiolìo delle ossa' [the crushing of her teeth and the creaking of her bones.][47] Indeed, as she drags her lacerated body up the stairs to give birth, Marietta seems almost to be desperately struggling to escape a pursuer: 'Su, su tenendosi alla ringhiera della scala con la sinistra e arrovesciandovisi sopra sino a stringere coi denti la bracciaiola, andò nello sgabuzzino dove era la sua branda' [Up, up, holding on to the railing of the stairs with her left hand and curling herself over it in order to clutch the banister with her teeth, she went to the cubbyhole where her cot was].[48] In short, in Pascoli's narration the child's birth verges on murdering the mother. The repeated conflation of birth and death suggests that death immediately contaminates the original moment of life. The hole the mother digs and into which she commits her infant is hardly the protective nest or cradle but rather a suffocating tomb, thus deconstructing the neat dichotomies of inside/outside, safety/danger, home/foreign that critical readings of Pascoli seek to establish.

Marietta, whose name is a diminutive form of the Virgin's, and who gives birth, like her namesake, on Christmas, must clearly be seen as a shadowy double of the Blessed Mother. We might call her the Cursed Mother: as a neighbour comments upon the discovery of her body, 'She is alive, though it would have been better for her had she died.' Another incarnation of Marietta appears in the jarring poem 'L'etèra' ('The Courtesan'), discussed at some length in chapter 2. This poem opens with the death of the courtesan Myrrhine, and recounts the wandering of her soul in the afterworld. At the shocking climax of the poem, Myrrhine encounters the froglike souls of her 'children who died before they were born, who were chased away before they could ask for pity.' Pascoli here presents a confrontation between a would-be mother and the children she aborted. The juxtapositions of birth and death, of cursed mothers with blessed mothers, reveal the ambivalence of origins, an ambivalence that elicits and constitutes the 'uncanny.' Pascoli's interrogation of origins, then, mirrors Freud's own interrogation of the *unheimlich*: both reveal an essential bifurcation and coincidence of contraries. Pascoli's poetry not only stages a nostalgia for an original moment of purity and wholeness, a refuge in which to retreat and regress, but also dramatizes that moment's status as myth. In other words, Pascoli's work, permeated by ambivalence and a quasi-Gothic *inquietudine*, suggests not so much that the innocent and marvelling child creates true poetry but that poetry creates the *fanciullino*, who exists only as an artistic construction.

4 Envisioning Childhood: Memory, Desire, *Pietas*, and Play

> all he did was to remember like the old and be honest like children
> W.H. Auden, 'In Memory of Sigmund Freud'

Composed roughly at the same time, Giovanni Pascoli's essay *Il fanciullino* (*The Little Boy*, published in 1903) and Sigmund Freud's *Three Essays on the Theory of Sexuality* (1905, with revised and expanded editions appearing through 1924) seem to have little in common other than their dates of composition and the importance attributed to them as fundamental, programmatic statements of their respective authors.[1] The first offers reflections on poetics, the second proposes a theory of sexuality. Reading each with the other in mind, however, discloses fundamental concerns common to both authors. While significantly diverging on the issue of eroticism, Freud and Pascoli privilege childhood in order to universalize the relevance of their own discourse. Further, both authors approach their projects by way of the roles of memory and desire. For Freud, 'Infantile Sexuality' is the central essay of the 'three essays,'[2] while Pascoli uses the image of the little boy as a figuration of the poet. Before turning to an analysis of these particular texts, I will briefly situate them historically in light of nineteenth-century European views of and attitudes toward childhood.[3]

For historians of childhood in Western culture, the seminal work has been *L'enfant et la vie familiale sous l'ancien régime* (1960) by Philippe Ariès. The author argues that 'childhood' is a particularly modern concept, and that before the sixteenth century the unique nature of children was not recognized.[4] Though this study and its conclusions have been refined and criticized by later historians in the field, several recent scholars have shown that the concept of childhood seems to have had a notable development in the nineteenth century. These scholars draw on various forms of evidence to support this thesis. Linda A. Pollock, for example, studies diaries and autobiographies of parents and children, while others examine state legislation, the development of universal, compulsory, state-run education, religion-sponsored educational ventures, the growth of child-centred organizations such as the Boy Scouts, literary representations of children (notably in Wordsworth and Dickens), literature for children (such as *Alice's Adventures in Wonderland* and *Peter Pan*), published child-rearing guides for parents, and scientific-philosophical developments such as the work of Darwin, Piaget, and Freud himself.

Drawing on this evidence, scholars have delineated two coexisting yet in a sense antithetical notions of the child, both of which have roots in Christian thought. The first, most notably articulated by Rousseau, is that of the child as 'innocent' and as embodying and representing a pre-experiential purity and goodness. The opposing view sees the child as naturally aggressive, stained by 'original sin,' and thus in need of the curbs of education. Archard most clearly elaborates this dichotomy:

> In the first instance, children are seen as nearest to God, whilst adults, correlatively, are furthest away from Him. Children have a purity which derives from their having arrived only recently in the world. They are Nature which Society corrupts ... On the other hand, there is the view of children as vicious, requiring society's education and constraints to secure proper behaviour.[5]

Priscilla Robertson, studying popular child-rearing guides of the century, underscores the same dichotomy:

> Rousseau ... provided rationale for the view that children are born good, with a capacity for reason, and that their natural virtues need only be brought out. The opposite attitude, that children are born troublesome if not corrupt, implies that the remedy is *force majeure*. In the early 1800's Rousseau's ideas had the bloom of fashion, and several books of practical advice by popular women writers passed his theories along ... In France, the pejorative view of childhood, though less common, found expression from time to time. The *Livre de Famille*, a cheap paperback handbook available late in the century, described the child as cruelty and egoism personified – an angel only when he sleeps. Waking, he had to be brought into absolute submission.[6]

Summarizing her survey of diaries and autobiographies, Pollock remarks that, 'There are two distinctive features of the nineteenth-century texts: the appearance of nostalgia for childhood and also an increase in the proportion of texts (especially the British samples) which describe ambivalence.'[7] Pollock speculates that 'perhaps the wish to retain childhood was linked to the wish to revert back to a predominantly rural society rather than live in an urban, technological one?'[8] Finding that children are not referred to as 'innocent' in these texts until the eighteenth century, she suggests that 'It is also possible that the emergence of the concept of innocence was due to the ideas of Locke (1694) and Rousseau (1763).'[9] Finally, C. John Sommerville interrogates the role of industrialization in this question and proposes an interpretation of the idealized representations of children in Victorian England, an interpretation based on the notion of repression. He argues that 'In the 19th century [children] were asked to play just one role, in an unreal world. It was their task to symbolize the innocence which a severely repressed society felt it had lost.'[10]

Though Freud, a staunch atheist, clearly did not believe in the doctrine of original sin, his account of childhood participates in the less popular camp of thought which held that children were naturally depraved. While Freud focuses on and develops his notions of the aggressive instincts more thoroughly in his later works, in the *Three Essays* he does insist on 'cruelty' as a 'component' of the sexual instincts, a component that is to be found already in infancy, pre-dating the dominance of the genitals in sexual life and existing 'independently from the erotogenic zones.' He notes that 'Cruelty in general comes easily to the childish nature, since the obstacle that brings the instinct for mastery to a halt at another person's pain – namely a capacity for pity – is developed relatively late' (192–3). This darker view of the child's nature sets Freud's essay apart from Pascoli's idealized description of the 'fanciullino' and indeed from the more popular literary representations of children in the late nineteenth century.[11] However, his insistence on the sexuality of children, and his earnest call for their sexual education,[12] was his more revolutionary contribution to the public discourse on childhood at the time. Though this contribution was not a total novelty in Western thought,[13] Sommerville characterizes the impact of Freud's essay thus:

> The main block to acceptance [of psychoanalytic theory] was Freud's view of the child's nature. In 1905 his essay on 'Infant Sexuality' appeared, pointing out how much of the child's activity ran on the same kind of energy

that would eventually be devoted to sex. Indeed, he thought there was already a sexual dimension in the child's interests ... The outcry was tremendous. To a society which had valued children as symbols of sexual innocence, Freud's views seemed the height of perversion. Freud himself said that he had resisted these ideas for almost five years. Of course, he had defined sex very widely, to include pleasures that are not usually associated with that concept. But he had shown how they could be related to adult genital sexuality. So he was shunned as a moral degenerate ... his contemporaries assumed that he was degrading childhood ...[14]

In Pascoli's account, on the other hand, the gentle child whose vision defines the heart of poetry is entirely devoid of any sexuality or eroticism. Pascoli's essay, with its emphasis on and nostalgia for the fresh wonder of the *fanciullino*, clearly participates in the 'child as innocent' tradition explored by the above-cited historians, and the predominantly rustic themes and images of his poetry support the analyses of 'child' as a cipher for 'pre-industrial.' Of crucial importance to the development of Pascoli's poetics is James Sully's *Studies of Childhood* (1895). Maurizio Perugi has revealed that Pascoli possessed a French translation of this psychological tome (*Ètudes*, 1898), and richly annotated it during his revisions of *Il fanciullino*. Sully's analyses and (often charming) anecdotes of childhood speech provided Pascoli with a concrete framework for the articulation of his poetics.[15]

Pascoli's essay should be read as a culmination of a particular strain in Italian literary thinking that can be traced through the works of Giambattista Vico (writing in the early eighteenth century) and Giacomo Leopardi (from the early nineteenth century). This line of thought, roughly put, asserts poetry as an originary, primal, pre-logical form of thought and language, and the poet as a primitive or childlike figure.[16] This 'primitive' conception of poetry gained considerable currency in the nineteenth century, so much so that in 1924 the critic Francesco Flora complained that 'Troppo abbiamo abusato del detto che la poesia è la lingua primigenia e materna del genere umano' [We have abused too much the saying that poetry is the original and maternal language of the human race][17] and criticized those who would take this idea so far as to assert that learning and culture were antithetical to poetry and detrimental to its pure expression. Pascoli's impressive erudition – he was an accomplished Latin poet, Dante scholar, and translator of classical Greek and Latin and contemporary English poetry – clearly acquits him of the charge of equating poetry with ignorance. However, his revolutionary poetic practice, described by Contini as 'pre-grammaticality,' opened his poems to the criticism of being childish and even mawkish. Indeed, one must imagine that Flora had some of Pascoli's onomatopoeic poems in mind when he warned that, with the 'primitive' view of poetry, 'C'è il pericolo di arrivare a dire che i veri poeti sono gli animali, magari gli usignoli' [There is the risk of going so far as to say that the true poets are the animals, perhaps the nightingales].[18]

With *Il fanciullino*, however, Pascoli does not merely reiterate the ideas developed by Vico and Leopardi, nor does he posit the simplified view criticized by Flora. In his description of the wonder of the child's vision as the core of true poetry, Pascoli complicates the potentially simplistic thesis by suggesting the importance of a dynamic, or a doubled perspective. Deploying the same simile used disparagingly by Flora, Pascoli writes in the first section of *Il fanciullino*: 'Ma l'uomo riposato ama parlare con lui (i.e. il fanciullino) e udirne il chiacchiericcio e rispondergli a tono e grave; e l'armonia di quelle voci è assai dolce ad ascoltare, come d'un usignuolo che gorgheggi presso un ruscello che mormora' (25–6) ['But the older and peaceful man loves to talk with him, to listen to his noisy chattering and to answer back in tune with him and gravely; and the harmony of those voices is very sweet to the ear, like the voice of a nightingale trilling near a murmuring brook'].[19] Here, the harmony between the voices of the adult-at-peace and the inner child creates the poetic music. This simultaneity of voices, as in the double perspective of poems such as 'In ritardo,' rescues Pascoli's verse from the critiques of childishness.[20] More importantly, this simultaneity discloses the fundamentally relational and dynamic role of the 'child's voice,' one that derives meaning and value in its difference from the mature rationality of adult language.

Despite their fundamentally different views of childhood, for both Freud and Pascoli childhood represents a common starting ground, a period before one or another defining path was taken, and therefore a moment in which 'universals' among men are most clearly seen. For Pascoli, the cries of a baby are the same everywhere, before any specific cultural or national milieu trains the child to speak his or her native language.[21] He asserts, in short, 'Un fanciullino è fanciullino allo stesso modo da per tutto' (53) ['A child is a child in the same way everywhere'].[22] Similarly for Freud, the vigorous and polymorphous sexuality of the infant are universal, until his or her familial and cultural experiences teach the 'shame, disgust and morality' that will channel that libido into either 'perversions, neuroses, or normal sexuality.' By focusing on childhood, then, both authors get to the 'source,' as it were, of their objects of study, whether poetry or sexuality. In the process, both writers make strong assertions: because of this common starting ground, all human beings are all potential poets, as they are all potential 'perverts.' The universalizing gesture of turning to childhood implies an ethics of inclusion, one that aims to embrace all humankind within its purview. For Pascoli, the universal voice of true poetry, 'in quanto è poesia, la poesia senza aggettivo, ha una suprema utilità morale e sociale' (40) ['insofar as it is poetry, poetry unqualified, has a supreme moral and social usefulness'].[23] Here the 'adjective' that may attach itself to poetry would be any arbitrary cultural accretions that obscure the essential purity of poetry. By stripping away these accretions and unveiling the poetry without adjectives, Pascoli strives to speak with a voice of universal relevance. This is the root of the moral and social utility of poetry: its ability to transcend difference and remind people of their common bonds. Similarly for Freud, the return to infancy discloses the commonality of all subjects, however different their adult behaviours seem to be. Illness, for example, is not essentially different from health but a matter of degrees along a scale that is the same for everyone.[24] As Freud writes on the question of neurosis,

> we no longer think that health and illness, normal and neurotic people, are to be sharply distinguished from each other, and that neurotic traits must necessarily be taken as proofs of general inferiority ... We all produce such substitutive structures [neurotic symptoms] and ... it is only their number, intensity, and distribution which justify us in using the practical concept of illness ... (478)

Similarly, on the topic of sexual 'inversion,' or homosexuality, he insists that 'everyone, even the most normal person, is capable of making a homosexual object-choice, and has done so at some point in his life' (462).

While the universalizing epistemologies of Freud and Pascoli lay the groundwork for an ideal of understanding and even compassion by insisting on our ultimate (or, more precisely, our primitive) sameness, by the same token these gestures run the risk of obscuring irreducible otherness. Despite his revolutionary work on sexuality, Freud's theorization of female sexuality, and indeed femaleness in general, continues to be criticized for its patriarchal assumptions. Despite his sincerely pious calls for the quelling of greed, Pascoli energetically advocated Italy's militant attempts to acquire colonies in Africa. Although such gestures of marginalization and of privileging one group over another seem inconsistent with the ideal of inclusion I have been exploring, I think they can also be seen as yet another extension of those very theories. Inclusion slips over into homogenization and an insistence on essential (narcissistic) sameness. The challenge of theorizing female sexuality on its own terms reveals this dynamic in Freud's writings. Pascoli's call for the homogenizing effects of a colonial war discloses the same epistemology at work. By seeing past differences to the underlying sameness, both risk diminishing the importance and integrity of those differences.

Freud posits the imaginative failure of the young boy to 'guess that there exists another type of genital structure of equal worth,' that is, the failure to perceive otherness as difference rather than as lack. He argues that, 'It is self-evident to a male child that a genital like his own is to be attributed to everyone he knows, and he cannot make its absence tally with his picture of these other people' (195). This failure that Freud ascribes to boys repeats Freud's own struggles to understand the desires and sexuality of women. '[The erotic life] of woman – partly owing to the stunting effects of civilized conditions and partly owing to their conventional secretiveness and insincerity – is still veiled in an impenetrable obscurity' (151). The little boy's fantasy of the phallic mother clearly suggests the inferiority of the female genital structure and, more fundamentally, discloses the projection of the 'same' onto the 'other.' The inevitably male subject position of the 'universal' child generates the fantasy of the sameness of all subjects. The need for the mother once to have been 'whole' exemplifies what Weber has called the 'narcissistic narrative of origins.'[25] In discussing the *Three Essays*, Weber notes that 'The interests at work in the child's first "sexual theories" reveal the concern with origins to be part of the ego's narcissistic effort to consolidate its organization through the "temporalizing-temporizing," i.e. narrative articulation of alterity (as origin, loss, separation). The phantasm of the maternal phallus represents difference as absence, the Other as variant of the Same, repetition as recognition.'[26] In the *Three Essays* Freud proposes his notion of 'penis envy,' stating that girls experience 'envy for the penis ... culminating in the wish to be boys themselves' (195).[27]

The drive to consolidate the integrity of the self through story-telling motivates Pascoli's colonialist discourse as well. Pascoli's famous and rhetorically skilled 'La grande proletaria si è mossa' appeared in the journal *La Tribuna* on 27 November 1911. According to the distinctions

Pascoli himself elaborates in *Il fanciullino*, he appears here as the orator and not the poet: he is quite explicitly advocating the Italian invasion and colonization of Libya (Italy had declared war on Turkey and invaded Libya on 29 September of that year).[28] He speaks from a position of national humility and even shame: fifteen years earlier, under the Crispi administration, Italy had been the first and only European power to suffer defeat by an African army. Pascoli refers briefly to the humiliation of the 1896 Abyssinian campaign, in which more than 4,000 Italian soldiers were killed in Adowa by Emperor Menelik's army. 'Quoting' the voices that mock Italy, he exclaims, 'Garibaldi? ma il vostro esercito s'è fatto vincere e annientare da africani scalzi! Viva Menelik!' (*Opere*, 608) [Garibaldi? But your army was conquered and annihilated by barefoot Africans! Long live Menelik!]. It is in part to erase the shame of this defeat that a new campaign is urged. The 'barefoot' Africans are cast, rather typically, as in need of the 'humanizing' and 'civilizing' effects that the Italians are indeed duty bound to bring. Having been recently 'redeemed' (i.e., unified) itself, Italy now must accept its role as 'redeemer' ('pur mo redenta, doveva a sua volta divenir redentrice'). Pascoli here envisages Africans as Freud envisages girls: as lacking ('scalzi') and as desiring to be made 'whole.'

Organizing the essay under the central metaphor of Italy as the proletarian nation of Europe, Pascoli makes very few references to the Africans themselves or to the Turks, who at the time occupied the land. The emphasis in the essay is not on the benefits colonization will bring to the colonized people, but on the advantages for the Italians. More than the shame of Adowa, Pascoli focuses on the humiliation of emigration and the need for so many Italians to leave their culturally rich and historically prestigious land to earn a living in foreign countries. It is Italy's 'maternal duty' to provide 'her sons' with what they want – work. And he is at pains to insist upon the existence of such a thing as an 'Italian.' Indeed, war for Pascoli plays a similar role to childhood: he evokes it as a space where differences are effaced and where we can see the underlying and essential bond of community among men who may otherwise appear very different. War erases geographic, physiological, and, most importantly for Pascoli, class distinctions, as all Italians become united against their common misfortunes: 'Il roseo e grave alpino combatte vicino al bruno e snello siciliano ... il popolo lotta con la nobilità e con la borghesia. Così là muore, in questa lotta, l'artigiano e il campagnolo vicino al conte, al marchese, al duca' [The rosy and serious northerner battles alongside the dark and slender Sicilian ... the working class fights next to the nobility and the bourgeoisie. And so they die there, in this struggle, the artisan and the rustic next to the count, the marquis, the duke].[29] Indeed the Italian army, fifty years after the birth of the unified nation, is held up as a sort of utopian community, a microcosm of what the entire nation ought to look like and a sign to the rest of the world of how far Italy has come in its mere fifty years of existence as more than a 'geographical expression': 'Chi vuol conoscere quale ora ella è, guardi la sua armata e il suo esercito' (612) [Whoever wants to know what she [Italy] is now, should look at her soldiers and her army]. The army (like childhood) appears utopian because it is unified: a family of brothers whose 'madre comune' is Italy 'herself,' 'pura e santa madre nostra Italia.'[30] Pascoli underscores that Italy is no longer defined only by geography, natural borders, or the land itself, but rather has become a true, whole nation.

On one of the few occasions when Pascoli does make reference to the 'enemy,' he chooses precisely a little girl to be the representative of the Arabs who inhabit the land Italy aims to possess. In this striking passage, Pascoli attempts to dismantle the negative image of the army as a band of violent brutes. He seeks to replace this connection of the military with the image of a gentle, strong, brave group of men who respond to their duty. To accomplish this, he *narrates the story* of the Italian soldier who finds, protects, and nurtures a little Arab girl on the battlefield. Having been thus rescued, she grows up as an Italian and is therefore not only saved but 'redeemed.' By both feminizing and infantilizing the 'other,' Pascoli's discourse diffuses the threat of difference: what could be more helpless, less threatening, than a little girl? In this fantasy story, the soldier offers the *bambina* protective 'heroic and maternal piety.' The soldier, then, becomes an ideally whole figure: fully Italian (rather than limited to a regional identity), both 'masculine' in his military bravery and 'feminine' in his maternal compassion.

Pascoli's familial metaphor clearly intervenes in the political and social situation of his time: the depiction of Italy as a family fosters a sense of 'natural' national unity in the recently constructed nation. In addition, we can detect here another link with Freudian thought: namely, the insistent return to the nuclear family as primary model. We have seen already the central importance for Pascoli of the 'nest' metaphor throughout his work, and the predominant concern with home and family intimacy persists even through the works that ostensibly go 'beyond' autobiography, such as the *Conviviali*. Freud as well, even when undertaking analyses that go beyond the personal psyche and reach into the historical and anthropological in scope (particularly the later works, such as *Totem and Taboo*), maintains his insistence on the familial Oedipal model as the underlying theoretical structure. Both writers, in short, insist upon the familial model in order to lend their work the potential of universal cogency and validity. More importantly, the glaring contradiction of proletarian speech, so grossly at odds with the Pascolian ethos of innocence, contentment, and simplicity, highlights an inner tension already at work in *Il fanciullino* and throughout the poetry. Pascoli's desire to locate a pure point of origin, a fully innocent voice, a poetry without adjectives, not only compels him to repress the cultural ambivalence concerning childhood that I outlined earlier but also repeatedly reveals the inescapable and irreducible ambivalence of that desired voice. In *Il fanciullino*, this ambivalence reveals itself through the motion of metaphors deployed to define the 'child's voice.' Described as a *harmony* of voices (as we have seen), and also as a *farmaco*, a theatre, a church, a playing child, a gardener, a pair of binoculars, a truce, and a nursing infant (as I will explore below), the 'purity' of the *fanciullino*'s voice can be theorized only as relational, contingent, and ambivalent.

The centrality of the parent-child relationship necessitates the gesture of turning back. To be a true poet, Pascoli insists, one must turn back to the wonder of the child's vision and allow the voice of that 'inner child' to return. The 'moral and social' task of the poet is to bring back the voice of the marvelling child, a voice repressed by the demands of rational adult discourse, and to evoke the same wonder in readers: 'mirabili dovevano parere [i fatti] anche agli altri bambini come lui, che erano nell'anima di tutti i suoi uditori' (30) ['they had to seem wonderful to the other children like him, who were in the souls of all his listeners'].[31] For Freud, because 'symptoms are substitutes' of undesirable behaviours for repressed mental processes, analysis proceeds 'by systematically turning these symptoms back ... into emotionally cathected ideas' (164). The task of the analyst is to bring back these repressed, cathected ideas into the consciousness of the analysand, who can then begin to 'work through' them. In both projects the role of memory is essential.

In his preface to *Primi poemetti*, composed as a letter to his sister Maria, Pascoli equates poetry with memory, asserting that 'Il ricordo è poesia, e la poesia non è se non ricordo.'[32] The connection between poetry and memory appears explicitly in *Il fanciullino* as well, 'eccoli i fanciullini che si riconoscono, dall'impannata al balcone dei loro tuguri e palazzo, contemplando un ricordo e un sogno comune' (33) ['there the Eternal

Children will gather, and recognize each other, from the poor ragged curtains of their hovels to the balconies of their palaces, contemplating a common memory and a common dream'].[33] Specifically, Pascoli insists that the poet does not create something new, but reminds readers of what they already know but have forgotten. Poetry's task is one of recovery and re-cognition. 'Soltanto questo tu vuoi, seppure qualche cosa vuoi dal diletto in fuori che tu stesso ricavi da quella visione e da quel sentimento' (34) ['This is all you want, if you want anything at all, other than the delight you yourself gain from that vision and that feeling'].[34] To paraphrase Shelley, the *fanciullino* becomes the 'faculty' that helps us 'to remember that which we know.'[35]

The role of memory in psychoanalysis is fraught with complications, as Freud's early essay on 'Screen Memories' (1899)[36] reveals, almost in spite of itself. Freud here starts with the assumption that, for the most part, people tend to remember episodes from their past that are significant and to forget unimportant events. When a subject does have a vivid recollection of an event that is seemingly unimportant or 'innocent,' Freud suggests that the unconscious has been at work. The remembered scene is indeed highly significant but with a hidden meaning to be decoded, precisely as a dream, symptom, or parapraxis. The unconscious has grasped the innocent memory and, because of various elements in it that can be overdetermined, has charged it with suppressed fantasies. Freud structures the essay on 'screen memories' in a highly literary way, as a dialogue between himself and a patient. Together, they work out an interpretation of a specific memory and in the course of this exemplum articulate the theory of screen memories. It is generally agreed that this 'patient' is in fact a 'screen' for Freud himself, and that the details discussed are largely autobiographical. The problem that arises and fails to be fully resolved involves not the 'truth' of the unconscious fantasy that attaches itself to the otherwise irrelevant memory, but the status of that memory itself. Could it be that this memory, like Freud's 'interlocutor' himself, is an entirely constructed fiction? Freud suggests the possibility that what a subject may experience as a memory could be in fact the equivalent of a waking dream: 'You projected the two fantasies on to one another and made a childhood memory of them ... I can assure you that people often construct such things unconsciously – almost like works of fiction.'[37] The patient responds to the suggestion of unconscious fabrication with some disbelief, at least in this particular case, arguing that 'A feeling tells me, though, that the scene is genuine.' Freud then agrees that it indeed may very well be so and proposes that, instead of a process of fabrication, one of selection may have taken place: that is, the unconscious hit upon an actual memory that was particularly well suited to express, in a coded way, its illicit fantasies, and therefore charged that memory with particular strength. Finally, between complete fiction and mere selection, a third possibility is suggested: namely, that the memory was chosen from the store of actual childhood experience but was worked on and adapted to fit the unconscious phantasm.

Freud does not offer any universally applicable formula for determining which of the three possibilities pertains to the status of any given 'screen memory': complete fiction, accurate record, or modified account. He suggests only that the subject can rely on the 'feeling' that the scene is genuine, or can try to contact the other people who appear in the memory for validation. For the particular memory that he analyses in this essay, the precise status of it is not as important as the unconscious ideas it conveys, and thus the issue can remain unresolved without much damage to the main point of the theory.[38] In the formulation of the female Oedipal complex, Freud does resolve the issue, judging that the sheer number of patients with 'memories' of infantile seduction precludes the possibility that those memories refer to real events. In his essay 'Femininity' from 1932, Freud recapitulates the evolution of his theories on the etiology of neurosis. He explains how his clinical research persuaded him to modify his 'seduction' theory, convincing him that his patients had not in fact actually experienced sexual trauma in infancy but rather were describing repressed infantile fantasies. He writes, 'In the period in which the main interest was in discovering infantile sexual traumas, almost all my women patients told me that they had been seduced by their father. I was driven to recognize in the end that these reports were untrue and so came to understand that these hysterical symptoms are derived from phantasies and not from real occurrences' (349).[39] However, we can easily think of instances in which it becomes very important to determine whether the image one has in mind is a reliable memory or not. From the courtroom to the clinical encounter, the ethical questions at stake in the reliability of memory are enormous.[40] Psychoanalysis finds itself enmeshed in a paradoxical bind: Freud's postulation of the unconscious and its workings destabilizes any facile faith in the transparency of memory as an innocent image-record of past experiences. At the same time, given the fundamental role of childhood experiences in determining adult behaviour and in creating the unconscious itself, analysis finds itself dependent on the very structure its theories destabilized.[41]

The problems with which the role of memory is fraught in analysis constitute a metonymy for further issues that arise from the postulation of the unconscious. To return to our comparison with Pascoli, we can see a structural parallel between the *unconscious* (created by the repression of childhood sexuality, the 'memories' of which are no longer accessible to consciousness) and the *fanciullino* who exists in all of us. Both writers propose a kind of 'split self' or double subject, in which the experiences of childhood (whether sexual or poetic) constitute a kind of shadow self that persists throughout adult life. Pascoli brings this issue to bear directly on questions of morality: the *fanciullino* can see only the good and the beautiful (that is, only the truly poetic) even if the person within whom the *fanciullino* resides is depraved. Pascoli's metaphor of a symbiotic relationship ('colui che ti ospita') underscores the image of two coexisting beings:

> Così, caro fanciullo, hanno gran torto coloro che attribuiscono, per ciò che tu non vedi se non il buono, qualche merito di bontà a colui che ti ospita. Il quale può essere anche un masnadiero, e aver dentro sè un fanciullo che gli canti le delizie della pace e dell'innocenza. (47)

> [Thus, my dear Child, very wrong are those who, just because you see only what is good, attribute some merit of goodness to the person in whom you dwell. Such a person could even be a bandit and have within him a Child who sings to him the delights of peace and of innocence.][42]

This general and hypothetical speculation follows the specific example of Virgil's poetry and the specific issue of slavery. Unlike the practical prose writers of his time, Virgil nowhere in his poetry represents slaves, or even uses the word 'slave.' A true poet, he never wrote about slavery because his inner child recoiled from it as unpoetic, that is, as not good and not beautiful: 'Per questo non Virgilio proprio, ma il fanciullino che egli aveva in cuore, non voleva gli schiavi nei campi' (46) ['That is why, not Vergil himself, but the child in his heart, did not want slaves in the fields'].[43] But Virgil himself may have been 'inconsapevole' [unaware] of this inner judgment, and of the 'liberty he was proclaiming.'

Again, Pascoli and Freud begin with diametrically opposed premises: for Freud, man is 'naturally' cruel and driven by desire for pleasure and aggression. To exist productively in society, he must be taught shame, disgust, pity, and morality.[44] For Pascoli, man is naturally attuned to the good and the beautiful, and later may fall away from this, usually through a failure to be content and a subsequent maliciousness based on avarice.

In both cases, however, the primitive, primordial nature remains within the individual and may have occasion to speak. These occasions fall outside the norms of daily discourse, and, in fact, are the privileged occasions to which our writers devote their attention and their theories. For Freud, the unconscious speaks in dreams, symptoms, parapraxes, and screen memories. For Pascoli, the *fanciullino* speaks in poetry. Pascoli's essay emphasizes this imaginative split in its structure as a dialogue between himself and his inner *fanciullino*. While the majority of the text consists of Pascoli's prose explications of what poetry is (or should be), at various points he poses questions to the *fanciullino*, addressed in the informal '*tu.*' The *fanciullino* 'responds' in poems. Indeed, the dialogic form of this essay, in which both participants are representations (more or less fictive) of the writer himself, mirrors the form Freud gives to his essay on 'screen memories.' The literary device in both cases is not mere decorative flair but emphasizes the way in which our primordial existence continues to live within us in quasi-independence and continues to interact and 'speak' to, with, and through us.

The anxiety elicited by this doubling of the self is given voice in the horror evoked by such Gothic tales as Mary Shelley's *Frankenstein* (1818) and Poe's 'The Murders in the Rue Morgue' (1841). The atrocities committed by Frankenstein's monster and by the sailor's orang-utan demonstrate a crisis of responsibility. Both these pairings (the doctor and his creation, the Frenchman and his ape) participate in the topos of the 'double.' Indeed, it has often been noted that the monster has usurped his creator's name in the popular idiom, 'Frankenstein' often being used to designate the creation rather than the creator. As 'doubles,' the beasts might be read as externalizations or personifications of the human 'id,' detached from the 'superego' and so unfettered in their cruelty. Poe's French sailor, for example, believed that the wild ape was under his control, safely locked within a cage. But the beast escapes. Having stolen the sailor's razor blade, the orang-utan commits his horrific crimes in a grotesque mimicking of his master's shaving. The sailor watches helplessly as 'this thing of darkness' parodies him in a murderous frenzy:

> The Frenchman followed in despair; the ape, razor still in hand, occasionally stopping to look back and gesticulate at its pursuer ... As the sailor looked in, the gigantic animal had seized Madame L'Espanaye by the hair, (which was loose, as she had been combing it,) and was flourishing the razor about her face, in imitation of the motions of a barber ... Its wander-

ing and wild glances fell at this moment upon the head of the bed, over which the face of its master, rigid with horror, was just discernible. The fury of the beast, who no doubt still bore in mind the dreaded whip, was instantly converted into fear. Conscious of having deserved punishment, it seemed desirous of concealing its bloody deeds ...[45]

Of particular interest in this passage are the details pertaining to acts of personal grooming. The animal holds a razor and apes the actions of a barber, and the woman has been interrupted in the act of combing her hair. Shaving and combing are both civilizing activities and, specifically, activities that seek to remove, arrange, or otherwise control the natural growth of hair. In other words, the scene of the visual confrontation between the animal and its owner contains seemingly unimportant (even parenthetical) references to civilizing rituals. In particular, such rituals seek to erase or at least minimize the visible links (hair) between the human subject and its uncanny double, the primate. Rather than reading the tales as allegories of certain Freudian concepts, I would suggest that these stories dramatize the same anxieties evoked by the Freudian theorization of the unconscious. Both suggest a structure of transgressive action for which the subject both is and is not responsible: '"My friend," said Dupin, in a kind tone ... "I know perfectly well that you are innocent of the atrocities in the Rue Morgue. It will not do, however, to deny that you are in some measure implicated in them."'[46] In these tales, the horror derives not merely from the cruelty in itself but from the uncontrollability of that cruelty and from the irreducible ambiguity in locating its true agent. Both the monster and the ape are dependent on and subordinate to their masters. But both subhuman creatures are simultaneously independent from and uncontrolled by these humans. Thus they dramatize the same terrifying tensions inherent in the concept of the unconscious as radically alienated from and yet intimately part of the subject. Both the Gothic dramatizations and the Freudian theorization open up the unsettling and unsettled question of where to attribute agency.[47]

Freud's discussion of infantile amnesia in the *Three Essays* powerfully dramatizes, in a different context, the theme of the subject's self-estrangement. Freud opens the essay on infantile sexuality with a discussion of his theme's novelty. He suggests that our own inability to remember our early childhood plays a role in the dearth of scientific scrutiny of this topic. He remarks, 'What I have in mind is the peculiar amnesia which, in the case of most people, though certainly not all, hides the earliest beginnings of their childhood up to their sixth or eighth year ... For we learn from other people that during these years, of which at a later date we retain nothing in our memory but a few unintelligible and fragmentary recollections, we reacted in a lively manner to impressions, that we were capable of expressing pain and joy in a human fashion ...' (174). Freud goes on to argue, of course, that repression is the root of this amnesia. Whatever its cause, however, the result 'turns everyone's childhood into something like a prehistoric epic' (176). In other words, our own most formative experiences are foreign to us, and we rely on the narration of other people to enlighten us about ourselves. We cannot gain direct access to the root of our subjectivity but must read it in other people's stories about us.

For Freud, the unconscious traces of these formative years, however, remain and, indeed, play a decisive role. In the *Three Essays*, Freud postulates the intrinsic link between memory and desire. Desire, he asserts, is grounded in the memory of pleasure, a memory that demands its repetition. 'This satisfaction must have been previously experienced in order to have left behind a need for its repetition' (184). While adult sexuality has its roots in childhood eroticism, even early manifestations of desire, such as childhood thumb sucking, have their roots in previous, infantile experiences. Thus, the analysis of childhood eroticism, itself a 'source,' generates yet another inquiry that delves farther back in time: 'Furthermore, it is clear that the behaviour of a child who indulges in thumb-sucking is determined by a search for some pleasure which has already been experienced and is now remembered' (181). Ultimately, this repeated regression backwards through time, in which every stage of sexual activity is revealed as the repetition (with a difference) of an earlier experience, comes to a kind of halt in the earliest possible experience of satisfaction: 'No one who has seen a baby sinking back satiated from the breast and falling asleep with flushed cheeks and a blissful smile can escape the reflection that this picture persists as a prototype of the expression of sexual satisfaction later in life' (182). What adults experience as desire arises first out of the pleasure the infant feels when a biological need is met (most notably, the need for nourishment). The subject ever after wants to *repeat* that pleasurable satisfaction. Pascoli, too, deploys the same image as the 'prototype' of his object of analysis. Speaking to the 'fanciullino,' he states, 'fai come tutti i bambini i quali non solo, quando sono un po' sollevati, giocano e saltano con certe loro cantilene ben ritmate, ma quando sono ancora poppanti, e fanno la boschereccia, con misura e cadenza balbettano tra sè e sè le loro file di *pa pa* e *ma ma*' (36) ['You sing like all children who jump and play at some well timed sing-song of theirs, not only when they are somewhat grown, but even when they are still nursing and making wild woodland sounds, and babble to themselves in measured rhythm their long strings of *pa pa* and *ma ma*'].[48] Later in the essay, Pascoli claims, 'Egli [the poet] ... unisce i suoi pensieri con quel ritmo nativo, che è nell'anima del bimbo che poppa e del monello che ruzza' (49) ['He connects his thoughts with that inborn rhythm which is in the soul of a suckling babe and of a carefree urchin'].[49] The nursing infant, in both accounts, becomes an arrival point in the process of regression that seeks to locate an original moment of wholeness and satisfaction. Both poetry and sexuality, then, find their source in an infantile experience that is neither poetic nor sexual but relational and dependent upon another for the fullness of the self. Furthermore, neither author ultimately comes to a complete, full, satisfying halt in his regressive search for an origin. For Freud no sooner offers the image of the satisfied infant at the mother's breast than he must add, 'or at substitutes for it' (181). Reading this account literally, we can assume such substitutes would include bottles or the breast of a wet nurse. However, the comment, made in an almost offhand manner and bracketed by commas, reveals the possibilities of 'substitutes' already at the 'origin,' subtly undermining the satisfying sense of having located a singular, distinct, and universal source. In Pascoli's text, the image of the nursing infant, though chronologically prior to that of the playing child, shares the stage with this other image as a source of poetry. Both the 'bimbo che poppa' and the 'monello che ruzza' provide metaphors for the essence of poetic language – neither one is sufficient in and of itself.

More than an experiential, temporal, or literal moment, the 'nursing and playing' evoked by Pascoli register a differential function, a mode that finds its value in its difference from other, dominant modes of being. Freud groups the various manifestations of infantile sexuality (oral, anal, etc.) under the rubric 'pre-genital' and emphasizes that this phase of sexuality is not aimed at reproduction. The auto-eroticism of the infant or the four-year-old does not perform any useful function, nor is it motivated by any such teleology: 'organization and subordination to the reproduction function are still absent' (199). To accept these infantile behaviours as 'sexual,' then, one must be willing to separate sexuality from reproduction. These auto-erotic pleasures seek not to procreate but to re-create previous pleasurable sensations experienced unexpectedly and by chance. Pascoli's playful, 'pre-grammatical' use of language mirrors Freud's 'pre-genital' phase of sexuality in that it, too, resists being enlisted into the service of a function, goal, or use. The auto-eroticism of the infant shares the self-sufficiency of Pascoli's onomatopoeic verse, whose phonic qualities provide a pleasure independent of the words' meanings. More substantially, where Freud imagines a kind of sexuality freed from (and beyond) the demands of the species' needs (reproduction), Pascoli envisages a use of language freed from (and beyond) the demands of social needs (the conveying of information, persuasion). In this regard, Pascoli can indeed find the prototype of poetry in Sully's accounts of the rudiments of infantile speech: 'The child hears the sounds he produces and falls in love with them. From this moment he begins to go on babbling for the pleasure it brings' (137).

Pascoli employs several telling images to emphasize poetry's rejection of quantifiable utility. He opens the essay by insisting on both childhood and old age as the privileged domains of poetry, because these periods exist outside of the 'productive' period of life: the young child and the old sage can stand outside the demands of work, exchange, and productivity. But here we see that poetry cannot be simplistically equated with play; it is characterized, rather, by the simultaneity of play and contemplation, 'innocence' and 'experience,' *meraviglia* and sagacity.[50]

Explicitly opposing the realm of poetry to the world of work, Pascoli envisages the settings in which the inner children of all, of whatever profession or social class, can emerge and connect. 'Siano gli operai, i contadini, i banchieri, i professori in una chiesa a una funzione di festa; si trovino poveri e ricchi, gli esasperati e gli annoiti, in un teatro a una bella musica: ecco tutti i loro fanciullini alla finestra dell'anima ...' (32–3) ['Let the laborers, the farmers, the bankers, the professors be in a church at the celebration of a feast; let the poor and the rich, the weary and the annoyed, be gathered in a theater, listening to beautiful music: there will come, also, all their little children at the window of their soul'].[51] The church and the theatre share the quality of housing 'weekend' activities – Mass and musicals are attended outside the typical work week. Church and theatre, furthermore, offer experiences that transport participants from the quotidian to another realm of perception, thus providing the opportunity for respite and recreation. Clearly, Pascoli seeks to imply that poetry, too, offers this kind of experience. Finally, we should note that church and theatre are both communal spaces; spaces of social gathering rather than of solitude (Pascoli emphasizes the 'feast day' celebration in the church rather than its role as a space for private meditation). Thus, the metaphors imply that poetry plays a fundamentally social and communal role.

For Pascoli, poetry's inherently social task is to speak to and condition the subject's desires. Reading true poetry, individuals learn to be satisfied with the small and humble things that surround them and that they already have. Poetry teaches us to appreciate what is already present rather than long for what is absent: 'le cose assenti, o non visti mai, sono sempre a tutti meravigliose ... intenso il sentimento poetico è di chi trova la poesia in ciò che lo circonda' (41) ['what is far away, or never seen, is always an object of fascination for everyone ... intense is the poetic feeling of the one who finds poetry in what is near at hand'].[52] In his preface to *Primi poemetti*, Pascoli tells a 'fable' about a 'rondone' who brings food to a nest full of baby *rondini*, feeding the offspring of another bird from another species. We are to learn from this example 'international charity' and, Pascoli urges his readers, 'Uomini, insomma, contentatevi del poco' [Men, in short, be content with just a little]. Similarly, Pascoli tells another 'fable' or parable in the preface to the *Poemi conviviali*, a preface that takes the form of a letter addressed to his colleague Adolfo de Bosis (the editor of the literary journal *Convito*, in which several of the 'Convivial' poems originally appeared before being issued in this collection). Here he tells of the thirsty person who believes that his thirst is so great that not even an amphora of water will satisfy him, when in reality a mere cupful would do. Pascoli then lists a series of increasingly 'worse' scenarios that may arise from the thirsty man's desire. Because of his desire, he may take the jug from another, or go so far as to break the jug if he cannot have it all himself, gaining at least the gratification of making others as miserable as he. Finally and 'infinitely worse,' all the thirsty people may kill each other, so that no one may drink. Again, Pascoli urges that the way to avoid suffering is 'col contentarci. Ciò che piace è sì il molto, ma il poco è ciò che appaga' [with being content. That which pleases, yes, is having a lot, but that which satisfies is having a little].[53] Poetry's efficacy lies in its ability to teach us this contentment. Even in its role as a memory of former grief and suffering, as Pascoli describes to his sister, it enables us by contrast to appreciate what we have now. If all the ills of the world ultimately derive from this lack of contentment, then poetry's revolutionary power derives not from specific political engagement but from its ability to remedy the very roots of avarice. 'E sommamente benefico è tale sentimento, che pone un soave e leggiero freno all'instancabile desiderio, il quale ci fa perpetuamente correre con infelice ansia per la via della felicità' (42) ['And exceedingly beneficial is this [poetic] feeling, which sets a light and gentle restraint on the unremitting desire that makes us perpetually run, full of wretched longing, in search of happiness.'][54]

The critic Guido Guglielmi has analysed Pascoli's 'L'ultimo viaggio' (in *Poemi conviviali*) in a way that responds directly to the question of the role of desire. Guglielmi contrasts the figures of Femio, the bard, and Odisseo, the hero, in light of their desires. He writes, 'Femio rappresenta la poesia come consolazione. Ascoltare il mare nel cavo di una conchiglia lo appaga. Gli basta l'eco ... Ma Odisseo vuole la cosa, non l'ombra: Il fatto, non il detto.' [Femio represents poetry as consolation. He is satisfied with listening to the sea in the hollow of a shell. The echo is enough for him. But Odysseus wants the thing, not the shadow: the deed, not the word].[55] Femio's desires are limited to what the world of representations and shadows can actually offer, and thus are able to be satisfied. Odysseus's desires mark a 'dismisura' – he desires all, or, to use Lacanian terminology not adopted by Guglielmi but I think appropriate to his analysis, he desires the 'real.' Femio becomes the foil of Odysseus, who is critiqued in the poem. In his praise of the humble and satisfiable desires embodied in the bard Femio, Pascoli, argues Guglielmi, 'tesse un velo di *pietas*, un velo etico' [weaves a veil of piety, an ethical veil].[56]

Pascoli marks out a rather utopian ethical project for poetry, a project that could, without adopting an explicitly engaged socialist stance, go so far as to alleviate the suffering brought about by class conflict. Pascoli cites Virgil as the model of this ideal: 'Egli insegnava ad amare la vita in cui non fosse l'ostacolo né doloroso della miseria né invidioso della richezza: egli voleva abolire la lotta tra le classi e la guerra tra i popoli. Che volete voi, o poeti socialisti, che dite cose tanto diverse e le dite tanto diversamente da lui?' (42) ['He taught how to love the kind of life in which there might be neither the painful spectacle of wretched poverty nor the offensive spectacle of wealth: he wanted to abolish class struggles and wars. What do you want, oh socialist poets, who say such different things and in a way so different from his?'].[57] Pascoli himself invites us to read the essay as an ideal goal when, in the final footnote, he explains that, rather than a confession, the thoughts expressed are a 'warning' to himself, who is 'ben lontano dal fare ciò che pur credo sia da fare!' (71) ['quite far from doing what, in faith, I truly believe should be done'].[58] Already within *Il fanciullino*, however, Pascoli reveals the ambivalent role poetry plays in this idealistic agenda. The shortcoming, in other words, derives not primarily from any personal, individual defect but from the inherent, structural ambiguity of this poetics, in particular in its relation to desire. Intrinsically linked to memory, to the recuperation of lost infantile joys, poetry becomes as well a Lethean experience, numbing us to the pains and anger of the adult world: 'Tu sai che ti amo, o mio intimo benefattore, o invisibile coppiere del farmaco *nepenthès* e *àcholon,* contro il dolore e l'ira' (35) ['You do know that I love you, my intimate benefactor, invisible cup-bearer of *nepenthès* and *acholon* against pain and anger'].[59] Poetry as a *farmaco,* then, can both heal and poison, as Derrida has argued. More specifically in this case, as the cupbearer of the Homeric drugs *nepenthès* and *acholon,* poetry relieves the pain and anger of our daily adult lives with its soothing, childlike visions. But in providing this comfort and forgetfulness, poetry may risk becoming the opium of the people, preaching a contentment with the status quo that would dissuade progressive action.[60]

Pier Paolo Pasolini has examined Pascoli's poetics in the light of his unorthodox socialism. For Pasolini, Pascoli remains an essentially conservative poet, despite the linguistic innovations he offers. Although he experiments in a revolutionary way with local dialects, 'spoken' diction (*parlata*), and other linguistic novelties that seem to rupture the poetic tradition, Pascoli, according to Pasolini, remains firmly inserted within the tradition of the enclosed, privileged, elite, poetic self: 'Nel Pascoli quell'allargamento lingusitico è sempre in funzione della vita intima e poetica dell'io, e, quindi, della lingua letteraria nel suo momento centralistica e in definitiva ancora tradizionale' [In Pascoli that linguistic expansion is always a function of the intimate and poetic life of the self, and therefore, of literary language in its centralizing and clearly still traditional moment].[61] He opposes this centrism of the lyric self to the works of Verga and Manzoni. These writers, Pasolini claims, enlarge their literary diction to include the voices of the oppressed, thus enacting an 'ideologically motivated realism.' Pasolini, of course, is not asking how well Pascoli's poetry measures up to the standards of the ideal socialism expressed in *Il fanciullino.* Rather, he questions how effectively this poetry (which incorporates the language and depicts the experiences of the poor agricultural classes) breaks down the barriers that enclose 'literature' as an elite enterprise. Thus he poses a different, and in a sense more concrete, socialist standard against which to evaluate Pascoli's work, and judges it to have fallen short of this ideal.

Pasolini asserts that Pascoli's poetry remains focused on the intimacy of the poet's subjectivity. In this sense, his political critique parallels a common critique of the Freudian undertaking. Here, too, the relentless focus on the individual's interiority and inner life shifts attention from the social to the personal. Citing the socialist psychoanalyst Joel Kovel, Sarah Winter summarizes one such political-minded critique of psychoanalysis. She notes that 'Kovel argues that seeing one's fate as a product of the psychological struggles of the "inner self" means that the social, economic, and political causes of human suffering under advanced capitalism cannot be perceived and therefore cannot come under the kind of political pressure that might generate social change.'[62] The core of the inner self, however, in both Freudian and Pascolian discourses, is revealed to be not cut off from but rather radically open to and indeed dependent on 'other people.' It would clearly be naive to claim that Pascoli's lyrics compel us to undertake revolutionary anticapitalist action. However, the reading of Pascoli's texts disarticulates the neat dichotomy between 'inner self' and 'social' implicit in the above critiques.

The moving preface to *Myricae*, Pascoli's first collection of verse, takes up again the question of poetry's moral and social efficacy. In this brief and striking passage, Pascoli articulates with a slightly different slant his vision of poetry's power, a vision less grandiose yet more potent than the quasi-socialist agenda of *Il fanciullino*.

> Rimangano rimangano questi canti su la tomba di mio padre! ... Sono frulli d'uccelli, stormire di cipressi, lontano cantare di campane: non disdicono a un camposanto. Di qualche lagrima, di qualche singulto, spero trovar perdono, poichè qui meno che altrove il lettore potrà o vorrà dire: Che me ne importa del dolor tuo?
>
> Uomo che leggi, furono uomini che apersero quella tomba. E in quella finì tutta una fiorente famiglia. E la tomba (ricordo un'usanza africana) non spicca nel deserto per i candidi sassi della vendetta: è greggia, tetra, nera.
>
> Ma l'uomo che da quel nero ha oscurato la vita, ti chiama a benedire la vita, che è bella, tutta bella; cioè sarebbe; se noi non guastassimo a noi e a gli altri. Bella sarebbe; anche nel pianto che fosse però rugiada di sereno, non scroscio di tempesta; anche nel momento ultimo, quando gli occhi stanchi di contemplare si chiudono come a raccogliere e riporre nell'anima la visione, per sempre. Ma gli uomini amarono più le tenebre che la luce, e più il male altrui che il proprio bene. E del male volontario dànno, a torto, biasimo alla natura, madre dolcissima, che anche nello spegnerci, sembra che ci culli e addormenti. Oh! lasciamo fare a lei, che sa quello che fa, e ci vuol bene.

Questa è la parola che dico ora con voce non ancor ben sicura e chiara, e che ripeterò meglio col tempo; le dia ora qualche soavità il pensiero che questa parola potrebbe esser di odio, e è d'amore.

[May they remain, may they remain, these songs, on the tomb of my father! ... They are the fluttering of birds, the rustling of cypresses, the far-off singing of the church bell: they do not ill become a cemetery. For some tears, for some sighing, I hope to find pardon, since here less than elsewhere will the reader want or be able to say, 'What does your grief matter to me?'

Man who may be reading, they were men who opened that tomb. And within that tomb ended an entire flowering family. And the tomb (I remember an African custom) does not stand out conspicuously in the desert for its white rocks of vengeance: it is grey, gloomy, black.[63]

But the man whose life has been darkened by that blackness calls you to bless life, which is beautiful, all beautiful, or it would be if we would not ruin it for ourselves and for others. Beautiful it would be, even in the tear that could be a serene dew rather than the pelting of a tempest. Life would even be beautiful in its last moment, when the eyes, tired of contemplation, close as if to collect the vision and place it back in the soul, forever. But men loved the darkness more than the light, and the harm of others more than their own good. And for willing evil they wrongly accuse nature, our sweetest mother, who even in extinguishing our lives seems to rock us gently and put us to sleep. Oh! May we let her be – she who knows what she is doing and who loves us.

These are the words that I speak now with a voice not yet very sure or clear. I will repeat it better with time. May you take some comfort now in the thought that these words could be of hate, but instead are of love. (my translation)]

The collection of poems is dedicated to and commemorates Ruggero Pascoli, the poet's father, whose assassin was never brought to justice. Though the father's death was a crippling blow to the 'flowering family,' Pascoli presents his poems not as flowers of hatred but as songs of love. He explicitly renounces the project of vendetta (though by announcing this renunciation he implies that he does indeed have cause for vengeance), substituting commemoration for vengeance. In so doing, he attempts to bring a halt to the cycle of evil and grief that men bring upon themselves.

He quotes St John's gospel ('gli uomini amarono più le tenebre che la luce' [men loved darkness rather than light (John 3: 19)]) in underscoring the role men have in bringing about their own sorrow. The quotations he chooses lead us not only to the evangelist, but also to the romantic poet Giacomo Leopardi, the only Italian poet, other than Dante, to whom Pascoli devoted major works of scholarship. Pascoli here quotes the same passage from St John that Leopardi uses as an epigram for his long poem 'La ginestra.' In this deeply pessimistic poem, an apostrophe to a broom flower growing in the volcanic ash on the slopes of Mt Vesuvius, Leopardi depicts nature as a heartless 'matrigna' or stepmother. Pascoli refutes this notion, insisting that nature, on the contrary, is our 'madre dolcissima.' It is not she who is responsible for our grief and pain but we ourselves. In place of the violent, unnatural death of the father brought about by men, Pascoli envisages a sweet death in the arms of the mother. Indeed, in the absence of the father all nature rises up as a universal, protective mother. Pascoli deploys chthonic imagery in his equation of dying and being gently rocked to sleep: the tomb becomes the cradle and finally the universal womb as the earth mother welcomes us back inside herself.[64] The depiction of nature as our mother leads to the conclusion that we are all her children. Thus Pascoli once again undertakes a universalizing argument that rests upon the assertion of the commonality of childhood as a bond among men.

In the opening of the preface, Pascoli cites yet another monumental Italian poet, Francesco Petrarca, in his desire to find 'pardon' among his readers for the sighs and tears that will follow in the form of poems. For Petrarch, of course, the tears and sighs were over his beloved Laura, and he asks his readers for 'not only pardon but pity' ['spero trovar pietà, non che perdono,' line 8] in the first sonnet of the *Canzoniere*, or song book of 366 love poems. It is surprising that Pascoli should choose to evoke Petrarch's prefatory poem in his own preface, since the themes of erotic love and amorous passion that define that Renaissance collection are so absent in this volume. I suggest that the choice of this citation is not, however, arbitrary nor mere rhetorical flourish. Rather, I believe Pascoli wishes to elicit a parallel: Pascoli's collection of poems, like Petrarch's, centres on and is dedicated to a figure beloved and lost – Laura / Ruggero Pascoli. The poems grow out of the absence of these figures, commemorating and in a sense resuscitating them. Most importantly, the poems mark the desire of the poets for these lost figures.

The evocation of the Petrarch of the *Rime sparse*, at the same time, seems discordant with Pascoli's project, which is not at all concerned with romantic love. Indeed, as mentioned earlier, Pascoli underscores in his programmatic essay that the *fanciullino* has no interest in the romantic aspect of the adult world. He is devoid of eroticism, and, as a consequence, so is all true poetry: 'Non sono gli amori, non sono le donne, per belle e dee che siano, che premono ai fanciulli; sì le aste bronzee e i carri da guerra e i lunghi viaggi e le grandi traversìe' (28) ['It is not love, not women, however beautiful and goddess-like they might be, that matter to children; but bronze lances and war chariots and long journeys and great adventures'].[65] In a footnote to this passage, Pascoli elaborates that depictions of 'the erotic and feminine element' make a composition more 'dramatic' but less 'poetic.' Indeed, according to his line of argument 'love poetry' (in precisely the Petrarchan sense) becomes an oxymoron. Pascoli does not belabour the notion that children are asexual in this essay, because it could be taken for granted as a matter of fact, whereas Freud, writing at the same time, does need to argue for his opposite opinion. It is not such an obvious and accepted fact, however, that true poetry cannot be about romantic love.

We should notice in this brief passage that it is not only sexuality that Pascoli posits outside the realm of poetry but explicitly the feminine. In speaking of Homer, Pascoli notes: 'E la sua fanciullezza parlava per ciò piú di Achille che d'Elena, e s'intratteneva col Ciclope meglio che con Calipso' ['That is why his childhood spoke more of Achilles than of Helen, and preferred to linger with the Cyclops rather than with Calypso'].[66] Pascoli, in short, unquestioningly equates the erotic with the feminine (he speaks of 'l'elemento femminile e erotico'), a link clearly derived from his heterosexual male point of view. He proceeds to dismiss both, in theory, from the domain of poetry.[67] Pascoli, as we have seen, does in fact populate his poetry with female characters, all of whom are explicitly de- or non-eroticized, most notably, his sisters and his mother.[68] In fact, the very two Homeric characters whom Pascoli here names as exemplars of the erotic make appearances in his *Poemi conviviali*: Helen in 'Antìclo,' and Calypso in 'L'ultimo viaggio.' Chapter 2 of this study examines the uncanny nature of these appearances, noting in both cases the woman's role as harbinger of death. Read alongside *Il fanciullino*, which excludes the feminine-erotic, the *Convivial Poems* stage a return of the repressed in the figures of these uncanny women.

For Pascoli, poetry does not depict, celebrate, or lament erotic love because, as we have seen, poetry must teach satisfaction rather than fuel desire. The poetic sentiment, 'che pone un soave e leggiero freno all'instancabile desiderio,' reins in gently the frenzied search for satisfaction among objects that can never fully replace the missing One, halting the metonymic displacement of desire that is doomed to failure from the start. And indeed, Pascoli's poetry does, in a sense, evoke satisfaction: the only fully satisfying relationship, the only moment of fully experienced *jouissance* – figured as the infant's satisfaction in its mother.[69] The polymorphous infantile sexuality postulated by Freud, a sexuality that encompasses the mother not so much as its object but as a completion of its own subjectivity, becomes the figure of a repression that returns and resonates in the tolling bells, the uncanny women, the assonances and rhythms of Pascoli's work. But, as the uncanny figures of Calypso and Helen suggest, the fulfilment of that desire entails the death of the subject. We remember that, in the preface to *Myricae*, the characterization of nature as a mother immediately elicits a meditation on death. We can employ the terminology of Kristeva here and say in other words that Pascoli concerns himself not with objects of sexual desire but with desire for the 'Thing': 'This "something" would be previous to the detectable "object": the secret and unreachable horizon of our loves and desires, it assumes, for the imagination, the consistency of an archaic mother, which, however, no precise image manages to encompass.'[70]

Giorgio Agamben elaborates this dynamic on a linguistic level, analysing the structural role played by desire in Pascoli's poetry. In an introductory essay to *Il fanciullino*, Agamben undertakes a linguistic analysis of the most prominent and distinctive features of Pascoli's *linguaggio*, dedicating the essay to Contini, who was the first systematically to enumerate and examine these features and term them 'pre-grammatical.'[71] Evoking the Augustinian notion of desire as the 'volontà di sapere,' Agamben maps out three kinds of utterances and the role of desire in each. First he describes utterances with a clear meaning – normal words, as it were. At the other extreme, there are utterances that have no meaning, that are 'pure sound.' In between are sounds that clearly signify something but whose meaning remains unknown. The listener knows *that* they mean something but does not know *what* they mean. It is in this class of utterances that desire figures most prominently, because it is here that we most want to know. Pascoli's poetry is suspended precisely here, unfolding in this space of desire and ambiguity. Agamben goes on to designate two kinds of motion in Pascoli's poetry. Extremely precise or technical words as well as foreign words (especially English and local dialect) are moving from clear meaning to no meaning. For the typical (Italian) reader, such words clearly have a meaning, but that meaning itself is obscure. Agamben characterizes these technical and foreign words as 'dying' from word into sound and suspended by poetry in the middle space of desire. In the other direction, Pascoli's hallmark onomatopoeic rendering of church bells and animal noises seems, in the context of poetry, to take on significance. Agamben points to these phonemes as dying from sound into speech, again suspended in the realm of desire. According to this scheme, the opposing directionality of glossolalia and onomatopoeia meet in the desiring 'linguaggio di Pascoli.' Agamben opens his essay with the paradoxical statement by Pascoli, who composed extensively in Latin, that 'la lingua dei poeti è sempre una lingua morta ... curioso a dirsi; lingua morta che si usa a dar maggior vita al pensiero' [the poet's language is always a dead language ... strange to say; a dead language that is used to give a fuller life to thought]. Agamben maintains the metaphor of death in the notion of a vocabulary that is dying. A vivid example of this kind of movement or dying from word into sound can be found in *Myricae*'s 'Dialogo,' in which the 'sparrow,' addressing the 'swallows,' says 'v'è di voi che vide ... vide ... vide ... videvitt?' Here a standard verb form ('who sees') gradually transforms into a non-semantic onomatopoeic rendition of a bird noise ('videvitt'). As such – as 'dying' – the words are kept in a kind of motion.[72] To reach definitively one end point or the other (clear sense or non-sense, in this schema) would represent a kind of stasis or death.

Agamben's emphasis on 'dying' as motion and process repeats, I think, Weber's exploration of the present particle as an articulation of necessary repetition – that is, process rather than stasis, continual motion of displacement always already from the beginning. This reading suggests that Pascoli develops a poetics of desire, alongside his agenda of teaching contentment with the 'little,' because even the originating moment of satisfaction that forms the paradigm or 'core' of the *fanciullino*'s voice – a voice dispersed within the discourse of the adult – is already contingent, open, and dependent on the other. Pascoli promises in his *Myricae* preface that he will *repeat* his words of love, because this collection cannot possibly be sufficient. Pascoli's poetry enacts a primordial drive for lost infantile satisfaction, and his poetry unfolds just on this side of that satisfaction, in the space of motion ('tremare'), life ('resuscitation'), and desire. Pascoli wrote no love poetry, he claims, because children have no sexuality; yet every one of his verses is a love poem.

The reference to Petrarch, I think, has a second motivation that develops this question. Petrarch underscores that he seeks not merely pardon (for the 'varied style' of the 'fragments' he presents) but *pity*. Pascoli omits this specific request in his preface, but it is this omitted word that is written through the entire collection. The desire for pity, not explicitly expressed in the prose, is enacted through the poems themselves, because 'here less than elsewhere people will be able or want to say, "What does your grief matter to me?"' Poetry elicits compassion: it can communicate grief in a way that makes it relevant to those who are not directly involved in the speaking subject's loss. Thus, it is able to create a bond of compassion and understanding among readers where otherwise there would be indifference. The unlikely pairing of Ruggero and Laura helps elucidate this possibility.[73] A link between Pascoli's lost father and Petrarch's lost lover introduces the register of sexuality into a relationship devoid of it. But pursuing this line of thought opens the possibility that a certain kind of desire does obtain in this case and that its evocation in Pascoli's poetry is precisely what enables it to fulfil its ethical task of forging a compassionate bond with its readers. Pascoli here presents, and in many poems dramatizes, his specific biographical trauma – namely, the loss of the father through assassination – and his subsequent precipitation into a world of financial and emotional deprivation. But, through the poetry, he translates this trauma in such a way as to evoke the figure of a shared, structural trauma: the child's loss of the imagined 'phallic mother' and his/her subsequent precipitation into the symbolic world of deprivation. Pascoli's particular tragedy – his personal, unique loss – elicits the compassion of readers who have no connection to it because the poetry resonates with a more universal longing.

5 Remembering the Golden Age

> The world's great age begins anew
> The golden years return
>
> Percy Bysshe Shelley, 'Hellas'

In 'L'era nuova' (1899) and *Future of an Illusion* (1927–8),[1] as the titles indicate, Pascoli and Freud adopt a kind of prophetic stance, contemplating the future course of civilization. In particular, they consider the relationship between faith and science, characterizing religious faith as an 'illusion' and modern science as its foil.[2] Both writers posit their own discourse (poetry, psychoanalysis) as the bearer of a sober 'truth,' in contrast to the comforting illusions offered by religion. In so doing, both Pascoli and Freud construct a temporal scheme of revelation or demystification that unfolds both phylogenetically (from primitive illusions to modern rationality) and ontogenetically (from infantile illusions to adult rationality). Both writers cast themselves as demystifiers who, by unveiling the illusory foundations of earlier belief systems, seek to promote a more mature and realistic basis for future ethical and moral conduct. In this final chapter, then, I consider both Giovanni Pascoli and Sigmund Freud in their roles as social thinkers. Their cultural writings allow us to survey the vision each proposes of the general scope, goals, and contributions of their enterprises. More specifically, these prophetic, forward-looking essays reveal yet another manifestation of the writers' exploration of origins, namely, their use of the ancient myth of the golden age.

'L'era nuova,' delivered on the eve of a new century, takes up again the question of the moral scope of poetry. While in *Il fanciullino* Pascoli emphasized the wonder of the child, newly arrived in the world and marvelling at all around him, here in this somewhat darker essay he considers the relative merits of science and faith in the face of man's mortality and inevitable death. Pascoli, then, in discussing the goals of poetry chooses to focus on the two points that allow him to speak in a universalizing key: birth (infancy) and death – the two end points of existence that all people have in common, whatever other differences may divide them. Pascoli here argues insistently that poetry's role in the dawning century is to become the 'coscienza di scienza' – the conscience of science. That is, poetry must make readers truly integrate and feel what science has intellectually revealed about mankind: namely, our mortality. Similarly, in *Future of an Illusion*, Freud argues that religion derives from man's universal need to feel protected and loved in the face of the threatening and overwhelming natural world. The image of God the Father, he claims, is a primitive and infantile illusion, based in Oedipal ambivalence, created to assuage this profound sense of helplessness.[3] Religion, in short, is society's shared 'obsessional neurosis,' and Freud calls for mankind to grow up.

Beginning in the fourth chapter of *Future*, Freud adopts a dialogic form in which he gives voice, in quotation marks, to an imagined dissenter. At various points in the essay, this 'other' voice points out what appear to be logical inconsistencies in Freud's argument and offers other criticisms and rebuttals of Freud's claims. Freud, I suggest, sets up this 'dialogue' in order to contrast his own 'scientific' discourse ('which is no illusion,' he asserts in the closing sentence of the essay) with religion. Freud notes that religion admits of no open dialogue and no discussion, but instead relies on monologic authority. Freud, then, by creating and incorporating this questioning voice, underscores that *his* discourse has no fear of being interrogated. At the same time, the dialogue sets the stage for further elaboration and clarification of his arguments as 'responses' to this interlocutor. This strategy stands in stark contrast to that of religion, which does not permit such dialogic intercourse because, Freud claims, it cannot answer any questions that may challenge it.

Pascoli employs a similar rhetorical strategy. He imagines the collective voice of his fellows ('si dice') and allows that voice to address science directly as 'tu' – 'you.' In this manner, the voice speaks *to* science as if in dialogue (and, in fact, 'science' has the opportunity to speak in its own defence) rather than speaking only *about* it. Interestingly, Pascoli's voice in speaking to science anticipates precisely the imaginary question put to Freud by his interlocutor:

> Oh! tu sei fallita, o scienza: ed è bene: ma sii maledetta, che hai rischiato di far fallire anche l'*altra*! La felicità tu non l'hai data, e non la potevi dare: ebbene, se non distrutta, hai attenuata, oscurata, amareggiata quella che ci dava la fede. (*Opere*, 2: 443)
>
> [Oh! you have failed, o science! and it is well: but may you be cursed, because you have run the risk of making the *other* fail, too! You did not, and could not, give us happiness: and this would be fine, if you had not destroyed, darkened, embittered that which faith used to give us.]
>
> I think I have now shown that your endeavours come down to an attempt to replace a proved and emotionally valuable illusion by another one, which is unproved and without emotional value. (*Standard Edition*, 21: 52)

The intervening, invented voices accuse both 'science' and Freud, science's advocate, of having stripped men of religion's consolations by revealing those comforts to be illusory and also of having failed to offer anything of comparable consolation in the place of discredited religion, thus leaving men bereft. While these texts engage the same debate and consider many of the same details, the dialogic form reveals how Pascoli strives to adopt a more transcendent viewpoint. Pascoli permeates his text with a multiplicity of voices. He quotes, for example, Horace, Virgil, Homer, and Vincenzo Monti at various points throughout the essay and embeds 'quotations' from 'science' and the 'public' in the course of his exposition. In some passages his critique of 'primitivism' becomes so nostalgic and impassioned that one wonders whether he is debunking or advocating this view. For example, in quoting the 'public' and their frustration with the alleged advances of the modern age, Pascoli writes, 'Siamo costretti di sofisticare con tuoi colori, o scienza, gli ingenui prodotti della fede' (*Opere* 2: 443) [We are forced to adorn in your colours, O science, the ingenuous products of faith]. Naive, childlike faith must be dressed up in the robes of sophisticated science to be legitimated. Throughout 'L'era nuova,' such strategies of quotation and empathy make it difficult at times to locate precisely Pascoli's own voice. Where Freud speaks as the scientist, articulating one of the two sides from within the debate, Pascoli takes a perspective that includes and is simultaneously outside of the two competing discourses: the position of poetry.

Dwelling on the failure of scientific advances to conquer death, Pascoli asserts that the goal of poetry in the new century will be to make men face their mortality: *science* cannot overcome death, it can only make life more convenient and easy, and *faith* gives us only an illusion of immortality. Poetry should make us fully human by allowing us truly to feel our smallness and mortality. In this way, it prevents us from attempting to escape back into bestial unconsciousness. Poetry must be the 'coscienza di scienza.' It does not offer the illusory consolation that religion once did, but it does fill the emotional gap left by science when it dismantles that consolation. Since the essay focuses on the finality of death, the 'fede' Pascoli refers to is the belief in the immortality of the individual soul and an afterlife. What science has revealed, and what poetry must make us truly realize, is the illusory foundation of that belief. Death, in short, becomes the bottom line. The truth of its finality serves as the foil not only to religion, which tries to offer a transcendence, but also to science, which has discovered no cure for it, as Freud acknowledges when he writes, 'and finally there is the painful riddle of death, against which no medicine has yet been found, nor probably will be' (*Standard Edition*, 21: 16).

As a corollary to humanity's mortality and the finitude of death, the texts emphasize man's smallness in the face of the infinite cosmos. For Pascoli, while science has established the knowledge of humanity's relative impotence, it is poetry's job to make us integrate that knowledge into our 'conscience.' He speaks of 'l'infinita piccolezza nostra a confronto dell'infinita grandezza e moltitudine degli astri. Ricordo il Leopardi e il Poe, e potrei ricordare molti altri. Tuttavia sulle nostre anime quella spaventevole proporzione ... non è ancora entrata nella nostra coscienza' (*Opere*, 2: 448-9) [our infinite smallness in comparison to the infinite grandeur and multitude of the heavenly bodies. I recall Leopardi and Poe, and I could recall many others. Nevertheless on our souls that frightening proportion ... has not yet entered into our consciousness]. Freud, too insists on the relative insignificance and non-centrality of humanity:

> Critics persist in describing as 'deeply religious' anyone who admits to a sense of man's insignificance or impotence in the face of the universe, although what constitutes the essence of the religious attitude is not this feeling but only the next step after it, which seeks a remedy for it. The man

who goes no further, but humbly acquiesces in the small part which human beings play in the great world – such a man is, on the contrary, irreligious in the truest sense of the word. (*Standard Edition*, 21: 32–3)

From these considerations, an ethical purpose to their projects emerges: that of freeing their contemporaries from illusion, of adopting the pose of a clear-sighted rationalist unafraid of the truth. In this regard, both writers take aim at one of the most popular manifestations of irrational illusions of the time, the séances of the spiritualists. Pascoli vividly contrasts the sublimity of Old Testament visions (here specifically Ezekiel 1: 1–28) with the absurdity of the conjurers studied by such eminent scientists as William Crookes:[4]

> Siamo costretti di prendere in prestito da Crookes le fotografie degli spiriti immateriali e materializzati, per rinforzare la vecchia metafisica: a far la riprova con un tavolino che gira, della sublime visione di Ezechiele. (*Opere* 2: 443)
>
> [We are forced to borrow Crookes's photographs of immaterial spirits which have materialized, in order to support the old metaphysics: to confirm the sublime vision of Ezekiel with a spinning table.]

Freud does not spare the mediums his disdain:

> The proceedings of the spiritualists meet us at this point; they are convinced of the survival of the individual soul and they seek to demonstrate to us beyond doubt the truth of this one religious doctrine. Unfortunately they cannot succeed in refuting the fact that the appearance and utterances of their spirits are merely the products of their own mental activity. They have called up the spirits of the greatest men and of the most eminent thinkers, but all the pronouncements and information which they have received from them have been so foolish and so wretchedly meaningless that one can find nothing credible in them but the capacity of the spirits to adapt themselves to the circle of people who have conjured them up. (*Standard Edition* 21: 27–8)

The venom with which Freud and Pascoli mock the spiritualist movement may be motivated in part by the proximity of their own projects to the derided séances and photographed ghosts. Freud's own work with hypnosis, and Pascoli's poetic resuscitations of his *cari morti* resemble the spiritualists' practices closely enough to stimulate the dismissive gestures quoted above, and the reassertions of the rational bases of their own work.

Both carry the conviction that, rather than safeguarding morality, illusion-based belief systems actually stunt moral development. The disillusioning of people will not bring about a chaotic collapse of civilized or moral behaviour, but will open the way for a truly enlightened code of civility, based on the knowledge that all share a common fate, one that is irreparable and inevitable. Pascoli insists that '*saremo più buoni* ... e riconosceremo, a questo segno, a quest'aria di famiglia, a questa traccia di dolore immedicabile, i nostri fratelli per nostri fratelli' (*Opere*, 2: 451–2) [we will be better ... and we will recognize, with that sign, with this sense of family, with this trace of incurable grief, our brother as our brothers]. In fact, the phrase 'saremo più buoni,' printed in italics, appears earlier in the essay (as the conditional, 'saremmo più buoni,' also in italics), and thus becomes a sort of refrain. In a similar way, Freud discusses at length the social advantages of realizing that moral codes and prohibitions were not divinely and arbitrarily imposed but serve a logical function for communal benefit.[5] Both Pascoli and Freud, then, cast themselves as rationalists who want to expose the inadequacy of religion as a compensating illusion in the face of death.[6] Both advocate a replacement of that illusory defence mechanism with a courageous stance of confronting the 'truth.' Such a stance, rather than pulling the rug from under all moral precepts, will ultimately encourage a more mature, developed, and human morality. In other words, psychoanalytic theory and poetry serve as antidotes to narcissism, revealing the self as neither immortal nor primary.

Furthermore, both writers draw on a chronological construct in which 'illusion' temporally precedes rational knowledge. In this way, they posit scientific, rational knowledge as an advance in a developmental process. This temporal construct, moreover, obtains in both a phylogenetic and an ontogenetic scheme. Freud makes this parallel explicit throughout his text. To give just one example, he points out this isomorphic relationship in explaining the psychological motivations for the construction of the fantasy of a protective and paternal god. In his explanation, Freud makes reference (as he does several times throughout the text) to his earlier anthropological study *Totem and Taboo*. He writes 'man makes the forces of nature not simply into persons with whom he can associate as he would with his equals ... but he gives them the character of a father. He turns them into gods, following in this, as I have tried to show, not only an infant prototype but a phylogenetic one' (*Standard Edition*,

2: 17). Indeed it is the central thesis of the text that religion is a stage of arrested psychological development in society; thus, the infant/primitive parallel is implicit throughout the entire argument. Pascoli is equally explicit in constructing and deploying this parallel. In *Il fanciullino* he writes, 'I primi uomini non sapevano niente; sapevano quello che sai tu' (35) ['The first men knew nothing; they knew what you know, Child'].[7] In this regard, Giuseppe Nava has summarized succinctly that 'Il fondamento teorico dichiarato è la ben nota equazione pascoliana, e ancor prima leopardiana e vichiana, tra infanzia dell'uomo, mondo antico come infanzia dell'umanità, e facoltà e linguaggio della poesia' [The theoretical foundation is the well-known equation asserted by Pascoli, and by Leopardi and Vico before him, among the infancy of man, the ancient world as humanity's infancy, and the poetic faculty and language].[8]

The parallel drawn between the development of the individual and the evolution of the species in these writers is not a new one. Nava points out the precedents for such parallels in Vico and in Leopardi.[9] Furthermore, David Archard has pointed out the influence of Darwin's 1877 essay, 'A Biographical Sketch of a Child,' as well as the work of Ernst Haeckel (1834–1919) on late nineteenth-century thinking.[10] He explains that, 'An explicit formulation of the relationship between the development of the individual and that of the species, Darwinian in spirit and employed by Darwin himself, was made by Ernst Haeckel. His "biogenetic law," which can be briefly summarized as "ontogeny is the short and rapid recapitulation of phylogeny," was embraced by many late nineteenth-century evolutionary thinkers.'[11] Archard points out that while the 'strict' or literal interpretation of the 'law' was 'widely discredited,' the looser interpretation, which posited an isomorphic parallel between the two kinds of 'development,' became a widespread notion. Archard cites Freud as one of the inheritors of this view.

This infantile/primitive isomorphic construct is not restricted to Darwinian-influenced evolutionary thought, however.[12] A similar parallel exists in Christian thinking. As we saw in the previous chapter, eighteenth- and nineteenth-century philosophers, poets, and child-raising experts invested the 'child' with a pre-lapsarian innocence and purity, thus suggesting a parallel between the individual's infancy and the infancy of mankind, each progressing from innocence to knowledge. The book of Genesis, of course, provides the Judaeo-Christian model of mankind's fall from primal innocence (Genesis 3: 1–24). Pascoli discusses this biblical story in some detail in his critical essay on Dante's

Divine Comedy entitled 'Minerva oscura' (published in instalments in the journal *Convito*). In his analysis of Dante's exposition of the sins of usury and sodomy, he meditates upon the consequence of Adam's first sin. In the Edenic world, production (of food) and reproduction were effortless, whereas, as a consequence of original sin these activities were burdened with pain and necessitated work. In his Dantean exegesis, then, Pascoli asserts that the sinfulness of usury and sodomy derives from their defiance of productivity and of work: the realities of the postlapsarian, adult world (*Opere* 2: 748–50).

The biblical model describes the movement from primal purity to present pain as loss – as a movement from ease to work and from plenty to deprivation. In 'L'era nuova,' the moment of 'knowledge' is just the opposite: the 'unhappy discovery' (echoing, I think, Eve's eating of the fruit of the Tree of Knowledge) is the knowledge of death that elevates us above the animals. He writes 'la lugubre ma benefica scoperta ... che siete mortali. Perchè fu quella ... la vostra *ascensione*' (ibid., 439) [the lugubrious but beneficial discovery ... that you are mortal. Because that was ... your *ascension*]. The animals evoked in 'L'era nuova' are not the sparrows, owls, and other delicate creatures we often find lovingly described in the poems, but vicious predators with destructive fangs and claws: 'Ogni volta che scendete dall'inamabile altezza, alla quale eravate ascesi, voi vi trovate nelle dita i vecchi artigli e nelle mandibole le vecchie zanne e nel cuore la vecchia ferocia di cannibali' (ibid., 440). [Every time you descend from the bitter height to which you had ascended, you find on your fingers the old claws, in your jaws the old fangs and in your heart the old ferocity of cannibals']. This essay highlights the ferocity rather than the fragility of the primordial (note the anaphora of *vecchio*), and calls poetry to a humanizing mission: to make us truly remember our smallness and the finality of death. *Fede*, Pascoli (like Freud) argues, would have us 'forget' this discovery.

As Pascoli asserts in *Sotto il velame* (1900), classical antiquity offers similar accounts of a perfect originary state in its myths of the golden age – the 'sogno pagano dell'Eden cristiano' [pagan dream of the Christian Eden].[13] Pascoli engages several texts throughout his works that elaborate this myth, including Hesiod's *Erga* (*Works and Days*, eighth century BCE), Virgil's 'Ecloga IV' (the fourth or 'Messianic' eclogue, 40 BCE), and Horace's 'Carmen saeculare' ('Hymn for a New Age,' 17 BCE). In *Sotto il velame*, Pascoli analyses in detail Dante's medieval deployment of this myth as embodied in his image of the Old Man of Crete (*Inferno* XIV).[14]

Hesiod emphasizes the ease and plenty enjoyed by the people of the earliest historic era. Opening his account of the succession of golden, silver, bronze, heroic, and iron ages, he writes:

> In the beginning, the immortals who have their homes on Olympos
> created the golden generation of mortal people.
> These lived in Kronos' time, when he was the king in heaven.
> They lived as if they were gods, their hearts free from all sorrow,
> by themselves, and without hard work or pain; no miserable
> old age came their way ...
> the fruitful grainland yielded its harvest to them
> of its own accord; this was great and abundant, while they at their pleasure
> quietly looked after their works, in the midst of good things. (lines 109–19)[15]

In contrast to this blissful past era, the narrator himself lives in the miserable present. The greater part of the poem offers concrete, practical counsel to his brother 'Perses,' insisting on the advantages of hard work and foresight and supplying maxims and technical advice on topics from agriculture to clothes making to marriage. The necessity of work in the current age provides the unifying theme to the poem.

Virgil's eclogue heralds the return of Saturn, god of the golden age, to mark the treaty between Marc Antony and Octavian. Antony's marriage to Octavian's sister, the poem suggests, will produce a son whose birth will inaugurate a return of the golden age. Virgil, in depicting the effect the child's birth will engender, offers the following fantasy:

> At tibi prima, puer, nulo munuscula cultu
> errantis hederas cum baccare tellus
> mixtaque ridenti colocasia fundet acantho.
> ipsae lacte domun referent distenta capellae
> ubera ...
> molli paulatim flavescet campus arista
> incultisque rubens pendebit sentibus uua
> et durae quercus sudabunt roscida mella. (lines 18–22, 28–30)

> [But first, as little gifts for you, child, Earth untilled
> Will pour the straying ivy rife, and baccaris,
> And colocasia mixing with acanthus' smile.
> She-goats unshepherded will bring home udders plumped
> With milk ...
> Soft spikes of grain will gradually gild the fields,
> And reddening grapes will hang in clusters on wild brier,
> And dewy honey sweat from tough Italian oaks.][16]

As in Hesiod, the Virgilian images of the golden age emphasize bounty and, specifically, the *spontaneous generation* of the earth's abundance, without recourse to work: 'non rastros patietur humus, non uinea falcem' (line 40) ['The soil will suffer hoes no more, nor vines the hook' (trans. Lee, 59)].

Roughly twenty-five years after Virgil's hopeful pastoral, inspired by Octavia's betrothal, Octavian (now Augustus) commissioned Horace to write his joyful 'Carmen.' This hymn to Apollo and Diana accompanied the celebration of the 'secular' games, that 'would mark the achievements of the Augustan regime and inaugurate a new age (*saeculum*) in Roman history.'[17] Horace depicts the reign of Augustus as a revival of the golden age for the Seven Hills. The chorus rejoices that 'iam Fides et Pax et Honos Pudorque / priscus et neglecta redire Virtus / audit, apparetque beata pleno / Copia cornu' (lines 57–60) ['Now Good Faith, Peace, and Honour, along with old-fashioned Modesty and Virtue, who has been so long neglected, venture to return, and blessed plenty with her full horn is seen by all' (trans. Rudd, 267)]. While references to agricultural abundance and to 'Mother Earth, who is fertile in crops and livestock' ['fertilis frugum pecorisque tellus / spicea donet Cererem corona,' lines 29–30] are not absent here, they are overshadowed by the emphasis on Rome's power and its destined right to that power.

Following Horace, Dante depicts the reign of the 'buon Agosto' as a near-embodiment of the golden age in the *Divine Comedy*, a time of peace and good government. But, of course, from Dante's perspective, this Augustan golden age has become almost as distant a cultural memory as Saturn's golden age was to Virgil and Horace. As the pilgrim and his guide continue through the seventh circle of Hell, following their encounter with the violent against God, they discuss the origin of the infernal rivers. Dante here offers, through 'Virgil,' a provocative and enigmatic image of the succession of ages, an image in which one man's body encapsulates the whole mythical course of human history. Virgil explains to Dante: "'In mezzo mar siede un paese guasto,"/ diss'elli allora, "che s'appella Creta,/ sotto 'l cui rege già 'l mondo casto. // Una montagna v'è che già fu lieta / d'acqua e di fronde, che si chiamò Ida; or e diserta come cosa vieta"' (*Inferno* XIV: 94–9) ['In the midst of the sea lies a ruined land,' he said / then, 'called Crete, under whose king the world once was chaste. A mountain is there that once was happy with / water and foliage, called Ida; now it is desolate, like / an outworn thing'].[18] In the mountain of Crete, which, we are reminded, provided Rhea with a hiding place for Jupiter, stands an old man with a head of gold, arms and chest of silver, a brass abdomen, iron legs, and a clay right foot, on which he rests most of his weight. From his neck down is a crack from which tears drop. The reader, along with the pilgrim, discovers that this extraordinary mountain is the origin of the infernal rivers. The image itself, as Durling points out, has 'a double origin' in both classical poetry (Ovid) and scripture (Deuteronomy).[19] As such, the image serves as a synecdoche of the whole Dantean project, an imaginative synthesis of pagan and Christian traditions. The old man is not so much a metaphor for the course of human history as an embodiment of the *figurations* (Ovidian, biblical) of human corruption.

Pascoli mobilizes all these representations of the golden age in his works. Hesiod appears as the central character in 'Il poeta degli Iloti' ('The Poet of the Helots,' referring to Hesiod as the poet of the Spartan serfs). This poem, divided into two parts, contains many direct allusions to Hesiod, both the *Erga* and the *Theogony*. It is an imaginative tale in which Hesiod, returning victorious from a poetry competition, travels home with a humble slave. Although his winning composition had been a poem of war, by the end of his journey with the wise and honest slave, he renounces the false world of epic and devotes himself to singing of honest, humble work: 'Ma poi mi piacque, non cantare il vero, / si la menzogna che somiglia al vero. / Ora il lavoro canterò, né curo / ch'io sembri ai re l'Aedo degli schiavi' (lines 152–5) ['it pleased me not to sing of truth, but of the lie that resembles the truth. / Now I will sing of work, nor do I care / that I seem to the kings a Bard of slaves'].[20] The character of Hesiod, then, emerges as the counter to the Odysseus of 'L'ultimo viaggio': where Odysseus attempted to leave behind the tiresome, quotidian life of Ithaca and voyage back to the epic adventures of his heroic and bellicose youth, 'Hesiod' undertakes the opposite trajectory in his choice of thematic content for his poetry. Ultimately, both characters arrive at a realization of the illusory nature of that epic world. Bàrberi Squarotti has pointed out the various direct echoes of Hesiod's *Erga* in 'L'ultimo viaggio,' particularly in the image of the 'well-wrought steering-oar' hanging 'over the smoke of the fireplace.'[21] Such echoes smuggle Hesiod into Pascoli's Homeric poem, confronting the two characters ('Hesiod' and 'Ulysses') and underscoring the antithetical relationship between them. Hesiod embodies the subject reconciled to the adult realities of the world of work, while Ulysses dramatizes the captivation of infantile illusions.

Freud telescopes the golden age myth from the ages of man to personal history, and at the same time gives it a materialist reading. It is no longer the gods who ordain that the earth should burst forth in a burgeoning of nourishment for the race of men, but rather the mother, who provides the necessary sustenance for the infant. The fall from this 'golden age' becomes the loss of her gratuitous nourishment – as he writes in 'Femininity,' 'The child ... never gets over the pain of losing its mother's breast' – and the realization of the mother's 'castration.' In 'Family Romances' (1909), Freud considers the fantasies of neurotic children that seem aimed at their parents in 'revenge and retaliation' (239). Such fantasies, like the dreams of normal adults in which emperor and empress appear, seek to re-evoke the infant's perception of his or her parents as omnipotent. He writes,

> For a small child his parents are at first the only authority and the source of all belief ... But as intellectual growth increases, the child cannot help discovering by degrees the category to which his parents belong ... Indeed the whole effort at replacing the real father by a superior one is only an expression of the child's longing for the happy, vanished days when his father seemed to him the noblest and strongest of men and his mother the dearest and loveliest of women. He is turning away from the father whom he knows to-day to the father in whom he believed in the earlier years of his childhood; and his phantasy is no more than the expression of a regret that those happy days have gone. (*Standard Edition*, 9: 237, 240–1)

Freud here adumbrates in very clear terms the notion of a happier past grounded not in objective reality but in a certain perception of reality. Such a 'happy' period 'vanishes' with the accumulation of knowledge (the ability and opportunity to compare one's own parents with other adults). In sketching his own myth of a golden age and subsequent fall, Freud claims that the bygone era of plenty and abundance is grounded in illusions, the most fundamental and primary of which is the illusion of the pre-Oedipal, phallic mother. When reality makes it impossible to maintain such illusions about our own individual parents, the fantasy is transferred onto God the Father and Mother Nature, omnipotent and protective.

The call to move beyond such fantasies motivates Pascoli's 'secular' speech (and here both senses of the adjective can be applied). Pascoli opens his 'L'era nuova' with Italian translations of both Horace and Virgil. Lamenting that the sybil's prophecies have been scattered in the winds (another Virgilian echo, of course), he redeploys the Augustan poets' words as an expression of hope for the promise of the twentieth century. He quotes (in Italian translation) lines six and seven of Virgil's Latin eclogue: 'torna la Vergine già, il buon tempo è già di Saturno: / genere d'uomini nuovo dai ceruli culmini scende' ['iam redit et uirgo, redeunt Saturnia regna, / iam noua progenies caelo demittitur alto']; 'Now too returns the Virgin; Saturn's rule returns; A new begetting now descends from Heaven's height'].[22] Invoking these lines, Pascoli wonders what the dawning century will bring, and if, indeed, there will be a 'renaissance' of 'justice and peace, bounty and wealth' (*Opere*, 2: 438).

Pascoli frames the lines from Virgil with two quotations (in Italian translation) from Horace's 'Hymn.' Should we at this turning of the century, he asks, raise a hymn to the sun? Horace's poem provides an apostrophe to the 'old and young god of our people': 'Sol di vita che con il fiammo carro / porti e celi il giorno, che sempre un altro e / quello sei, non veder di Roma / nulla più grande!' ['alme Sol, curru nitido diem qui / promis et celas aliusque et idem / nasceris, possis nihil urbe Roma / visere maius' (lines 9–12); 'Life-giving Sun, who with your shining car bring forth the day and hide it away, who are born anew and yet the same, may you never be able to behold anything greater than the city of Rome!' (trans. Rudd, 263)]. The invocation of the sun lends a certain classical *gravitas* to the text. Yet Pascoli immediately questions the appropriateness of this borrowed apostrophe. The first two sentences of the speech are, in fact, questions, and the speech, furthermore, was delivered in Messina, not Rome. Later in the speech (Part VI), Pascoli redeploys this same quotation, revealing, precisely, its out-of-placeness, its anachronism. Today, he explains, we know quite well that the sun is not 'always other' – we know that the sun we see rising in the east is the self-same physical body that appeared to set in the west. The 'primitives,' however, saw the sun as simultaneously other and the same. They imagined that it must travel in a carriage from one end of the globe to the other. Horace 'rendered in a memorable formula' the primitive, poetic illusions of an earlier age.

Pascoli returns to Horace again just after the Virgilian quotation, to illustrate further what the desired golden age would bring: 'Fede e Pace, Onore e Costume antico ed / osa la negletta Virtù tornare e / già si mostra l'universal Rocchezza / piena di doni' (lines 57–60; the Latin is cited, with English translation, at page 144 above). The Roman images of the new age foregrounds that this *era nuova* is in fact the returning of an ancient, originary model. Hope, in other words, is grounded in memory and repetition. As a poet citing poets, Pascoli elicits the expectation of parallelism: readers might assume that he, Pascoli, wants to imply that he is adopting the role and voice of the Augustan poets. Instead, the citations serve an *ubi sunt* motif: 'Oh! gli uomini si guardano attorno, cercando l'Orazio migliore che canti l'Augusto più benefico e la Roma più magnifica ...' (*Opere*, 2: 438) [Oh! men look around searching for a better Horace who may sing of a more beneficial Augustus and a more magnificent Rome]. Pascoli is not the 'better Horace,' because the advances of the *scienza nuova* and the realities of modern warfare ('guerre coloniali, nazionali ed etniche') have precluded the return of those ancient illusions.

The citations that open 'L'era nuova,' then, stand in an antithetical rather than epigrammatic relationship to the speech that calls for a move away from such primitive illusions. These quotations, I think, are equally telling in what they omit. In both cases, Pascoli leaves off precisely where Virgil and Horace invoke Lucina, the goddess of childbirth. Virgil's fourth eclogue, in lines that immediately follow Pascoli's citation, goes on to predict the coming of a new golden age with the birth of the emperor's son: 'tu modo nascenti puero, quo ferrea primum / desinet ac toto surget gens aurea mundo, / casta faue Lucina' (lines 8–10) ['O chaste Lucina, look with blessing on the boy whose birth will end the iron race at last and raise a golden through the world' (trans. Lee, 57)]. Later in the poem, the pain inherent in childbearing is alluded to parenthetically. Horace, too, immediately following the invocation to the 'life-giving sun' quoted by Pascoli, goes on to ask 'rite matures aperire partus / lenis, Ilithyia, tuere matres, / sive tu Lucina probas vocari / seu Genitalis' ('Carmen,' lines 13–16) ['You whose gentle function it is to open the way for the births in due season, protect our mothers, O Ilithyia, or Lucina if you prefer that name, or Genitalis' (trans. Rudd, 263)]. Earth's burgeoning plenitude, in both Roman writers, becomes intimately linked with human reproduction. In fact, both original compositions are epithalamiums of a sort: Virgil's celebrates the promised marriage of Antony and Octavia, and Horace's condones the new marriage laws (the 'lege marita' of line 20) approved by the senate, which will result in a return to family values and healthier offspring. Hovering behind the images of a prolific Mother Earth spontaneously bringing forth her fruits and vegetation is the mystery of human procreation. The figure of Lucina, furthermore, casts a shadow on the golden imagery of Saturn's reign.[23] Virgil's symmetrical references to 'mater' and 'pater' highlight that the role of 'Genitalis' is predicated on difference, and Horace's allusion to Augustus's 18 BCE dictate implies that her power, which needs to be regulated by laws, is potentially disruptive.

In these golden age poems, the difference and disruption of human origins underlie the images of peace and plenty. The quotations chosen by Pascoli as banners to his speech omit the original poems' considerations of human fertility and reproduction, but the role of Lucina re-emerges in the last of Pascoli's *Convivial poems*, to be discussed below.

'L'era nuova' is not the only occasion on which Pascoli deploys Virgil's fourth eclogue. Fragments from the same poem appear as epigrams to the following collections of Italian verse:

Myricae and *Canti di castelvecchio*: 'arbusta iuvant humilesque myricae' [they delight in trees and lowly tamarisks]
Primi poemetti and *Nuovi poemetti*: 'paulo maiora' [slightly greater]
Odi e inni: 'canamus' [let us sing]
Poemi conviviali: 'non omnes arbusta iuvant' [not all delight in trees]

In their complete form, the opening two lines of the fourth eclogue read as follows: 'Sicelides Musae, paulo maiora canamus!/non omnis arbusta iuvant humilesque myricae' ['Sicilian Muses, grant me a slightly greater song! / Not all delight in trees and lowly tamarisks' (trans. Lee, 57)]. In these opening lines, Virgil begs the Muses for the power to compose a weightier poem, more lofty than the other eclogues, whose simple pastoral themes are implied by the 'trees and lowly tamarisks.' The fragmentation of the lines dramatizes the fracturing of the wholeness of the 'original.' These fragments, broken out of their original context, signify differently. In *Myricae* (whose very title is a quotation from Virgil) the epigram, by omitting the negation, implies the very opposite of Virgil's sense: in Pascoli's context, the humble pastoral theme does bring 'delight,' for example. Even when regrouped, as in the preceding list, the epigrams do not 'add up' to the full verses of the original. Rather, there are repetitions and omissions that, when brought together, do not reconstruct the whole. Pascoli's fragmented citations, I believe, highlight a constitutive fragmentation inherent in the 'whole original.' Although overtly praising the glories of the golden age and heralding its return, Virgil's eclogue is riven by 'vestiges' that undermine the Edenic imagery. References – fleeting and parenthetical – to pain, deceit, and war run like hairline fractures through the poem: 'si qua manent sceleris uestigia nostri' (line 13) ['if traces of our sin remain']; 'pauca tamen suberunt priscae uestigia fraudis' (line 31) ['traces, though few, will linger yet of the old deceit']; '(matri longa decem tulerunt fastidia menses)' (line 61, parentheses in original) ['Ten lunar months have brought your mother long discomfort']. These contaminating 'vestiges,' or 'traces' or fractures anticipate the *fessure* of the Old Man of Crete, fractures that are not restricted to the fallen body but are already there in the golden head.

Like Freud's reading of Hoffmann as described by Cixous, Pascoli's analysis of Dante vigorously seeks to establish identities and dispel doubt.[24] On a rhetorical level, the preponderance of the copulative (*è* and *sono*) and the repetition of the 'così ... come' structure announce this strategy. Throughout his discussion of the Old Man of Crete, (which follows the general methodology of the entire essay), he repeatedly asserts a series of allegorical identities and correspondences among diverse images. His first equation, mentioned above, identifies Crete with Eden. Both sites, he reminds us, were fruitful forests that became the birthplace of humanity. To reinforce the seamless equation of pagan and Christian imagery, Pascoli later asserts, 'l'età dell'oro era innocente, non c'è da dubitare' (*Opere*, 2: 475) [the golden age was innocent, this is not to be doubted]. He goes on to assert that 'il Veglio è il genere umano stesso' [the Old Man is the human race itself], and that the Old Man's body is composed of elements that 'sono le quattro età del genere umano' [are the four ages of the human race]. Pascoli turns his attention to the wound that begins where the golden head ends, and, drawing on St Thomas, identifies the wound as 'vulneratio naturae' [wound of nature] ('La fessura è molto probabilmente, dunque, codesta vulneratio', ibid., 473) [the fissure is quite probably, then, this wound]. This weakness resulted when original sin unhinged the human potentials from reason's control. These wounded human potentials (*la ragione, la volontà, l'irascibile, il concupiscibile*), consequently, are no longer oriented towards the virtues (Prudence, Temperance, Justice, and Fortitude). Pascoli strives to clarify the allegorical significance of each of the rivers (Acheron, Styx, Phlegethon, and Cocytus) and other infernal landmarks by aligning them with theological concepts (Bede's four injuries, the four virtues, etc.). Even in the face of irregularities, Pascoli persists in explaining away disruptions so that the text continues to coordinate with his systemizations. Categories are sometimes subdivided, and sometimes conjoined so as to add up to the requisite numbers. For example, he writes in this section, 'Il peccato originale indebolì queste quattro potenze dell'anima, sì da agevolare quelle quattro specie di peccati. Quattro? Ma sono tre. Sì, tre disposizioni: incontinenza, malizia con forza e malizia con frode. Ma l'incontinenza è duplice, di concupiscenza e d'irascibile. E così sono quattro' (ibid., 475) [Original sin weakened these four potentials of the soul, so as to facilitate those four kinds of sin. Four? But there are three.

Yes, three dispositions: incontinence, malice with force, and malice with deception. But incontinence is double, that of lust and that of anger. And so there are four]. At points such as this, the readings feel forced.

All the titles of his Dante essays ('Minerva oscura,' 'Sotto il velame,' 'La mirabile visione') imply the faculty of vision. The essays demonstrate the desire to see through the haze, to discern clearly the truth beyond veils and obscurities. In constructing his elaborate series of equations, Pascoli seeks to close holes, to find in Dante's masterpiece a comprehensive system of congruities – 'una perfetta corrispondenza,' as he puts it. His methodology strives to re-create a pristine, golden whole free of difference, like the Old Man's head before the fissures of time after the fall and the fractures of sin. This vigorous systemization responds to the uncanny qualities of Dante's images by attempting to neutralize them. Pascoli's reading of Dante, I suggest, strives to force equations where the figurative language and metaphorical imagery suggest rather than equate, to dispel the haze and see clearly, to establish identity and negate differences. In other words, his reading attempts to conjure up a golden age by exorcising the uncanniness of figurative language and asserting pure allegory in its place.

Recalling Freud's analogy of having located the 'source of the Nile' in his search for the origins of hysteria, Pascoli insists that 'I fiumi dell'inferno hanno una sola e unica fonte: la fessura del gran veglio'(ibid., 475). The rivers of hell have one single and unique source (*una, sola, unica*): the wound of the Old Man of Crete who 'is' the human race. Pascoli, like Freud, seeks here a single, unified point of origin. But the origin of the hellish waters is a wound, an opening, a fracture: the bleeding out of the human race after its fall from perfect justice and innocence. The pure golden head, on the other hand, as the realm of perfect correspondences, does not secrete anything.[25] The rivers of hell flowing from the Old Man's wounds recall the inspirational springs flowing from the 'wound' in Mt Helicon created by Pegasus. Where the springs were sacred to the Muses, no poetry flows from the seamless, silent golden age.[26]

As an accomplished Latinist and Dante scholar, Pascoli knew both Virgil's poem and the role this eclogue plays in Dante's *Purgatorio*. Here, this 'messianic' pastoral serves as the salvatory text for the poet-character Statius. In the *Purgatorio*, Statius claims that he became both a poet and a Christian through reading Virgil's works. Specifically, he explains how he read Virgil's fourth eclogue not as a celebration of the birth of the pagan child but as a prophecy of the birth of Christ. Pascoli invokes precisely this Christian 'misreading' as the capstone of his *Poemi conviviali*. Having cited a fragment of the eclogue as his epigram, he concludes this collection of classically inspired verses with a moving poem depicting the Nativity of Christ, 'La buona novella.' This poem, I believe, can be read as Pascoli's translation of Virgil's fourth eclogue. (The *terza rima* of the entire composition announces the Dantean presence as well.) The piece emphasizes the *fessure* of the original and re-evokes the image of Lucina in its depiction of the Nativity.[27] The poem opens 'In the east,' where the shepherds, some tending their herds by the babbling springs and others by the silent tombs, sing of life and of God. An angel leads them to the manger in Bethlehem, where they encounter a humble Mary and a fragile Christ. The shepherds' songs recall the pastoral pieces of Virgil and at the same time embody the poetic vision of the *fanciullino*. The second half of the poem is set in Rome, in the cloyed and exhausted lull immediately following the winter celebrations of the 'Saturnalia,' the feasts honouring Saturn. In the final section of the poem, an angel arrives in Rome from Judea to announce 'peace.' However, the dissolute and violent Romans, 'drunk with blood,' are deaf to the message. Only a humble, wounded gladiator hears the angel, and then 'chiuse gli occhi in pace' ['he closed his eyes in peace' (2: 143)].

The two parts of the poem echo each other without, however, becoming mirror images. In the east, Bethlehem 'dormiva' while in the west Roma 'dormiva.' Each part opens with a sort of panoramic, impersonal overview (marked by the grammatically impersonal and imperfect verbs), then focuses on particular characters and specific events (marked by a transition to the *passato remoto* and named subjects: Maath, the shepherd, and 'il Geta,' the gladiator-slave). The humility and simplicity of the Virgin in Part One contrasts sharply with the powerful yet cold and distant Cibele/Rhea pagan goddess.

Pascoli unites the two parts by recourse to images of falling. The first and most striking of these images compares the meek song of the shepherds to the chirping of a fledgling fallen from its nest (interestingly, given Pascoli's hallmark imagery, the *nido* this time is implied but not named). 'E il canto, sotto i cieli arsi dal lume, / a piè dell'universo, era sommesso, / era non più che un pigolìo d'implume // caduto, sotto il suo grande cipresso' (I, lines 19–22) ['The song 'neath the heavens burning / with light lay meek under the universe, / was no more than a chirping of a fledgling // which has fallen beneath a great cypress' (2: 129)]. The vastness and abstractness of the 'cieli' and 'universo' on the one hand, contrasted with the concrete image of the fallen baby bird on the other, emphasize the smallness of the fledgling and, by implication, of the shepherd. The song becomes a specific, precise point in the oceanic expansiveness of the universe, seeming not just *sommesso* but almost *sommerso*. Pascoli's brilliant use of an adjective ('implume') and a past participle ('caduto') with no substantive to indicate the bird powerfully figures weakness: the creature is defined by what it lacks (*im-plume*, without feathers) and what it has lost (having fallen). The *enjambement* enacts what it describes, as if 'caduto' had fallen off the end of the previous poetic verse. The location 'under his great cypress' – the tree traditionally associated, of course, with death – casts the shadow of mortality onto the image of weakness and fragility.

The motif of falling is picked up (as it were) in several other verses. 'Dio! Che la nostra vita cader / fai, come pietra, dalla tua gran fionda.' In this truly daring poetic move, Pascoli, through the shepherd, compares God to a child with a slingshot, who lets human life fall like a rock down to earth. Contemplating the course of human life and the inevitability of death, the shepherd goes on to lament, 'Vedo qualche smarrito astro che cade: / muore anche l'astro' – even the stars fall and die. In Part Two, 'Le corone / eran cadute' while the spent revellers finally sleep. Meanwhile, only the wounded and dying gladiator lies awake, and the dripping of his blood echoes in the profound silence: 'Rantolava; il silenzio era profondo: / il cader lento d'una goccia rossa / solo restava del fragor del mondo' (III, lines 7–9) ['The death rattle; the silence was profound: / the slow falling of a red drop / alone remained of the din of the world' (2: 139)]. These numerous, repeated fallings evoke the theology of the poem's theme: God descending to earth in the person of His son, Jesus Christ, and the mission of the incarnated Christ to redeem fallen humanity. While the suffering and sinful images of humanity in both parts of the poem bespeak the post-lapsarian condition, the work does not simply versify orthodox doctrine. The poem's images of falling, often associated with images of death, contrast with the 'rising up' described in the contemporary 'L'era nuova.' In this speech, we recall, the knowledge of death was, Pascoli insists, 'la vostra *ascensione*.' In 'La buona novella,' the downward motion dramatizes a drive to return to bestial ignorance, a desire to descend.

Indeed the most direct connections between the poem and the contemporary speech concern the depiction of the beasts as unaware of their mortality. Rather than taking pride in their superior human knowledge, however, the shepherds clearly envy the fullness of life enjoyed by the ignorant animals: 'Addì cantava: – Tu, sola tu, vivi, / o greggia, che non mai dalle tue strade / vedi la Morte ferma là nei trivi' (II, lines 13–15) ['Addi sang: – You alone live, flock that never / sees from your paths Death standing motionless / where the roads of life and death cross each other' (2: 131)]. Three times in the poem, Pascoli depicts the herds as chewing, using the same verb: 'il dolce uguale ruminar del branco' (II, line 9) ['the sweet, calm ruminating of his herd' (2: 129)], and 'Ma tu, / pago il cuore, / stai ruminando sotto le rugiade' (II, lines 17–18) ['But you, your heart content, / keep on ruminating under the dews' (2: 131)]; and the bleeding gladiator is described as having to die far from 'suoi bovi ch'ora / sdraiati ruminavano pian piano' (III, lines 17–18) ['his oxen / who now rested, chewed, then chewed again' (2: 141)]. These images of peacefulness and satisfaction (*dolce, pago, piano*) contrast strongly with the suffering of the shepherds and gladiator. The beasts' contentment, Pascoli implies, lies in their exclusively literal relationship to the verb that describes them. That is, they 'ruminar' only in the literal sense – they chew and munch, but do not mull, think, ruminate. Not only does the more abstract sense of the verb not apply, but it is precisely because they have no access to the figurative meaning of the word that the beasts are envied by the shepherds, that they are more 'alive.'

The other object of the shepherds' wonder (and, consequently, the other addressee of their songs' apostrophe) is God. God shares with the sheep a fullness of life denied to humanity. The shepherd, who had earlier envisaged God as playing with a slingshot, is seeking 'il Dio che vivi tutto in sè.' The formulation recalls the vision that the entrapped Gog and Magog maintained of the godlike Zul: 'è sempre ciò che fu.' This awesome, marvellous image of God as self-sufficient, omnipresent, and eternal, along with the playful notion of the slingshot, casts the shepherd (who is also a composer of songs) as a *fanciullino*-figure. The shepherd's childlike perspective confronts, in dialogue, the perspective of Mary, who reveals in direct simplicity the knowledge that her child will die. The poem validates the shepherd's vision of a powerful, eternal God by enlisting our empathy for this perspective, and at the same time undercuts that vision by the poverty and fragility of Jesus and by Mary's sober truth.

Part Two deploys several images that allude to the golden age myth. The Saturnalia festival evokes the god of the golden age, and the temple of Rhea recalls that goddess's association with Crete, the 'pagan Eden.' The historical event (Christ's birth) unfolds in the 'time of the good Augustus,' praised by Horace as a return of the golden age. Finally, the detail of the gladiator's bleeding neck and his foot 'bianco di *creta*' [white with clay] recall, both in the visual image of a foot of clay and in the phonic evocation of the word *creta*, Dante's Old Man of Crete.[28] More than a trace of deceit and sin, however, contaminates this golden age. Pascoli vividly describes a post-orgiastic scene of extravagant violence ('Dischiuso il tempio era di Giano,' I, line 20) ['The temple of Janus was open' (2: 137)], lust ('In sogno le matrone / ora vedean gladiatori ignudi,' II, lines 2–3) ['In their dreams the matrons / now saw the gladiators naked' (2: 137)], slavery, and inebriation.[29] Into this fallen world, the angel arrives bearing its message of peace.

The concluding words of the poem, and of the collection, 'O catacombs,' darken the hopeful message of the angel's proclamation, alluding to the historical violence and injustice that continued to reign on earth after the birth of Christ. The conclusion implies that the golden age will not rain down or 'fall' from heaven, nor will justice be returning anytime soon. Ultimately, a true realization or fulfilment of the longed-for golden age comes only in death. The final lines of this poem and of the entire *Conviviali* collection echo with this point: 'Sol esso udì; ma lo ridisse ai morti, / e i morti ai morti, e le tombe alle tombe; / e non sapeano i sette colli assorti, / ciò che voi sapevate, o catecombe' (IV, lines 19–22) ['He alone heard; he said it to the dead, / the dead to the dead, the tombs to the tombs; / and the seven hills did not know, immersed / in sleep, that which you knew, O catacombs' (2: 143)].

Both Pascoli and Freud depart from the biblical Eden and the classical golden age by infusing that primary state with a fundamental ambivalence. They recast the fall from Edenic innocence into the knowledge of death as an ascent from a bestial to a human existence. Pascoli insists that it is our knowledge of our own inevitable death that separates us from the beasts. To try to deny or repress that knowledge amounts to a regression to an animal existence. For Freud, the repression of instinctual satisfaction marks the difference between bestial and human life. Both, in short, underscore that the process of surmounting the bestial state is double-edged. For these writers, the primordial, pre-lapsarian state is, furthermore, a state that threatens to obliterate the precarious grounds of individual human subjectivity as much as it affords a tempting mode of transcendence. Freud does not exhibit the same degree of nostalgia for that primordial, albeit illusory, state as Pascoli does: Pascoli's depiction of the dawning of the new era, evoking the meeting of the sunrise of the new and sunset of the old ('alba e tramonto'), aptly describes his position at the hazy point of contact or overlapping between the old religious faith in and longing for a transcendent Eden and the materialist position exemplified by Freud ('L'era nuova,' *Opere*, 2: 445). Pascoli, who classes himself as a poet of the older, primitive age, evokes 'nostalgia for the impossible,' as Guido Guglielmi elegantly puts it.[30] Throughout the poetry, Pascoli valorizes, mourns, and strives to recapture this pre-rational visionary capacity. An important departure from the classical and Christian myths is the shift in emphasis from the environmental (the beautiful garden, the burgeoning vegetation) to the perceptual. The primordial state was 'golden' not because the world was different but because the subject perceived it differently. For Pascoli, the revision of the myth is to envision a childlike transrational state of mind in which the 'plenty' derives not from a superabundance offered by nature but from a satisfaction with the little that is offered.

Pascoli's and Freud's writings refigure innocence as ignorance and wholeness as a loss of individual human identity – as a bestial existence. Pascoli claims that the new task of poetry is to make its readers feel their smallness and the finality of their death, to reconcile readers, in short, to the demands of the adult world and their own moral agency in that world. His poetry, on the other hand, becomes a space for the dead to go on living, a space for the transrational world of infantile perceptions, valorized because vanishing. However, such a recuperation does not present itself in a facile, celebratory way but in a deeply ambivalent mode. I have shown how the poetry enacts a turning back to pre-difference, to fullness, to 'pre-grammatical,' maternal wholeness. This turning back marks desire, the desire for the 'Thing,' as Kristeva puts it, and its realization threatens to annihilate the self. This primordial, maternal wholeness, which functions as a 'golden age' for Pascoli, is always already lost, while the poetry in some measure recuperates it, thematically and formally. The seeming disparity between the poetic project of recuperating the primordial past and the prose essay's agenda of promoting a mature acceptance of modern, adult rationality should not be ascribed to a simple generic distinction (i.e., poetry vs prose). Even in this prose piece, which calls for progress rather than for regression, we witness a deep and pervasive nostalgia for the primitive. In many passages, indeed, the essay becomes a hymn to the very forces it ostensibly seeks to 'surmount,' if not 'repress.' Such sympathy and even nostalgia for the older, primitive vision of the world emerges quite strongly in the passage that describes a shepherd's reflections on the mysteries of life: the motion of heavenly bodies, the world of dreams, and death.[31] Pascoli does not merely describe this vision, but personalizes and even identifies with it. First, he ascribes the reflections not to an anonymous 'them' ('primitive man') but to a particular shepherd. Pascoli does not simply record the shepherd's speculations but narrates his actions as well, creating a sort of vignette that allows the reader to enter more fully into this primitive consciousness. Finally, at the conclusion of the passage, Pascoli identifies with this consciousness by adopting the first-person-plural form of the verbs: 'we hide [the dead man's body] underground, and we put next to him all his necessary utensils and his beloved objects so that when he awakens, or when he returns, he may find them' (*Opere*, 2: 446). Such ambivalence and nostalgia serve as a means to promote Pascoli's program of compassion. Furthermore, by underscoring that the wholeness experienced derived from subjective perception rather than from external abundance, Pascoli can advocate a reining in of desires for that illusory plenitude.

Freud, true to his complete 'faith' in the rationalist-materialist world view, refers in the closing paragraphs of his essay to 'our god Logos.' His enterprise, indeed, can be seen as an apotheosis of 'Logos' – the word as logic, rationality, intelligence. 'Logos,' for example, would not permit the coexistence of contraries, such as the sun being simultaneously 'alius et idem.' In contrast to Freud's relentless rationalism, the fantastic and often grotesque literature of the *scapigliatura* emerges as an exponent of unbridled 'mythos.' Pascoli puts these two discourses into play, overriding the temporal model of chronological progression with a poetic model of simultaneity. Pascoli creates a 'hazy' perspective from which the rational ideology of 'Logos' speaks but is permeated with the nostalgic echoes of 'mythos.' To hark back to the structural 'compromise formation' discussed by Orlando, 'repression over repressed,' I submit that in Pascoli's poetry (and his poetic prose) a relationship of 'Logos over mythos' obtains.[32] Pascoli's poetry enacts a return of the repressed, and its uncanny effect reveals the intervention and the incorporation of the perspective of the rational, repressing 'Logos.'

We recall that Freud points out in his essay 'The "Uncanny"' that the effect of the uncanny derives not only from encounters that elicit a repressed infantile fear but also from encounters that seem to confirm surmounted infantile and primitive thought patterns. The effect of the uncanny that I have underscored in Pascoli's poetry, then, does not emerge spontaneously, as a product of Giovanni Pascoli's unconscious wishes or repressed libidinal energies. Nor is it merely a descriptive category to designate a general tone in the poetry or the dominant effect elicited by it, though this is part of its use. Rather, Pascoli deploys the uncanny, linguistically and thematically, as the central poetic and moral agenda of his work. By revealing that the threat to the subject is already inside the nest, that the mother is not only the protective and nurturing Madonna but also the murderous Marietta or Myrrhine, by depicting the cosy home as also haunted, the soothing womb as a threat of drowning, Pascoli signals the impossibility of such a return and the need to go beyond the mythical, primitive world of the infant. But by singing the praises of the child's vision and mourning the loss of that visionary world, he underscores, first, the power of transrational thought to override the logical distinctions and divisions that cause discontent and, second, the universally shared grief suffered by all humankind, whatever their individual life stories may be. Evoking the fear of and the nostalgia for the impossible dissolution of the self, Pascoli dramatizes and attempts to intervene in the universal tragedy of humanity and pleads for an ethic of *fratellanza*, of compassion, among those who have irretrievably lost their protective home.

Conclusion: Reading beyond the Family Romance

The goal of moving 'beyond' the family romance alludes to the methodological path undertaken in this study, which aimed to engage psychoanalysis in a way not limited to the classical model of applied psychoanalytic literary criticism. That is, the study proposes a structural and comparative approach that examines the significance of Pascoli's work beyond its role as either evidence or symptom of his personal family relationships. Pascoli's exceptional life story, from the tragic losses of his youth to the unusual living arrangement with his sisters, clearly had a deeply formative impact on every level of his psyche and his writing. However, the very uniqueness of his life runs the risk of exciting morbid curiosity and idle speculation, speculation that can be fuelled by some of the critical apparatus offered by psychoanalysis. More importantly, applied biographical psychoanalytic criticism, even when undertaken responsibly, runs the risk of a vicious circularity of argument, as discussed in the introduction. This study, then, intended to go beyond such biographically centred speculation and 'explanation.'

In his analysis of the genre of 'fantastic' literature, Todorov examines Freud's essay 'The "Uncanny"' and concludes that psychoanalysis opens two major epistemological paths for the literary critic: the structural (or 'poetics'), and the thematic (or 'hermeneutics').[1] In adopting a primarily structural model, informed by Orlando's notion of the 'compromise formation,' I have not, however, neglected the thematic material. Rather the structure is the dynamic relationship between the various elements of thematic content. As Samual Weber, whose close readings of Freud's texts have provided a methodological model for this study, asserts, 'If, as Freud's conclusion suggests, das Unheimliche has a privileged relation to literary "fiction," it is surely not to the mere contents represented "in" or "by" texts, but to their "formal," textual structure itself.'[2] In examining Pascoli's texts, I have attempted to demonstrate how his poetry puts into play a structural model that might be designated using the Kristevan notion of 'symbolic over semiotic,' where the 'semiotic' is the repressed element that returns in all its essential ambivalence. In comparison with the scientific, 'log-istic' enterprise of Freud, I reiterated Pascoli's project as a compromise formation of 'Logos over mythos,' where the ambivalent mythical elements are given voice and valued precisely because they are revealed to be logically impossible.

The project's title refers also to Freud's call for society to move beyond the mythical world of infantile illusions, one of which he articulates in his brief essay on the 'Family Romance.' Pascoli, too, particularly in his turn-of-the-century speech on the 'new era,' encourages his fellow men to move beyond the world of illusions and bravely face the fact of their mortality. However, my title also invokes another of Freud's essays, the daring *Beyond the Pleasure Principle*. Just as, in this Freudian text, the postulated death drive goes beyond the pleasure principle but does not negate or refute it, so for Pascoli the uncanny world of mythos must be surmounted but not forgotten. By evoking and enacting that pre-rational state, Pascoli aimed to intervene in the moral arena of his society at the deepest level, that of subjective perception, and to advocate an ethos of compassion and contentment. Pascoli has long been recognized as one of the foundational voices of Italy's twentieth-century poetic idiom. As we look back on the events of the twentieth century from its close, mindful of how Pascoli had looked forward with hope at its dawning, we can only regret that his project did not realize more fully its noble aims.

Notes

Introduction: Nesting Instincts

1 See also Gay, *Freud*, 87–96.
2 Bàrberi Squarotti, *Simboli e strutture*.
3 See Mario Moroni's 'Estetismo/modernismo in Italia,' in which he closely analyses Pascoli's 'La siepe' and suggests it as emblematic of the Pascolian notion of (defensive) subjectivity. He argues that the 'poetic self,' centralized behind the hedge that serves as a 'filter,' makes contact with the outside world but protects itself from its harshness by 'naturalizing' or 'mythicizing' that world.
4 Vazzana, *La struttura psicologica dell'opera pascoliana*.
5 Fiorenza Weinapple (in 'La "via crucis" del Pascoli') perceptively points out that the poem records the fatal date with the Roman numeral for ten: 'X.' She links this to both the rhetorical figure of 'chiasmus,' or crossing, which she traces through several poems, and to the physical figure of the cross, particularly as marking a gravesite. She suggests that the proliferation of these rhetorical crosses makes of the poems a kind of 'camposanto.'
6 Bàrberi Squarotti, *Simboli et strutture*, 100.
7 Ibid., 97–8.
8 Freud, 'The "Uncanny"' (1919), in *Standard Edition*, 17: 219–52.
9 For a discussion of Freud's development of the theories of repetition-compulsion and the death drive in the period 1919–20, see Hertz, 'Freud and the Sandman,' in *End of the Line*, 97–121. Hertz associates the uncanny with the anxiety of 'literary priority,' and emphasizes the inextricable link between Freud's figurative language and the 'pure concept' of repetition per se which this language seeks to make visible.
10 The last paragraph reads, 'Concerning the factors of silence, solitude and

darkness, we can only say that they are actually elements in the production of the infantile anxiety from which the majority of human beings have never become quite free. This problem has been discussed from a psycho-analytic point of view elsewhere' (Freud, 'The "Uncanny,"' 252).
11 Freud to Andreas-Salomè, 7 July 1914. Cited in Gay, *Freud*, 216.
12 Cixous, 'Fiction and Its Phantoms,' 536.
13 Ibid., 528.
14 The recent publication of *The Uncanny* by Nicholas Royle (New York: Routledge, 2003) attests to the text's continuing role as a hermeneutical tool in literary criticism.
15 Parkin-Gounelas, *Literature and Psychoanalysis*. See especially chapter 5, 'The Uncanny Text.'
16 Ibid., 119.
17 Ibid.
18 Weber, *The Legend of Freud*, 215–17. The title of the present study refers to Weber's reading, and my chapter titles seek to echo his discussion of the present participle.
19 Ibid., 24.
20 Ibid., 10.
21 *Il fanciullino* ('The Little Boy,' 1903) is the title of a well-known essay by Pascoli in which he develops his theory of poetry. (See Giovanni Pascoli, *Il fanciullino*, intro. and ed. by Agamben. This edition reproduces the 1907 text.) I discuss this essay at greater length in the fourth chapter.
22 The collection *Poemi conviviali* was first published in 1904 and includes twenty poems all treating classical themes, a preface in the form of a letter to Adolfo De Bosis, to whom the collection is dedicated, and a closing Greek phrase, which follows the last poem and reads: 'Those who delight in anxieties.' Several of the poems ('Solon,' 'Gog e Magog,' and 'Alexandros') were originally published in the literary journal *Convito*, in which also appeared the essay 'Minerva oscura,' one of Pascoli's studies on Dante. De Bosis edited and wrote for the journal, which also boasted Gabriele d'Annunzio as a major contributor. Twelve issues of the journal were published between 1895 and 1907. For studies on the *Convito* see Carlo Salinari, *Miti e coscienza*, and Emanuella Scarano, *Dalla* Cronaca bizantina *al* Convito. The *Poemi conviviali* is the only collection of Pascoli's poetry that has been translated into English in its entirety: *Giovanni Pascoli: Convivial Poems*, translated by Egidio Lunardi and Robert Nugent. The two volumes contain original text, translation, a brief introduction, and notes. The Italian edition of *Poemi conviviali*, edited by Giuseppe Leonelli, 1996, I have found very

useful particularly for its introductory comments and ample notes to each poem.
23 Cesare Garboli, 'Pascoli.' The two-page article in this widely circulated newspaper emphasizes the need for a fresh critical appraisal of the poet.
24 Fausto Curi, 'Eros e senilità,' in *Il possibile verbale*, 151–85.
25 Ibid., 176. Pascoli never married and had no children. He spent most of his adulthood living with his sisters: Ida, until her marriage; and Maria, who survived him and wrote his biography.
26 Curi (*Il possibile*) offers detailed readings of 'Solon,' 'L'ultimo viaggio,' and 'Il cieco di Chio,' all from the *Conviviali*.
27 Bàrberi Squarotti, *Simboli e strutture*: see his notes to chapter 1.
28 Ibid., 60–1.
29 '[E]gli era indubbiamente vittima di una vera e propria *phobie du marriage* ...' Elio Gioanola, 'Tre letture di testi poetici,' in *Psicanalisi, ermeneutica e letteratura*, 222.
30 Patrizio Rossi, 'I fiori del male.'
31 Stefano Agosti, 'Su un verso di Pascoli: Calcoli della tessitura sonora ed effetti a-significanti,' in *Critica della testualità*, 257.
32 See especially Orlando's *Towards a Freudian Theory of Literature*, a translation by Charmaine Lee of his *Per una teoria freudiana della letteratura*.
33 In the case of Racine's *Phèdre*, Orlando offers several levels of analysis, identifying and exploring such compromise formations as rationality/myth, law/desire, and Minos/Pasiphae.
34 Kristeva, *Revolution in Poetic Language*, trans. Margaret Waller.
35 Ibid., 22.
36 Ibid., 60.
37 I would associate this linguistic oscillation or dialectic with the thematic dialectic of 'breve' and 'illimite' described by Vazzana in *La struttura psicologica*.
38 Gianfranco Contini, 'Il linguaggio di Pascoli' (1955), in *Giovanni Pascoli: Poesie: Volume primo*.
39 Flora, 'Pascoli e la poesia moderna,' in Petrucciani et al., eds, *Materiali critici per Giovanni Pascoli*, 14.
40 Katja Liimatta, 'Impressionismo.' Umberto Eco, in his novel *La misteriosa fiamma della regina Loana*, draws on the thematic importance of 'fog' and the linguistic effect of haziness in Pascoli's poems. Eco cites several verses from four of Pascoli's poems in this novel, in which fog – literal and metaphorical – plays a central role in the life of the protagonist.
41 Ibid., 70.

42 Freud, *New Introductory Lectures* (1933), *Standard Edition*, 22: 79.
43 Guglielmi, 'Per una lettura dei Conviviali,' in Pazzaglia, ed., *I Poemi conviviali di Giovanni Pascoli. Convegno di Studi di San Mauro Pascoli e Barga*.
44 Ibid., 174.
45 Ibid., 175.
46 Bàrberi Squarotti, 'Appunti sulla sintassi pascoliana.'
47 Freud, *Jokes and Their Relation to the Unconscious* (1905), *Standard Edition*, 8: 122.
48 *Convivial Poems*, trans. Lunardi and Nugent, 75.
49 Freud writes in 'The "Uncanny,"' 'To some people that idea of being buried alive by mistake is the most uncanny thing of all. And yet psycho-analysis has taught us that this terrifying phantasy is only a transformation of another phantasy which had nothing originally terrifying about it at all, but was qualified by a certain lasciviousness – the phantasy, I mean, of intra-uterine existence' (244). An earlier version of this discussion of 'La voce' appears in my article 'Giovanni Pascoli's Ventriloquized Female Voices,' *Romance Review* 8 (1998) 29–37. The passage is reprinted here with kind permission of the journal.
50 The image of the oral cavity filled with dirt illustrates the analyses of Copjec and Dolar, who claim that the uncanny is elicited by a confrontation with a 'lack of lack.' See Copjec, 'Vampires, Breast-feeding and Anxiety,' and Dolar, '"I Shall Be with You on Your Wedding-Night": Lacan and the Uncanny.'
51 As Maud Ellman succinctly explains, 'When Freud speaks of the infant's incestuous desire for the mother he is referring to a welter of libidinous imaginings, unrestricted to the genitals and including the sadistic drives to devour or eviscerate the mother's body' ('Introduction,' *Psychoanalytic Literary Criticism*, 12).
52 Freud, 'Medusa's Head' (1940 [1922]). *Standard Edition*, 18: 273–4.
53 The repetition of nest imagery parallels what Weber calls Freud's 'mustering' of examples and illustrations of the uncanny (*Legend of Freud*, 207–35).
54 Freud, 'The Aetiology of Hysteria' (1896): 'I therefore put forward the thesis that at the bottom of every case of hysteria there are one or more occurrences of premature sexual experience, occurrences which belong to the earliest years of childhood but which can be reproduced through the work of psycho-analysis in spite of the intervening decades. I believe this is an important finding, the discovery of a *caput Nili* in neuropathology' (*Standard Edition*, 3: 203).
55 See the summary in *In Dora's Case*. 'Memory and fantasy supplement and subvert each other in such an equivocal and undecidable fashion that no single origin, be it an empirical event or an unconscious desire, can ever be conclusively determined' (15). In Bernheimer, 'Introduction, Part One.'

1. Foreshadowing: The *Scapigliati* and Psychoanalysis

1 The term literally means 'dishevelled hair.' Cletto Arrighi was the pen name of Carlo Righetti. His novel is published as *La scapigliatura: Romanzo sociale contemporaneo*, edited by Giuseppe Farinelli. Arrighi's novel was first published in 1862 as *La scapigliatura e il 6 febbraio*.
2 See Tessari, ed., *La scapigliatura*.
3 Tarchetti, 'Idee minime sul romanza' (1865), in *Tutte le opere*, 2: 522–35 (my translations throughout).
4 Tarchetti, *Fosca*, 16. The English rendering is from *Passion: A Novel*, translated by Lawrence Venuti, 16.
5 Gioanola, ed., *La scapigliatura*, 40.
6 Ibid., 108.
7 For a compelling discussion of this theme, see Tessari, 'L'immagine della morte nell'opera di Tarchetti e nella scapigliatura.' Citing, for example, from Boito's 'A Giovanni Camerana' the lines 'Alzan le pugna e mostrano a trofeo / dell'Arte loro un verme ed un aborto, / e giuocano al paleo / colle teste da morto' [they raise their fists and show them a worm and an abortion as a trophy of Art, and they play on the grass with skulls of the dead], Tessari argues that the *scapigliati* display such grotesque images of death ('rifiuti umani') in order to shock the intellectually and spiritually dead bourgeoisie with a sort of 'carnevale macabro.' But in Tarchetti, he claims, such necromancy spills over into an obsessive necrophilia.
8 Cixous, 'Fiction and Its Phantoms,' 542–3.
9 Ibid., 543.
10 What I perceive as a direct link between Tarchetti's 'io son morta, rispose, e tu nol sai' and Pascoli's 'non lo sai tu? ... Io non son viva ... Morta! Sì, morta!' has not, to my knowledge, been noted before.
11 On the prominence of the demonic as a characterization of the *scapigliatura*, we can turn to the titles of several critical works, including Fabio Finotti's 'Arrigo Boito,' and David del Principe's *Rebellion, Death and Aesthetics in Italy*. In anticipation of the argument I undertake in this chapter, we can note that Freud characterizes the unconscious drives he studies as 'demons from hell.'
12 I.U. Tarchetti, *Fantastic Tales*, 9.
13 Ibid., p. 13. For a very thorough historical account of the theme of the anatomist who works upon the bodies of the socially dispossessed, see Cristina Mazzoni's 'Is Beauty Only Skin Deep? Constructing the Female Corpse in Scapigliatura.' She undertakes a feminist-historical analysis of two other texts from this period: Camillo Boito's short story 'Un corpo' and Arrigo Boito's poem 'Lezione d'anatomia.'

14 Del Principe, *Rebellion, Death*, 96.
15 Finotti, 'Arrigo Boito,' discusses at length the strong Dantean influence on this poem and compares it with the comically grotesque demons of Malebolge.
16 Del Principe, *Rebellion, Death*, 96. See Mario Praz's *Romantic Agony*, 76–8, for a catalogue of the history and development of the vampire figure. Praz reads the vampire as an extension of the Byronic 'Fatal Man,' a figure who, in turn, derives from Marino and Milton's portrayals of Satan. Later in his study, Praz quotes D.H. Lawrence's assessment of vampirism as a defining characteristic of the writing of Edgar Allan Poe: 'The tales of Poe, as D.H. Lawrence observed, are always a symbolical, mythological translation of the same thirst for unrealizable love ... and of the desire for that complete fusion with the beloved that ends in vampirism' (145). This last, symbolic reading (there are, in Poe as in Tarchetti, no literal vampires) relates vampirism to the yearning for the dissolution of the boundaries of the self – a desire originating in love but, in its extreme form, spilling over into death. Baudelaire's 'Le Métamorphoses du vampire' (1851) dramatizes this same equation of sex and vampirism. Such a longing for 'complete fusion' is clearly connected to the uncanny depiction of the joined twins in the poem of Praga analysed above. Indeed, in his discussion of Madeline and Roderick Usher, Lawrence argues that twins are the most conducive to the ecstatic loss of self desired by the vampiric drive, since they provide the 'least resistance' to the opening of 'sympathetic nervous vibration' (*Studies in Classic American Literature*, 88). The simultaneous desire for and fear of this dissolution underlies many of the uncanny images of Gothic literature (notably, in Poe, that of being buried alive), the psychoanalytic prototype of which is the ambivalent memory of the womb. See also on this topic Joan Copjec, 'Vampires, Breast-feeding and Anxiety.'
17 Freud, *Civilization and Its Discontents* (1930), *Standard Edition*, 21: 64–148.
18 Freud, *The Ego and the Id* (1923), *Standard Edition*, 19: 3–66.
19 W.P. Day, *In the Circle of Fear and Desire*, 177. See the entire section, 'The Science of Fear: Sigmund Freud Meets Dracula,' 177–90. Harold Bloom adopts a similar line of reasoning in the specific case of Edgar Allan Poe, asserting that 'Poe is himself so reductive that the Freudian translations [of the thematic kind as undertaken first by Marie Bonaparte] are in his case merely redundant' (4). Bloom passionately argues against Poe's literary merit, claiming that his work's sustained popularity is due entirely to its 'mythopoetic' quality ('Introduction,' *Edgar Allan Poe*).
20 Day, *In the Circle of Fear and Desire*, 181.
21 Mirella Agorni, 'The Female Gothic: The Italy of Anne Radcliffe.' Agorni

focuses on Radcliffe's *The Italian*. See especially fn 17 (32), which lists ten English Gothic novels (other than Radcliffe's) published between 1792 and 1810 that have a 'distinctive Italian setting.'
22 Freud, *Three Essays on the Theory of Sexuality* (1905), *Standard Edition* 7: 141.
23 Roman Jackobson, *Selected Writings III*.
24 Felman, '*On Reading Poetry*,' 140.
25 Tarchetti, *Passion*, 34.
26 Ibid., 20.
27 Ibid., 49.
28 Ibid., 13.
29 Ibid.
30 Ibid., 48.
31 Elio Gioanola, 'Clara e Fosca.'
32 Tarchetti, *Passion*, 17.
33 Tom's identification, while irrational, is not unmotivated. The word 'alfiere,' in this context, refers to the piece called the 'bishop' in English, but actually means 'ensign' in the military sense. Thus, the warlike connotations of the piece allow it to crystallize the aggression of the match, while at the same time evoking for Tom his brother's role in the violent attempts to gain freedom.
34 Weber, 'The Unconscious Chess Player' in *The Return to Freud*, 37.
35 The poem bears strong resemblances to Baudelaire's 'Une Charogne' (1857), which dwells graphically and even obsessively on the rotting flesh of a human corpse. In this brutal poem, the speaker reminds his beloved of the horrific sight encountered by the couple – 'Ce beau matin d'été si doux' – namely, a corpse swarming with maggots and being eyed by a hungry bitch. After eight stanzas of shocking, detailed description, the speaker pronounces a sort of 'moral,' warning his beloved that one day she too will be a corpse. The poem ends with a sardonic evocation of the topos of the immortality that poetry confers upon its subjects – hardly a consolation after the prolonged meditation on the physical condition of a body left to rot in the sun. Francis Scarfe points to this poem as a prime example of Baudelaire's 'unclassical ... anti-aesthetic' in which, he suggests, 'the roots of that element of Surrealism are to be found' (Baudelaire, *The Complete Verse*, 40). While the poem outdoes Tarchetti's in graphic description, it disgusts rather than terrifies, and does so under the aegis of an antimaterialist 'lesson,' so to speak: do not put much store in the things of this world. For Tarchetti, I believe, there is no transcendent moral to be inferred but merely the hollow eyes and gaping mouth of death to be confronted.
36 Tessari, ed., *La scapigliatura*, 204.

37 Ibid., 206.
38 Freud, 'Medusa's Head' (1940 [1922]), *Standard Edition*, 18: 273–4.
39 Gioanola, 'Clara e Fosca,' 157.
40 See Patricia Yaeger, 'Toward a Female Sublime.' Through readings of several poems by female writers, Yaeger develops the notion of a 'pre-Oedipal sublime,' which stands in contrast to the 'romantic' sublime epitomized by writers such as Percy Bysshe Shelley.
41 Peter Brooks, 'Freud's Masterplot.'
42 Bonaparte, 'Life and Works of Edgar Allan Poe,' 116.
43 Ibid., 109.
44 Dolar has called 'the uncanny,' which she identifies with Lacan's 'object small a,' the 'pivotal point around which psychoanalytic concepts revolve' (Dolar, '"I shall Be With You,"' 6).
45 See Mario Petrucciani's *Emilio Praga*, 167–74, for an analysis of Praga's stylistic and thematic influence on Pascoli. Arguing that the germs of many of Pascoli's hallmark characteristics appear in the work of Praga, he concludes that, 'Forse non è illecito supporre che delle proposte innovatrici del Praga – derivate, o no, d'Oltralpe – tenne conto il Pascoli, nella tecnica disgregante e impressionistica (suoni e colori "psicologici"), nel gusto della poesia ingenua e delle descrizioni minute, o quando si volse al mondo dei familiari affetti, alla piccola realtà domestica e campestre. Li accomuna l'accorato amore e l'immediata vivezza delle "cose piccole e care," l'ansia di novità che fa del Praga un poeta volto al futuro e del Pascoli un poeta del Novecento' (174) [Perhaps it is not inappropriate to suppose that Pascoli took into account Praga's innovative proposals, whether or not they came from beyond the Alps. In particular, we note the impressionistic (psychological sounds and colours) and disarticulating technique, the taste for naive poetry and minute description, the turn to the world of familial affection, and of humble domestic and rural reality. They have in common in the sorrowful love and the immediate vividness of 'humble and dear things,' the anxiety of novelty that makes Praga a poet facing the future and Pascoli a poet of the twentieth century].
46 See especially chapter 1, 'The Semiotic and the Symbolic,' of Kristeva's *Revolution in Poetic Language*. Her terminology has been usefully synthesized in *Feminism and Psychoanalysis: A Critical Dictionary*. Here the 'semiotic' is defined as the 'pre-signifying impulses and drives that chaotically circulate in and through the infant's body.' This non-signifying, rhythmic energy flows in and is organized by the 'chora,' the 'site of the undifferentiated bodily space the mother and child share ... the unnamable, unspeakable corporeality of the inextricably tangled mother/child dyad which makes the

semiotic possible.' For Kristeva, what distinguishes poetic language from the theologized, authoritative symbolic order and from the stasis of fetishism is the fact that '[t]he text signifies the unsignifying: it assumes [*relève*] within a signifying practice this function (the semiotic), which ignores meaning and operates before meaning or despite it' (*Revolution*, 65).

47 Dolar, '"I Shall Be With You,"' 23.
48 See Robin Lydenberg, 'Freud's Uncanny Narratives,' for a feminist appraisal of the scene of the 'painted women' and similar episodes from 'The "Uncanny."' Lydenberg examines the various shifts throughout the essay between scientific and literary prose – shifts that she claims are attempts at evasion – and stresses Freud's attraction to and fear of the uncanniness of literature.
49 Tarchetti, *Fantastic Tales*, 88.
50 To note briefly an example of the issues at stake in this question, Silvia Vegetti Finzi discusses the space of responsibility when 'man' is seen as enclosed by the 'omnipotence of desire,' the inevitability of death, and the omnipresence of the pre-existing and defining symbolic order. Rather than conceding 'victory' to the forces, identified and analysed by psychoanalysis, Finzi suggests that 'when the two limits conditioning us have been found (the one of life and death, which follows its course regardless of our consent, and the one of the symbolic axis that exists independently of our intentionality), we can narrate our own biography feeling like subjects and not just objects of the plot regarding us' ('Freud and the Dream of Dreams,' 71). Such questions are explored more thoroughly in my fourth chapter.
51 We are again brought to the stories of Poe for further examples of this haunting image. Variants on the theme of being buried alive abound in his works. In 'The Black Cat,' the protagonist walls up the body of his wife in their cellar after having killed her with an axe. The pet cat, which he had unwittingly walled up as well, reveals the crime to the police with its screeching. In 'The Cask of Amontillado,' Montresor walls up his enemy Fortunato in his wine cellar while the latter is still alive (and, as in the above Tarchetti poem, the victim tries to believe that it is 'joke'). In 'The Fall of the House of Usher,' Roderick and the narrator bury Madeline, whom they believe to have died from her mysterious nervous malady, in a crypt in the bottom of the house. Days later she escapes from her coffin and kills her twin brother, as the house falls in on them both. The last example underscores a component common to all the variants – that of the burial taking place *within the home* of the victim and/or perpetrator. A great deal of the terror derives from this explicit conflation of the homely and the unhomely, of the threatening being implanted in the place of security.

52 In a Lacanian rereading of Freud's essay, Mladen Dolar ('" I Shall Be With You"') suggests that the fear is not really the fear of loss but the fear of the 'filling in' of the lack, the eruption of the real, the 'object small a,' which is the uncanny, into the imaginary. The real threatens to destabilize the notion of the self established by our passage through the mirror stage into the symbolic, a passage marked by the castrating 'lack' that the uncanny real now promises and threatens to fill in. Similarly, Joan Copjec defines anxiety as signalling a 'lack of lack,' a too-near encounter with the 'object small a' ('Vampires, Breast-feeding, and Anxiety'). For Dolar, Frankenstein's monster is the apotheosis of the real, so foreign to the symbolic order that he cannot even be named.

53 Lydenberg, 'Freud's Uncanny Narratives,' 1078.

54 A literary precedent for this disturbing poem is Leopardi's bitterly pessimistic 'Nella morte di una donna fatta trucidare col suo portato dal corruttore per mano ed arte di un chirurgo' [On the death of a woman slaughtered with the child she was carrying by the corrupt hand and art of a surgeon]. The poem is among the 'Poemi rifiutati' or compositions rejected by the author, and the story is based on the contemporary 'cronaca nera' or crime news. In the poem we encounter a similar cast of characters: a pregnant young woman, a surgeon, and the woman's lover. Here, the lover has actually instructed the surgeon to murder the woman and her infant in order to dispose of the evidence of his illicit affair. Leopardi does not even address the surgeon, whom he dismisses as having become a mere instrument, like the metallic instruments of his trade. Instead, he turns in disgust to the cowardly lover and berates him for his hideous crime. Invoking Christological imagery he refers to the woman as a victim and accuses the lover of trying to wash clean his sins with her blood. ('tu col suo sangue lavi?'). Most of the poem is addressed directly to the woman, for whom he wishes to evoke pity. In the course of the poem, however, the specificity of the woman and her particular plight fade out as she becomes a case in point illustrating Leopardi's pessimistic philosophy. Her only consolation is to have died young, before tasting any more of the bitterness of this life, which has nothing but pain and disillusionment to offer (the same 'consolation' he offers the ailing woman in 'Per una donna inferma di malattia lunga e mortale'). Her sad story is yet another reason for grief, yet more evidence to support his tragic world view ('Ecco nova di lutto / Cagion s'accresce a le cagioni antiche,' 2–3) [Thus a new cause for grief is added to the old ones]. Boito, if he had Leopardi's poem in mind, seems to take a step back and inscribe 'Leopardi' into his poem as the character of the romantic who

grieves for the young girl. Indeed, Leopardi wonders in his own poem how the 'beauty' and 'youth' of the girl could have failed to move the surgeon's heart, thus sounding much like Boito's grieving romantic.

55 Arrigo Boito, *Opere*, esp. xvi; Gioanola, ed., *La scapigliatura*, 78–81.
56 Finotti, 'Arrigo Boito.'
57 Pointing to this poem, as well as to Camillo Boito's 'Un corpo' and several other texts, Tessari insightfully shows a recurrent structure in *scapigliatura* literature: the 'scientist-poet-reality' triangle. 'Reality' is almost always embodied in a woman, and specifically one 'spinta versa la propia condizione di ente degradato, di oggetto, di rifiuto' [forced into the very condition of a degraded entity, of an object, of trash]. The poet, a type of 'sacerdote dell'ideale' dedicated to beauty, becomes an impotent voyeur, while the scientist, usually an anatomist or embalmer, appears omnipotent in his cognitive ability to know reality. Tessari sees this structure as repeating, in a macabre way, the archetypal 'love triangle' (Tessari, *La scapigliatura*). In his *Jokes and Their Relation to the Unconscious* (1905), Freud analyses another permutation of this triangle: the telling of the dirty joke or 'smut' (*Standard Edition*, 8). This analysis strikingly parallels the episodes depicted by both Camillo and Arrigo Boito, namely, the reduction of the woman to a 'violated apparition.' In both cases her role is that of mere pretext for an exchange between men (see Maud Ellmann's introduction in *Psychoanalytic Literary Criticism*, 15). Boito's poem does not, in my view, recuperate the integrity of the effaced and socially dispossessed woman and thus can hardly be used as a feminist counter-model. However, the ghastly appearance of the fetus at the end of the poem serves to dismantle the homosocial exchange and to disrupt their agonistic relationship. The structure of Camillo Boito's 'Un corpo' as analysed by Mazzoni strongly resembles that of the Spanish tale 'No lo invento' by Emilia Pardo Bazán (translated by Robert M. Fedorchek as 'The Gravedigger' in *'The White Horse' and Other Stories*). In this chilling tale, the young and beautiful protagonist, Puri la Casta, dies of brain fever just days before her wedding. Visiting his beloved's grave the night of her funeral, Puri's honourable fiancé is horrified to discover the town's old gravedigger violating her body. At his trial, the gravedigger reveals, without remorse, that for the past thirty years he has committed such acts upon every deceased female of the town. Joyce Tolliver demonstrates the parallelism constructed by the text between the characters of the fiancé and the gravedigger, strikingly similar to the links between the artist and the anatomist in Boito's story. Tolliver further argues that the necrophilia confessed by the gravedigger should be seen as a social criticism: it represents the

logical extension of the valuation of female frigidity and the valuation of the female as the object rather than the subject of sexual desire (*Cigar Smoke and Violet Water*).

58 Seen as that which disrupts the symmetry of the two contrasting 'black and white' discourses, this image functions in the same way as the bleeding neck of the 'black bishop.'

59 The title translates as 'The Solitary Sparrow,' but this term refers specifically to the blue rock-thrush, a bird known for not gathering into flocks. In the introductory note to Leopardi's poem in the Garzanti edition of the *Canti*, Bandini notes that this bird appears in Psalm 102 of the Vulgate and again, in reference to that psalm, in Petrarch's *Rime* 226 (Leopardi, *Canti*, introduction by Fernando Bandini, 109–10).

2. Returning: The *Poemi conviviali* and the Uncanny

1 Wordsworth, 'We Are Seven,' lines 5–8, 13–24. *Oxford Authors: William Wordsworth*, 83–4.

2 For biographical accounts, see Nadia Ebani, 'La vita di Giovanni Pascoli (1855–1912),' lxi–lxxi; Mario Pazzaglia, 'Una vita difficile,' in *Pascoli*, 39–60; and Giulio Ferroni, 'Verso una nuova poesia: Giovanni Pascoli,' in *Storia della letteratura italiana*, 3: 509–29.

3 See Freud, 'Remembering, Repeating, Working Through' (1914), *Standard Edition*, 12: 155–6, and 'Inhibitions, Symptoms and Anxiety' (1926), *Standard Edition*, 20: 159–60.

4 I will discuss this important essay in more depth in chapter 4.

5 Pascoli's essay has been recently translated into English by Rosamaria LaValva in her study *The Eternal Child: The Poetry and Poetics of Giovanni Pascoli*. This quotation at page 19 of her study.

6 For the central importance of the image of the *nido* (nest) in Pascoli's poetry, see especially Giorgio Bàrberi Squarotti's *Simboli e strutture*, and the introduction to this study.

7 A footnote to this line in the Goffis edition explains that it represents an 'answer to the desire of the two swallows to remake the lost nest, and raises the episode to the level of a symbol of the life of the poet, who remade his nest late' (*Opere*, 1: 503 [my translation]). The episode, indeed, has certain parallels with Pascoli's nurturing of a close and jealously guarded home life with his surviving sisters, Ida and Maria, at Castelvecchio. However, to limit the interpretation to this biographical connection reduces rather than 'raises' the symbolic potential. Indeed, such a method would suggest an allegorization rather than a symbolization of the poem. For a discussion of

Pascoli as a 'symbolic' rather than an 'allegorical' poet, see Giuseppe Nava, 'I *Canti di Castelvecchio*: Simbolo o allegoria?' Nava also discusses at length how this collection is not merely a continuation of but a real development from *Myricae*.

8 It is interesting to note that Wordsworth's epigraph to the 1807 edition of this ode, taken from Virgil's fourth eclogue, reads 'Paulo majora canamus.' This is the same quotation ('Paulo maiora' [Slightly greater]) that Pascoli chooses as the epigraph for his 1904 collection, *Primi poemetti*, as well as for the *Nuovi poemetti*.
9 In this regard see Gianfranco Contini, 'Il linguaggio di Pascoli.'
10 Diego Vitrioli (1819–98) won the Amsterdam prize for his Latin poem 'Xiphias' in 1845. (Pascoli himself won twelve gold medals in this competition in the course of his career.)
11 Apostrophe and prosopopoeia are tropes that figuratively animate or revive an absent interlocutor. See Barbara Johnson, 'Apostrophe, Animation, Abortion,' in *A World of Difference*, 184–99, for a feminist-deconstructionist account of the deployment of apostrophe in poetry by men and by women. Here these devices serve to reanimate the 'poeta sepolto.'
12 LaValva, *Eternal Child*, 47, 49.
13 I am indebted to Ernesto Livorni for elucidating this comparison and for the evocative language with which to express it.
14 As Nava writes, Pascoli 'valorizza piuttosto i dati primari comuni con le altre specie, che i dati logico-razionali propri della specie umana' ('I *Canti*,' 338) [values the primitive abilities that we have in common with other species rather than the rational, logical abilities that are unique to the human species]. To put it in the terms developed by the neuroscientist Gerald Edleman, Pascoli valorizes 'primary consciousness' over 'higher-order consciousness.' Edleman suggests that 'primary consciousness' – possessed by animals and in the past by humans before they evolved and built socially and linguistically constructed self-consciousness upon it – is that state to which some mystics aspire (Edleman, *Bright Air*, 124). This suggests that the transcendent obliteration of self-awareness is simultaneously regressive and progressive.
15 Sigmund Freud, 'The "Uncanny,"' (1919), *Standard Edition*, 17: 219–52.
16 The last paragraph reads, 'Concerning the factors of silence, solitude and darkness, we can only say that they are actually elements in the production of the infantile anxiety from which the majority of human beings have never become quite free. This problem has been discussed from a psycho-analytic point of view elsewhere' (ibid., 252).
17 My reading of Freud's essay has been informed by Samuel Weber, Neil Hertz, and Hélène Cixous. These critics emphasize the processes of repeti-

tion, substitution, and incomplete return in their analyses of 'Das Unheimliche.' See my introduction for a detailed discussion of methodological issues.
18 Pascoli, *Convivial Poems*, trans. and ed. by Lunardi and Nugent, 2: 30. All subsequent translations of the *Convivial Poems* will come from this edition and be cited by volume and page number.
19 For recent readings of this poem, see Giuseppe Nava, 'Il mito vuoto: L'ultimo viaggio.' Nava positions the poems of Tennyson, Graf, d'Annunzio, and Pascoli within the context of a general revival of classical antiquity and Greek culture, one that, when compared to previous revivals, was particularly concrete, as shown in the fields of archaeology and philology. He argues that where the Ulysses of the other poets appears as a hero of will, Pascoli's Ulysses undertakes a backward voyage that is strongly Leopardian and that underscores the impossibility of recuperating past illusions. See also Rosamaria LaValva, 'Ritorno a Calypso.' She too emphasizes the sharp contrast between Pascoli's poem and the d'Annunzian model. She offers a Jungian-informed discussion of the '*puer-senex*' archetypal antithesis, and underscores the oneiric qualities Pascoli achieves in the poem.
20 Freud discusses the structure of the compromise formation in *The Interpretation of Dreams* (1900), *Standard Edition*, 5: 596–97, and in *Jokes and Their Relation to the Unconscious* (1905), *Standard Edition*, 8: 203–4. See especially Francesco Orlando, *Towards a Freudian Theory of Literature*, for a discussion of the structure of the compromise formation as a tool of literary analysis.
21 See also Giustiniani's 'Travel as Inspiration in Pascoli's Poetry.' He observes that Pascoli portrays travel as torment or despair and that 'Even returning home is not always a joy, nor is it a reward for the pain and effort expended. Very often it means disillusion instead' (142). Giustiniani's observations clearly apply not only to the literal homes but also to such psychical homes as that to which Ulysses here seeks to return.
22 An earlier version of this discussion of Anticlo appears in my article 'Giovanni Pascoli's Ventriloquized Female Voices,' *Romance Review* 8 (1998): 29–37. The passage is reprinted here with kind permission of the journal.
23 In her analysis of the poetry of Gerard de Nerval, Julia Kristeva has articulated a structure that obtains, I believe, in the poetry of Pascoli as well, and that appears markedly in the particular poems I am considering here. Discussing the poem 'El Desdichado' ('The Disinherited' – it is from the fourth line of this poem that Kristeva takes the title of her book, *Black Sun*), she writes,

> Such an avoidance of sexuality and its naming confirms the hypothesis that the 'star' of 'El Desdichado' is closer to the archaic Thing than to

an object of desire. Nevertheless, and although such an avoidance seems necessary for the psychic balance of some, one could wonder if, by thus blocking the way toward the *other* (threatening, to be sure, but also insuring the conditions for setting up the boundaries of the self), the subject does not sentence itself to lie in the Thing's grave. Sublimation alone, without elaborating the erotic and thanatoid contents, seems a weak recourse against the regressive tendencies that break up bonds and lead to death (158–9).

This characterization seems to 'apply' with surprising aptness to Pascoli's poems, which are known for their almost total lack of sexual and romantic content. But I cite Kristeva's analysis here not as a way of explaining the genesis of Pascoli's poems, whose polyvalent and phonosymbolic musicality do indeed embody what Kristeva labels the 'semiotic.' Rather than using Kristeva's elegant reading of Nerval as an interpretive key to the causal or biographical components of Pascoli's poetry, I read useful re-elaborations of the poetry's effects. That is, Kristeva's analysis puts Pascoli's poetry in other words, the words of clinical analysis rather than of symbolist poetry (though Kristeva's analytic prose is itself highly poetic). Pascoli's poetry, as I have been demonstrating, dramatizes, meditates upon, and enacts the 'regressive tendencies ... that lead to death,' elaborating and exploring both the seductive and the threatening possibilities of desiring 'to lie in the Thing's grave.'

24 Chapter 1 of this study explores the writings of the *scapigliati* in depth.
25 Ovid, *Metamorphoses*, 3: lines 407–510.

3. Positioning Pascoli in the Fin de Siècle: The Case of Infanticide

1 Silvio Pellico, 'Dei doveri degli uomini,' in *Prose e poesie*, 290.
2 Carolina Invernizio, *Storia d'una sartina*. The phrase 'madre snaturata' appears at least three times, on pages 38, 45, and 47. Giselda is described as 'un'enigma ...' on page 51.
3 For a provocative analysis of the trope of infanticide in Edgar Allan Poe's 'The Purloined Letter,' see A. Samuel Kimball, 'D-Ciphering Dupin's Facsimile Signature.'
4 Invernizio, in *Tre storie in giallo e nero*.
5 For a detailed comparative analysis of these two stories, see Anna Laura Lepschy, 'Carolina Invernizio's *Ij delit d'na bela fia* and *Storia d'una sartina*.' Lepschy shows that the tales are not so much an original and a translation as two distinct renderings. For an overview of Invernizio's work, see Lepschy, 'The popular novel, 1850–1920.' The Biblioteca Nazionale in Florence

houses editions of *Sartina* from 1892, 1901, 1905, and 1908, attesting to the popularity of the novel.
6 Mary Gibson, *Born to Crime*, 20.
7 Cesare Lombroso and William Ferrero, *The Female Offender*, 214. Mary Gibson and Nicole Hahn Rafter have provided a more recent and complete English translation of *La donna delinquente*, entitled (more accurately than the previous translation) *Criminal Woman, the Prostitute and the Normal Woman*. Gibson and Hahn include the many chapters that were omitted in the first English translation. However, in the interest of readability (the original text is more than 600 pages long), they streamline the prose by deleting the digressions into proverbs, anecdotes, and other examples. Thus, English readers can take advantage of both translations for the most complete understanding of this text.
8 Lombroso and Ferrero, *La donna delinquente*, 478; *The Female Offender*, 213.
9 *The Female Offender*, 213–17.
10 Lombroso and Ferrero, *La donna*, 359; *Female Offender*, 112–13.
11 Lombroso and Ferrero, 356; *Female Offender*, 107.
12 *Female Offender*, 151.
13 Ibid.
14 See also Nancy Harrowitz, *Antisemitism, Misogyny and the Logic of Cultural Difference*, 32.
15 Luigi Capuana, *Un vampiro*. Capuana mentions Lombroso's 'giubileo scientifico' celebrated 'last April.' My research indicates that he is referring to the Conference of Criminal Anthropology held in Turin in 1906 'to commemorate the life and work of Lombroso' (Gibson, 129). 1906 marked the thirtieth anniversary of the first edition of Lombroso's *L'uomo delinquente* (*Criminal Man*, 1876).
16 Capuana, *Un vampiro*, 5.
17 Ibid.
18 The definition is from *Garzanti linguistica*, available at www.garzantilinguistica.it. See in particular Cristina Della Coletta's 'Teoria realista e prassi fantastica: "Un vampiro" di Luigi Capuana.' Della Coletta argues that the vampire 'rappresenta allora l'*unheimlich* freudiano, il doppio che avrebbe dovuto rimanere nascosto, l'oggettivazione di quella familiare e insieme oscura parte di sè, che Lelio aveva censurato' (202) [represents then the Freudian *unheimlich*, the double that should have remained hidden, the realization of that familiar and at the same time obscure part of the self that Lelio had repressed]. She goes on to argue that the doubling of Lelio and the vampire signifies the mutual tension between realist theory,

which seeks to 'structure' the fantastic, and fantastic literature, which 'subverts' the order and stability of realism.
19 Capuana, *Un vampiro*, 9.
20 Ibid., 18. Harrowitz, *Antisemitism*, 1–14, discusses in depth the story of the quagga and the theory of telegony in the scientific discourse of the nineteenth century, emphasizing the issue of muddled paternity. She discusses at some length d'Annunzio's deployment of this theory in *L'innocente*. Capuana's character Mongeri does, in fact, end up marrying a widow.
21 Capuana, *Un vampiro*, 24–5.
22 A similar dynamic appears in Freud's discussion of occultism. In the *New Introductory Lectures*, he remarks, 'Of these conjectures no doubt the most probable is that there is a real core of yet unrecognized facts in occultism around which cheating and phantasy have spun a veil which it is hard to pierce. But how can we approach this core? At what point can we attack the problem?' (*Standard Edition*, 22: 36). The metaphors of 'spinning' and 'veils' cast the obscurity masking the truth as feminine, while Freud's own masculine and militaristic attempts to 'pierce' and 'attack' will eventually unmask the 'core' of truth. This 'core' (which evokes the ever-elusive 'core' of the uncanny, and the 'core' of psychoanalytic theory that must remain 'homogeneous,' discussed in the introduction), will prove not to be something different or 'other' but to accord with and indeed further demonstrate the validity of psychoanalytic claims.
23 Weber, *Legend of Freud*, 163.
24 Gibson, *Born to Crime*, 55–60.
25 Ibid., 56.
26 Ibid., 57.
27 Rachel G. Fuchs, 'Charity and Welfare.'
28 Ibid., 171.
29 Ibid., 178.
30 Ibid., 176.
31 'Orfano' illustrates Pascoli's strategy of producing poetry that can be read as naive, childlike verse, while at the same time offering a richly layered texture of literary allusions. This poem takes its chiastic opening and closing verses from Carducci's beautiful and haunting 1881 'Nevicata.' Compare: 'Lenta la neve fiocca, fiocca, fiocca. // La neve fiocca lenta, lenta, lenta ...' (vv 1 and 8 'Orfano') and 'Lenta fiocca la neve pe'l cielo cinereo: gridi / suoni di vita più non salgono da la città, / non d'erbaiola il grido o corrente rumore di carro, / non d'amor la canzon ilare e di gioventù. / Da la torre di piazza roche per l'aere le ore / gemon, come sospir d'un mondo lungi dal dì. /

Picchiano uccelli raminghi a' vetri appannati: gli amici / spiriti reduci son, guardano e chiamano a me. / In breve, o cari, in breve – tu càlmati, indomito cuore – / giù al silenzio verrò, ne l'ombra riposerò' [Slowly falls the snow through the ashen-gray sky: cries, / sounds of life no longer rise from the city, / neither the cry of the herb-seller nor the running noise of the carriage, / nor the happy song of love and of youth. / From the tower in the piazza the rough hours through the air / call, like the sigh of a world far from the day. / Baby birds strike against opaque glass: / my friends / are survivor spirits, they watch and call to me. / Soon, my dears, soon – calm yourself, fierce heart – / I will come down to the silence, I will rest in the shade (my translation)]. The echo of Carducci, then, becomes an echo of an echo: the voices of the 'cari' (the 'cari morti') calling the poet to join them in shadow and silence. The doubled evocation of the Carducci piece cradles Pascoli's brief composition in a call to death. In addition, we can hear an echo of Dante's *Paradiso*, XV, 121–3: 'L'una vegghiava a studio de la culla / e, consolando, usava l'idioma / che prima i padri e le madri trastulla' ['One woman watched with loving care the cradle / and, as she soothed her infant, used the way / of speech with which fathers and mothers play' (*Paradiso*, trans. Allen Mandelbaum, 135)]. Perhaps Pascoli is thus justifying his own poetic (public) use of dialect (intimate, private) words (here, the specific *zana* for the generic *culla*) through Dante's advocacy of the 'way of speech with which fathers and mothers play.'
32 Giovanni Pascoli, *Myricae*, 105.
33 Paolo Toschi, *Invito al folklore italiano*, 218. See also Toschi's discussion of Pascoli's poem 'La befana' in the context of the Epiphany customs in Italy, 256–8.
34 Ibid., 220.
35 Pascoli, *Opere*, 1: 103–4.
36 Ovid, Book VIII, vv 522–5, in *Metamorphoseon Libri XV*, 310–11.
37 Ovid, *The Metamorphoses*, trans. Gregory, 231.
38 Pascoli, *La befana e altri racconti*, 10.
39 Ibid., 11–12.
40 Ibid., 41.
41 Ibid., 33–4.
42 See Barbara Spackman, *Decadent Genealogies*, 23–32.
43 Pascoli, *La befana*, 36–7.
44 Ibid., 36.
45 Weber, *Legend of Freud*, 19, 21.
46 Pascoli, *La befana*, 33.
47 Ibid., 35.
48 Ibid.

Notes to pages 107–9   179

4. Envisioning Childhood: Memory, Desire, *Pietas*, and Play

1 The first version of *Il fanciullino* appeared in four instalments of *Marzocco* in 1897. It was revised as a single essay in 1903 (in *Miei pensieri di varia umanità*, Messina) and finally reissued with minor revisions in 1907 (in *Pensieri e discorsi*, Bologna). See the 'Avvertenza' by Giorgio Agamben in *Il fanciullino* (22) and Maurizio Perugi's critical summary in his study 'James Sully e la formazione dell'estetica pascoliana,' especially 227–8.
2 The three essays are entitled 'The Sexual Aberrations,' 'Infantile Sexuality,' and 'The Transformations of Puberty.' Freud, *Standard Edition*, 7: 130–243. Quotations will be cited hereafter by page number from this volume. Quotations from *Il fanciullino* will be from the Feltrinelli edition and cited by page number.
3 See Rosamaria LaValva, *The Eternal Child*, especially the chapter 'A Matter of Sources' (107–24), for a detailed discussion of romantic depictions and theories of the child, particularly in Vico, Foscolo, Wordsworth, and Leopardi.
4 Ariès's study was translated in 1962 as *Centuries of Childhood*. For more detailed critical summaries of the Ariès thesis, see David Archard, *Children: Rights and Childhood*, 15–20, and Linda A. Pollock, *Forgotten Children: Parent-Child Relations from 1500–1900* especially the first chapter.
5 Archard, *Children*, 37–8.
6 Priscilla Robertson, 'Home as a Nest,' 421–2.
7 Pollock, *Forgotten Children*, 110.
8 Ibid., 110.
9 Ibid., 107.
10 C. John Sommerville, *The Rise and Fall of Childhood*, 177.
11 LaValva notes the remarkable absence of cruelty by and towards the child in the Italian literary tradition. *The Eternal Child*, 101–2.
12 In addition to the essay under discussion, see also the open letter of 1907, translated as 'The Sexual Enlightenment of Children' – in which Freud insists upon the disadvantages of withholding sexual information from children – and the other essays contained in the collection of the same name. See Freud, *The Sexual Enlightenment of Children*.
13 As Archard writes, 'Freud is conventionally credited with persuading us that children are libidinous creatures whose polymorphous and perverse sexuality must be channeled and constricted in appropriate ways to make civilization possible. Yet the idea that before Freud children were viewed as sexless creatures is contestable. Michel Foucault in particular has argued that it is wrong to think children's sex had previously been passed over in silence. Indeed he claims the institutional discourse of eighteenth-century educa-

tional establishments to have presumed the existence of a precocious and active children's sexuality' (40). Archard insists on Freud and Piaget as important early contributors to a *developmental* mode of thinking about childhood.
14 Sommerville, *Rise and Fall of Childhood*, 215.
15 James Sully, *Studies of Childhood.* Perugi's meticulous philological essay ('James Sully') documents the many intersections between Sully's study and Pascoli's work, analysing the substantial influence of the British psychologist's observations on both *Il fanciullino* and the poetry. Throughout this chapter, I note some of the most relevant points of contact.
16 Giuseppe Nava has pointed out the affinities between Pascoli's description of Homer's poetic style in the second chapter of *Il fanciullino* and Vico's depiction of the 'heroic age.' Nava goes on to compare Leopardi's and Pascoli's thought, finding in both a sense of the 'mentalità magico-animistica, comune al fanciullino e al selvaggio, la cui perdita successiva si traduce in un impoverimento poetico' [magic-animistic mentality, common to the child and the savage, whose successive loss translated into poetic impoverishment]. But, Nava argues, where Leopardi sees this 'fall' as irreparable and the memory of the infantile/primitive state as additional pain, Pascoli attempts a 'recuperation' of this state through poetry. Giuseppe Nava, 'La struttura dei *Poemi conviviali*,' 233–48. Similarly, LaValva argues that, 'For Vico, childhood is a possible cyclical return. For the Romantics, and especially for Leopardi, it is a life-long regret, a memory of happiness linked ... to the blissful ignorance of disillusionment ... Pascoli invents the idea of the simultaneous presence of the real and the abstract child. When the real child is forced out of childhood the "other" must remain inside ... and he will thus safeguard the perennial and exciting source of poetic vision' (*The Eternal Child*, 120–1).
17 Francesco Flora, *Orfismo della parola*, 78.
18 Ibid., 76.
19 LaValva, *Eternal Child*, 3.
20 See chapter 2 for a discussion of this poem in the context of 'double perspectives.'
21 Following from this logic, Pascoli asserts the Crocean notion of 'poetry without adjectives,' 'la poesia senza aggettivo.' In a passage that Pascoli finds important enough to excerpt and quote again in the preface to the *Poemi conviviali*, he argues that there are no schools or genres of poetry, only 'poetry and ... non-poetry.' Other classifications are the constructions of scholars, not the poets themselves. He is constantly at pains to dissolve what he perceives as arbitrary and unnecessarily divisive barriers and distinctions.

22 LaValva, *Eternal Child*, 49. Perugi ('James Sully') notes that 'Nella stesura definitiva, la formula "La sostanza psichica è uguale nei fanciulli di tutti i popoli" è una dichiarazione, implicita quanto inequivocabile, della lezione appresa dal Sully' (239) [In the definitive draft, the formulation 'The psychic substance is the same in the children of all peoples' is a declaration, as implicit as it is unequivocal, of the lesson learned from Sully].
23 LaValva, *Eternal Child*, 27.
24 See chapter 1 for a discussion of illness in Freud's writing and in the Italian writers of the *scapigliatura*.
25 Weber, *Legend of Freud*, 163.
26 Ibid., 162.
27 Freud further elaborates on this theme in the later essay 'Femininity' (1932). Here the notion of the male as prototype or paradigm of the human is quite explicit. Freud insists that the female child, in her pre-Oedipal stages of development, is essentially 'masculine': she is ignorant of the vagina, and the phallic mother is her love-object, precisely as in the development of boys. With the discovery of 'castration,' 'girls hold their mother responsible for their lack of a penis and do not forgive her their being thus put at a disadvantage.' Their cathexis shifts from the now-hated mother to the father; they hope for a baby as a penis substitute and begin the psychical development of femininity, grounded in penis envy. The literature on Freudian psychoanalysis and various forms of feminism is enormous. For a brief overview of feminist critiques and uses of psychoanalysis, including accounts of the work of such figures as Simone de Beauvoir and Judith Butler, see the introduction to Ellmann, ed., *Psychoanalytic Literary Criticism*. Freud, *Freud on Women: A Reader* (edited by Elisabeth Young-Bruehl), is a useful anthology of Freud's writings on female sexuality arranged chronologically.
28 Antonio Gramsci, in a critique of Pascoli's 'socialism,' lists excerpts from his letters to Luigi Mercatelli, the *Tribune*'s correspondent in Eritrea (an Italian possession at the time). The letters reveal Pascoli's desire actively to encourage colonial expansion in Africa and his frustration with orthodox socialism, which limits its concerns to class rather than the nation as a whole. To give one example cited by Gramsci, Pascoli writes in a letter of 30 October 1899, 'I consider myself a socialist, profoundly socialist, but a socialist of humanity, not of a class. In as much as my socialism embraces all peoples, I do not feel it contrasts with the desire and aspiration for colonial expansion' (Petrucciani, et al., eds, *Materiali critici per Giovanni Pascoli*, 190). On Pascoli's colonialist views, see also Jared M. Becker, *Nationalism and Culture*, especially 90–100.

29 Pascoli, *Opere*, 2: 612. See also Carlo Salinari, *Miti e coscienza del decadentismo italiano*.
30 In *Il fanciullino* Pascoli links one's sentiments for the fatherland with one's affection for the mother, arguing that one should express these affections in poetry only in exceptional moments – specifically in moments of unusual joy or unusual grief. To proclaim such love overabundantly or too often is falsification at worst or unseemly at best (50). 'Non ci accorgiamo di lei, se non nelle sue feste e nelle sue – nostre! – disgrazie. E allora prorompe anche dal cuore del fanciullino il grido di gioa e il grido di dolore' ['We are not consciously aware of her except on her holidays and in her – and our – misfortunes. And then the cry of joy and the cry of grief bursts out even from the hearts of children' (LaValva, *Eternal Child*, 43)].
31 LaValva, *Eternal Child*, 11.
32 Pascoli, *Poesie: Volume primo*, 169.
33 LaValva, *Eternal Child*, 15.
34 Ibid., 17.
35 'We want the creative faculty to imagine that which we know.' Percy Bysshe Shelley, *A Defence of Poetry* (1821), in *Shelley's Poetry and Prose*, 502.
36 Freud, *Standard Edition*, 3: 303–22.
37 Ibid., 315.
38 In a similar vein, Sergio Benvenuto argues that the efficacy of any given psychoanalytic interpretation (in the clinical situation) does not rest upon its having revealed an event that actually occurred in the patient's past. Rather, the interpretation works when it discloses a subjective truth (always already an interpretation itself) and unbinds for the subject a previous, binding (neurotic) interpretation. In this way it can effect an encounter with a 'real' ('The Crisis of Interpretation,' 28).
39 Jane Gallop succinctly states the importance of this theoretical shift: 'It has become a commonplace in the history of psychoanalysis to mark as a turning point the moment in the 1890s when Freud stopped believing in a "real" seduction at the origin of hysteria and realized that the source of neurosis is the child's fantasies. This is the monumental break with the theories of traumatic etiology and the discovery of infantile sexuality' ('Keys to Dora,' 213–14).
40 Sarah Winter, for instance, points out that 'The use of "recovered memories" as evidence in legal cases involving murder or sexual abuse brought against parents by children has also garnered a great deal of media attention that has fueled a controversy over the accuracy of psychotherapeutic and psychoanalytic reconstructions of repressed unconscious material from childhood' (*Freud and the Institution of Psychoanalytic Knowledge*, 4). She cites

in this context Frederick Crews, *The Memory Wars: Freud's Legacy in Dispute* (New York: New York Review of Books, 1995).
41 Regarding memory, compare Sully: 'All recalling of past experiences illustrates the modifying influence of the later self in its attempt to assimilate and understand the past self; and this transforming effect is at its maximum when we try to get back to childhood' (*Studies of Childhood*, 15).
42 LaValva, *Eternal Child*, 39.
43 Ibid., 37.
44 The aggressive instinct becomes increasingly prominent in Freud's thinking over time, reaching a high point in the postulation of the death drive in *Beyond the Pleasure Principle* (1920).
45 Poe, *Complete Works*, 4: 189–91. See chapter 1 for a more detailed discussion of Freud's writings and the Gothic.
46 Ibid., 187.
47 Silvia Finzi, in discussing the possibility of retrieving agency from the apparently deterministic Freudian system, writes, 'Psychoanalysis, as a treatment and as an ethical horizon, takes the form of an exhaustion of impossibilities with which to tear out painfully those few residual degrees of freedom afforded to everyone. Freedom is not an original condition of man that can only be lost, but a conquest of knowledge and wisdom. When the two limits conditioning us have been found (the one of life and death which follows its course regardless of our consent, and the one of the symbolic axis that exists independently of our intentionality), we can narrate our own biography feeling like subjects and not just objects of the plot relating to us. Fate, if it is not recognized, goes on presenting us with the same events, at the insistence of the repetition compulsion. Individual responsibility instead produces the variations in the self-narration in which we can recognize the cipher of human freedom, all the more precious because of its rarity' ('Freud and the Dream of Dreams,' 71–2).
48 LaValva, *Eternal Child*, 21. Citing this line from Pascoli, Perugi notes that 'è esattamente il termine "gazouillement" [from the French translation of Sully that Pascoli mined so thoroughly] che egli [Pascoli] rende col romagnolismo "boschereccia"' (236) [it is precisely the term 'gazouillement' which Pascoli renders with the term from the Romagna region 'boschereccia']. Perugi goes on to quote the French version of Sully's passage that informs Pascoli's image. The original English of this excerpt from Sully reads, 'Along with this articulate sounds begin to appear in periods of happy contentment under the form of infantile babbling [*boschereccia*] or "la-la-laing." Thus the child will bring out a string of *a* and other vowel sounds [...]. This applies still more to the appearance of the

consonantal sounds which long before the end of the sixth month become combined with the vowels into syllabic sounds, as *pa, ma, mam,* and so forth' (*Studies of Childhood*, 135).
49 LaValva, *Eternal Child*, 43.
50 LaValva discusses the conjunction of the '*puer*' and '*senex,*' focusing on the archetypal qualities of these figures (*The Eternal Child*, 94–5). Throughout her discussion of Pascoli's writings, she is especially attentive to such archetypal images.
51 Ibid., 15.
52 Ibid., 29.
53 Pascoli, *Poemi conviviali*, 74.
54 LaValva, *Eternal Child*, 31.
55 Guido Guglielmi, 'Per una lettura dei *Conviviali*,' 179. See chapter 2 for a discussion of this poem.
56 Ibid., 183–4.
57 LaValva, *Eternal Child*, 31.
58 Ibid., 77.
59 Ibid., 19.
60 Later in the text, Pascoli emphasizes the importance of the figure of Matelda in Dante's *Paradiso*, asserting that Dante's 'art is incarnated in Matelda, who is primordial, happy, innocent human nature' (*Fanciullino*, 57). Matelda, of course, is associated with the heavenly river Lethe in Dante's poem.
61 Petrucciano, et al., eds, *Materiali critici per Giovanni Pascoli*, 116. It is telling that Pasolini should evoke two prose writers (Verga and Manzoni) as the foils to Pascoli's poetry. The comparison then seems to become a microcosm or case in point of the Bahktinian distinction between the novel (as a popular, open genre capable of providing heterogeneity of voices) and poetry (as an elite, closed genre dominated by the monolithic voice).
62 Winter, *Freud*, 16.
63 I have not been able to locate documentation of the specific African custom to which Pascoli alludes here. However, the implication seems to be that white rocks placed at a grave indicate that justice has been served and the party responsible for the death of the person buried has been appropriately punished. The fact that Ruggero's grave remains without such white rocks signals that his death remains unavenged.
64 The motion of the gently rocking cradle appears again, to give just one example from *Myricae*, at the conclusion of 'Il tuono' ('The Thunder'), a brief poem that picks up from the immediately preceding 'Il lampo' ('The Lightning'). This strongly alliterative poem ('E nella notte nera come il

nulla/ ... rimbombò, rimbalzò, rotolò cupo' [And in the night black as the void, it roared, it reverberated, it rolled darkly]) evokes the threatening sound of a sudden peal of thunder erupting in the 'night black as the void.' As the second thunderclap vanishes, the comforting voice of a mother in song emerges, along with the sound of a rocking cradle ('Soave allora un canto / s'udì di madre, e il moto di una culla' [Gently then one heard the mother's song and the cradle's motion]). The impersonal form of the verb 'one hears' along with the absence of any possessive pronoun modifying 'mother' (she is not 'my/your/her mother') lift the poem from the realm of personal memory and lend it an emblematic quality.

65 LaValva, *Eternal Child*, 7.
66 Ibid.
67 Although Pascoli, in this quotation, uses the word 'feminine,' it is more accurate to speak of his dismissal of the 'female,' and indeed he cites two female characters as exemplifying the erotic element that Homer does not treat in depth. Pascoli's poetry, on the most superficially thematic level, could be said to be extremely 'feminine' in light of its preoccupation with flowers, birds, and country domestic life. I am thinking here specifically of Toril Moi's distinction between 'female' as a biological fact and 'feminine' as culturally determined behaviours and characteristics ('Men against Patriarchy').
68 The *fanciullino* exists in a de-eroticized realm: 'Egli fa umano l'amore, perchè accarezza esso come sorella (oh! il bisbiglio dei due fanciulli tra un bramire di belve), accarezza e consola la bambina che è nella donna' (*Fanciullino*, 31) ['He makes love human, because he soothes it like a sister (oh! the whispering of the two children in the midst of the wild beasts bellowing), he caresses and comforts the little girl who is in the woman' (LaValva, *Eternal Child*, 13)]. The woman can only appear and interact with the poet at a double remove from sexuality, as both sister and child. The denied sexuality, however, seems to surface in the idyllic evocation of the two children whispering among the bellowing of animals. The juxtaposition of 'belve' with 'umano,' along with the clandestine tone created by the 'whispering' and by the parenthetical structure of the remark give the scene an illicit potential eroticism that subverts the insistence upon the purely platonic nature of the caresses.
69 As discussed in chapter 1, the encounter with the uncanny is the encounter not with lack, but with the lack of lack. The notion of 'satisfaction' (to make full) evokes this.
70 Kristeva, *Black Sun*, 145.
71 Agamben, 'Pascoli e il pensiero della voce.'

72 This motion should not be understood as emphatic dramatic or narrative action. Indeed, as Katja Liimatta has recently pointed out, action verbs are relatively rare in Pascoli's poetry, which gives predominance to linking and perceptual verbs such as 'seem' and 'appear' and even more so to nouns and adjectives. Liimatta underscores the sense of slowness in Pascoli's poetry, and his tendency to describe objects seen through haze, smoke, and fog ('Impressionismo di parole e suoni nella poesia di Pascoli'). Francesco Flora has observed the importance of motion in Pascoli's imagery: his language 'consiste in una capacità di rendere l'immagine in azione. L'immagine pascoliana non è mai qualcosa di fermo ... è sempre una cosa colta nel suo movimento dal reale' (Petrucciano, et al., eds, *Materiali critici*, 18–19) [consists of the ability to portray the image in action. The Pascolian image is never fixed ... it is always something captured in its movement from the real]. He goes on to stress the importance of 'tremare' (tremble) as a key word in Pascoli, both as a word that in its various forms appears with great frequency in the poetry, and as a description that captures the overall effect of the poetry. The kind of motion we find in Pascoli may be best described in general as a slow, indistinct trembling.

73 A linguistic motivation for this pairing derives from the word used by Petrarch for 'pity' – 'pietà.' In Italian, this word denotes both 'pity,' as Petrarch uses it in this context, and 'piety,' as in the concept of 'filial piety.' Pascoli himself dwells on the notion of *pietas* (citing Cicero, he uses the Latin form as well as the Italian) in his essay on Dante entitled 'Minerva oscura.' Here, he is at pains to align the Aristotelian division of sins in the *Inferno* with the 'Seven Deadly Sins' that structure *Purgatory* and also with the Ten Commandments of Exodus. He divides the commandments into two groups, those on the second tablet corresponding to 'Justice' and relating to behaviour towards one's neighbour, and those on the first tablet corresponding to 'Religion' and relating to behaviour towards God. The Fourth Commandment ('Honour your father and mother'), Pascoli claims, is the commandment of 'Piety.' It should be grouped with the first tablet commandments, as the parents are, in a sense, analogous to God in the respect owed to them (*Opere*, 2: 710–16). The word 'pietà' also appears as an end word in the poem 'L'etèra,' (in *Convivial Poems*) examined in the previous chapter. We are told that the courtesan's aborted children were spurned before they could even be born and ask for 'pietà' from their mother. Thus, in these other Pascolian texts, the idea of 'pietà' is defined exclusively in terms of the love that should exist between children and parents.

5. Remembering the Golden Age

1 *Future of an Illusion* (*Standard Edition*, 21: 5–58) in many respects anticipates the later *Civilization and Its Discontents* (1930). 'L'era nuova' is in *Opere*, 2: 435–42. Translations from 'L'era nuova' throughout the chapter are my own.
2 See Gay, *A Godless Jew*, for a consideration of this topic from the perspective of intellectual history. Gay argues that Freud's atheism, unlike his Jewish cultural heritage, was indispensable and fundamental to his creation of psychoanalysis.
3 Similarly, Julia Kristeva argues in her provocative essay 'Stabat Mater,' that 'Man overcomes the unthinkable of death by postulating maternal love in its place – in the place and in the stead of death and thought. This love, of which divine love is merely a not always convincing derivation, psychologically is perhaps a recall ... of the primal shelter that ensured the survival of the newborn' (*The Kristeva Reader*, 176). In this essay, Kristeva does not group together 'God the Father' and 'Mother Nature' (as does Freud) as illusory fantasy constructions. Rather, through an analysis of the cult of the Virgin, she is at pains to distinguish between the paternal god of law, authority, and prohibitions and the 'mother-goddess' of non-verbal love. Affection for and devotion to mother-goddess figures appear even in monotheistic cultures that officially deny the divinity of such maternal figures. In this regard, Kristeva writes, 'The mother and her attributes, evoking sorrowful humanity, thus become representatives of a "return of the repressed" in monotheism. They re-establish what is non-verbal and show up as the receptacle of a signifying disposition that is closer to the so-called primary processes' (172).
4 Sir William Crookes (1832–1919). According to the *Encyclopedia Britannica*, Crookes was a 'British chemist and physicist noted for his discovery of the element thallium and for his cathode-ray studies, fundamental in the development of atomic physics.' (**Crookes**, Sir William. [2006]. *Encyclopedia Britannica*. Retrieved 8 April 2006, from Encyclopedia Britannica Online http://search.eb.com/eb/article-9027981). Crookes investigated various forms of spiritualism, attending séances and documenting the work of mediums, in order to explore the possibility of previously unknown forces. In the early 1870s he published in three parts *Researches in the Phenomena of Spiritualism*. In Part II (*Psychic Force and Modern Spiritualism*) he refutes his critics, who claim (as Freud does in the cited passage) that 'mesmerism, clairvoyance, electro-biology, table-turning, spirit-rapping, and all the rest'

can be explained by 'unconscious cerebration' and 'unconscious muscular action' (46–7).
5 Freud, *Future of an Illusion*, 35 ff.
6 Pascoli considers 'faith' primarily in its manifestation as a belief in an afterlife. Freud concerns himself primarily with belief in any sort of divinity, particularly monotheistic notions of a paternal God, and in a secondary way with all the doctrines, behaviours, and institutions that follow from such a belief. Freud had earlier connected the performance of religious rituals with manifestations of obsessional neurosis ('Obsessive Actions and Religious Practices' [1907]). Both sets of 'ceremonial' behaviours, he argues, have symbolic or historical meaning, and are designed to protect the practitioner from the guilt and anxiety of repressed instinctual wishes.
7 Pascoli, *Il fanciullino*, section V (35). Further references to *Il fanciullino* will be by section and page number. The translation is from LaValva, *Eternal Child*, 19.
8 Giuseppe Nava, 'Il mito vuoto,' 109.
9 Pascoli cites Leopardi in 'L'era nuova' as having realized the new task of poetry, and he dedicated two significant essays of literary criticism to this romantic poet: 'Il sabato' and 'La ginestra.'
10 Charles Darwin, 'A Biographical Sketch of a Child,' in *The Collected Papers of Charles Darwin*, 191–9. In the essay, Darwin synthesizes and presents notes taken from personal observation of his own son. He discusses the child's development from birth to about age three, evaluating his motor, verbal, affective, and intellectual growth. At points, he compares and contrasts certain abilities of the developing child with those of various animals. James Sully (see previous chapter) draws on Darwin's essay in his *Studies of Childhood*.
11 David Archard, *Children: Rights and Childhood*, 32. According to the *Encyclopedia Britannica*, Haeckel was a 'German zoologist and evolutionist who was a strong proponent of Darwinism and who proposed new notions of the evolutionary descent of man ... Though his concepts of recapitulation were in error, Haeckel brought attention to important biological questions.' (Retrieved 8 September 2005 from Encyclopedia Britannica Online, http://search.eb.com/eb/article-2966).
12 In his 'Introductory Lectures,' Freud famously aligned psychoanalysis with the Darwinian and Copernican hypotheses as discourses that 'de-centre' humanity and that therefore meet with resistance. Here in *Future of an Illusion* Freud mentions with disdainful sarcasm the 'monkey trial' of 1925 in Tennessee (38).

13 Pascoli, *Sotto il velame*. In *Tutte le opere di Giovanni Pascoli., Prose II: Scritti danteschi, sezione seconda*, 470.
14 Robert Durling, in his edition of Dante's *Divine Comedy*, has pointed out Dante's use of Ovid in this image. Book I of the *Metamorphoses* recounts the succession of golden ('The first millennium was the age of gold ... Springtide the single season of the year'), silver ('After old Saturn fell ... Jove ruled the world with silver charm ... And it was then that Jove split up the year'), bronze ('And men in bronze were quick with sword and spear'), and iron ages ('Then came the age of iron ... Then land, once like the gift of sunlit air, Was cut in properties, estates, and holdings'), Ovid, *Metamorphoses*, 33–4. In Ovid's rendition, we can see that the degeneration of the world from its creation through the successive ages of man, culminating in the flight of Justice, corresponds to a progressive increase in and refinement of boundaries and distinctions (spring divided into four seasons; creation of homes, then of political borders, etc.).
15 Hesiod, *Works and Days*, trans. Lattimore, 31–2.
16 Virgil, *Eclogues*, trans. Lee, 57.
17 Niall Rudd, 'Introduction' to Horace, *Odes and Epodes*, 7.
18 Dante, *Divine Comedy*, ed. Durling, 223.
19 Ibid., 555. See Durling's excellent 'additional note' on the Old Man of Crete, 555–7.
20 Pascoli, *Convivial Poems*, trans. Egidio Lunardi and Robert Nugent, 2: 21. All translations of the *Convivial Poems* will come from this collection and be cited by volume and page number.
21 Giorgio Bàrberi Squarotti, 'Esiodo nei *Conviviali*' in Pazzaglia, ed., *I Poemi conviviali di Giovanni Pascoli*. The line cited is 629 from Hesiod's *Works and Days*, trans. Lattimore.
22 Pascoli, *Opere* 2: 437; Virgil, *Eclogues*, trans. Lee, 56, 57. The Virgin represents 'Justice.' (See Lee's notes, 114–16.)
23 Her shadow is darkened yet further by her role in the birth of Hercules, as recorded by Ovid. At the behest of Juno, Lucina attempted to kill Alcmena by preventing Hercules' birth while Alcmena was in the throes of labour.
24 See my introduction in this book for a discussion of Cixous's essay on Freud's '*The "Uncanny.*"'
25 I am thinking here of Cixous's provocative 'fiction is a secretion of death.'
26 See Ovid, *Metamorphoses*, Book V.
27 Indeed, Part One of the poem (first published 24 December 1899) is contemporary with 'L'era nuova,' which directly cites the eclogue. The poem and the 'secular' speech share thematic concerns, as I will show.

28 The foot marked with clay signified a slave for sale (Pascoli, *Conviviali*, 272n).
29 The open doors of Janus's temple indicate a time of war.
30 Guido Guglielmi, 'Per una lettura dei *Poemi conviviali*,' 183.
31 In this section, Pascoli illustrates the 'first, primitive conception' of life (which is in the process of being superseded by a new conception 'grounded in reality and science'). The thoughts of 'un pastore' are replicated to represent this conception. The passage opens with a meditation on the apparent nightly 'disappearance' of the sun, which gave rise to speculation that it must travel under the earth each night. It is here that Horace's lines are re-evoked. Pascoli then moves to a 'primitive' contemplation of the phenomena of sleep and dreaming: each person must have a shadowy 'double' who travels about during the night while the person's actual body lies motionless in his bed. Finally, Pascoli imitates how the shepherd's primitive mind might grapple with the experience of death: the shadowy double delays in returning – has, in fact, apparently disappeared. The deceased is put underground with his important objects so that he will have them when he awakens.
32 These terms allude to Pascoli's use of them in *Il fanciullino*, VI (38): 'Se tu conocessi Platone, ti direi che come egli ha ragione nel volere che i poeti facciano *mythous* e non *logous*, favole e non ragionamenti, così non ho torto io nel pretendere che i ragionatori facciano *logous* e non *mythous* [Platone, *Fedro* III B]. Ma pur troppo è difficile trovare chi si contenti di far solo quello che deve. E Platone stesso ... Ma egli era Platone' ['If you knew Plato, I would tell you that he is right when he insists that poets create *mythos* and not *logos*, tales and not discursive speech. Therefore I am not wrong in expecting discoursers to engage in *logos* and not in *mythos*. But unfortunately it is hard to find those who are happy to do only what they should. And Plato himself ... But he was Plato' (LaValva, *Eternal Child*, 25)]. The addressee here, as throughout the essay, is the 'little boy.'

Conclusion: Reading beyond the Family Romance

1 Tzvetan Todorov, *The Fantastic*, 149.
2 Weber, *Legend of Freud*, 218.

Bibliography

Agamben, G. 'Pascoli e il pensiero della voce.' In G. Pascoli, *Il fanciullino*. 3rd. ed. Milan: Feltrinelli, 1996.
Agorni, M. 'The Female Gothic: The Italy of Anne Radcliff.' In *Translating Italy for the Eighteenth Century*, 24–32. Manchester, UK, and Northampton, MA: St Jerome Publishing, 2002.
Agosti, S. *Critica della testualità*. Bologna: Il Mulino, 1994.
Archard, D. *Children: Rights and Childhood*. London and New York: Routledge, 1993.
Arrighi, C. *La scapigliatura: Romanzo sociale contemporaneo*. Ed. Giuseppe Farinelli. Milan: Istituto Propaganda Libraria, 1978.
Bàrberi Squarotti, G. 'Appunti sulla sintassi pascoliana.' *Lettere italiane* 12 (1960): 268–83.
– 'Esiodo nei *Conviviali*.' In Mario Pazzaglia, ed., *I Poemi conviviali di Giovanni Pascoli: Atti del Convegno di studi di San Mauro Pascoli e Barga*, 37–52. Florence: La Nuova Italia, 1995.
– 'Il fanciullino e la poetica pascoliana.' In *Giovanni Pascoli: Poesia e poetica. Atti del Convegno di studi pascoliani*, 19–56. Rimini: Maggioli, 1984.
– *Simboli e strutture della poesia del Pascoli*. Messina-Florence: D'Anna, 1966.
Bataille, G. 'Mouth.' In *Visions of Excess*. Minneapolis: University of Minnesota Press, 1985.
Baudelaire, C. *The Complete Verse*. Trans. and ed. Francis Scarfe. London: Anvil Press Poetry, 1986.
Bazzocchi, M.A. 'Il volto femminile del mito.' In Mario Pazzaglia, ed., *I Poemi conviviali di Giovanni Pascoli: Atti del Convegno di studi si San Mauro Pascoli e Barga*, 53–70. Florence: La Nuova Italia, 1995.
Beauvoir, S. *The Second Sex*. Trans. and ed. H.M. Parshley. New York: Vintage Books, 1989.

Becker, J.M. *Nationalism and Culture: Gabriele D'Annunzio and Italy after the Risorgimento*. New York: Peter Lang, 1994.
Benvenuto, S. 'The Crisis of Interpretation.' *Journal of European Psychoanalysis* 6 (Winter 1998): 19–46.
Bernheimer, C. 'Introduction, Part One.' In Bernheimer and Kahane, eds., *In Dora's Case*.
Bernheimer, C., and C. Kahane, eds. *In Dora's Case: Freud – Hysteria – Feminism*. New York: Columbia University Press, 1985.
Bloom, H. 'Introduction.' In *Edgar Allan Poe*. New York: Chelsea House Publishers, 1985.
– 'Freud and the Sublime.' In *Agon: Towards a Theory of Revisionism*. New York: Oxford University Press, 1982.
Boito, A. *Opere*. Ed. Mario Lavagetto. Milan: Garzanti, 1979.
Bonaparte, M. 'The Life and Works of Edgar Allan Poe: A Psycho-analytic Interpretation.' In John P. Muller and William J. Richardson, eds, *The Purloined Poe: Lacan, Derrida, and Psychoanalytic Reading*, 101–32. Baltimore, MD: Johns Hopkins University Press, 1988.
Brooks, P. 'Freud's Masterplot: Questions of Narrative.' *Yale French Studies* 55/56 (1977): 280–300.
Buhle, M.J. *Feminism and Its Discontents: A Century of Struggle with Psychoanalysis*. Cambridge, MA: Harvard University Press, 1998.
Capuana, L. *Un vampiro*. Florence: Passigli, 1995.
Carducci, G. *Poesie scelte*. Ed. Luigi Baldacci. Milan: Mondadori, 1983.
Cixous, H. 'Fiction and Its Phantoms: A Reading of Freud's *Das Unheimliche* (The "Uncanny").' *New Literary History* 7 (1976): 525–48.
Contini, G. 'Il linguaggio di Pascoli.' In *Giovanni Pascoli. Poesie. Volume primo*, xxiii–lviii. Milan: Mondadori, 1997.
Copjec, J. 'Vampires, Breast-feeding, and Anxiety.' *October* 58 (1991): 25–43.
Crookes, Sir William. *Researches in the Phenomena of Spiritualism*. Part II, *Psychic Force and Modern Spiritualism*. London: J. Burns, nd.
Curi, F. *Il possibile verbale*. Bologna: Edizioni Pendragon, 1995.
Dante. *The Divine Comedy*. Volume 1: *Inferno*. Ed. and trans. Robert M. Durling. Oxford: Oxford University Press, 1996.
– *The Divine Comedy*. Vol 2: *Purgatorio*. Ed and trans. Robert M. Durling. Oxford: Oxford University Press, 2003.
– *The Divine Comedy of Dante Alighieri. Paradiso*. Trans. Allen Mandelbaum. New York: Bantam Books, 1986.
Darwin, C. 'A Biographical Sketch of a Child.' In Paul H. Barret, ed., *The Collected Papers of Charles Darwin*, 191–9. Chicago and London: University of Chicago Press, 1977.

Day, W.P. *In the Circle of Fear and Desire: A Study of Gothic Fantasy.* Chicago: University of Chicago Press, 1985.
del Principe, D. *Rebellion, Death and Aesthetics in Italy: The Demons of Scapigliatura.* Madison, WI: Fairleigh Dickinson University Press, 1996.
Della Coletta, C. 'Teoria realista e prassi fantastica: "Un vampiro" di Luigi Capuana.' *MLN* 110.1 (1995): 192–208.
Dolar, M. '"I Shall Be with You on Your Wedding-Night": Lacan and the Uncanny.' *October* 58 (1991): 5–23.
Dör, J. *Introduction to the Reading of Lacan.* New York: The Other Press, 1998.
Ebani, N. 'La vita di Giovanni Pascoli (1855–1912).' *Poesie.* By Giovanni Pascoli. Ed. Augusto Vicinelli. Vol. 1, lxi–lxxi. Milan: Mondadori, 1997.
Edleman, G. *Bright Air, Brilliant Fire: On the Matter of the Mind.* New York: Basic Books, 1992.
Ellmann, M. 'Introduction.' In Maud Ellmann, ed., *Psychoanalytic Literary Criticism,* 1–35. London and New York: Longman, 1994.
Felman, S. 'On Reading Poetry: Reflections on the Limits and Possibilities of Psychoanalytic Approaches.' In John P. Miller and William J. Richardson, eds, *The Purloined Poe: Lacan, Derrida, and Psychoanalytic Reading,* 133–56. Baltimore, MD: Johns Hopkins University Press, 1988.
Ferroni, G. *Storia della letteratura italiana.* Vol. 3. Milan: Einaudi, 1991.
Finotti, F. 'Arrigo Boito: Il demone dello stile.' *Lettere italiane* 46 (1994): 395–421.
Finzi, S.V. 'Freud and the Dream of Dreams.' Trans. David Spafford. *Journal of European Psychoanalysis* 6 (Winter 1998): 47–73.
Flora, F. *Orfismo della parola.* Rocca San Casciano: Cappelli, 1953.
– 'Pascoli e la poesia moderna.' In Mario Petrucciani, Marta Bruscia, and Gianfranco Mariani, eds, *Materiali critici per Giovanni Pascoli,* 9–24. Rome: Ateneo, 1971.
Freud, S. *Freud on Women: A Reader.* Ed. Elisabeth Young-Bruehl. New York and London: Norton, 1990.
– *Gesammelte Schriften.* Vol. 10. Leipzig: Internationaler Psychoanalytischer Verlag, 1924.
– *The Sexual Enlightenment of Children.* Ed. Philip Rieff. 7th ed. New York: Collier Books, 1976.
– *The Standard Edition of the Complete Psychological Works.* Trans. and ed. J. Strachey. 24 vols. London: Hogarth Press, 1953–74.
Frye, N. *Anatomy of Criticism.* Princeton, NJ: Princeton University Press, 1957.
Fuchs, R. 'Charity and Welfare.' In David I. Kertzer and Marzio Barbagli, eds, *Family Life in the Long Nineteenth Century: 1789–1913.* Vol. 2, *The History of the European Family,* 155–94. New Haven, CT: Yale University Press, 2002.
Gallop, J. 'Keys to Dora.' In Charles Bernheimer and Claire Kahane, eds,

In Dora's Case: Freud–Hysteria Feminism, 200–20. New York: Columbia University Press, 1985.
Garboli, C. 'Pascoli: Sposo-fratello nel nido della poesia.' *La Repubblica.* 21 May 2000: 38–9.
Gay, P. *Freud: A Life for Our Time.* New York: Norton, 1988.
– *A Godless Jew: Freud, Atheism and the Making of Psychoanalysis.* New Haven, CT: Yale University Press, 1987.
Gibson, M. *Born to Crime: Cesare Lombroso and the Origins of Biological Criminology.* Italian and Italian American Studies. Westport, CT: Praeger, 2002.
Gioanola, E. 'Clara e Fosca: Eros e Thanatos nell'ultimo romanzo di Tarchetti.' In *Convegno nazionale su Igino Ugo Tarchetti e la scapigliatura.* San Salvatore Monferrato: Comune, 1979.
– *Psicanalisi, ermeneutica e letteratura.* Milan: Mursia, 1991.
Gioanola, E., ed., *La scapigliatura: Testi e commento.* Turin: Marietti, 1975.
Giustiniani, V.R. 'Travel as Inspiration in Pascoli's Poetry.' In *The Motif of the Journey in Nineteenth-Century Italian Literature*, 141–9. Gainesville: University Press of Florida, 1994.
Graf, A. *Le Poesie di Arturo Graf.* Turin: Giovanni Chiantore, 1922.
– *Roma nella memoria e nelle immaginazioni del medio evo.* Turin: 1882–3.
Guglielmi, G. 'Per una lettura dei *Conviviali.*' In Mario Pazzaglia, ed., *I Poemi conviviali di Giovanni Pascoli: Atti del Convegno di studi di San Mauro Pascoli e Barga*, 173–84. Florence: La Nuova Italia, 1995.
Harrowitz, N. *Antisemitism, Misogyny and the Logic of Cultural Difference.* Lincoln: University of Nebraska Press, 1994.
Hertz, N. *The End of the Line: Essays on Psychoanalysis and the Sublime.* New York: Columbia University Press, 1985.
Hesiod. *Works and Days.* Trans. Richard Lattimore. Ann Arbor: University of Michigan Press, 1959.
Homer. *The Odyssey.* Trans. Robert Fitzgerald. New York: Anchor Books, 1963.
Horace. *Odes and Epodes.* Ed. and trans. Niall Rudd. Cambridge, MA: Harvard University Press, 2004.
Invernizio, C. *Storia d'una sartina.* 1892.
– *Tre storie in giallo e nero.* Ed. Riccardo Reim and Bianca Spadolini. Rome: Armando, 2002.
Jackobson, R. *Selected Writings III.* The Hague: Mouton, 1981.
Jensen, W. *Gradiva.* Trans. Helen M. Downey. Los Angeles: Sun and Moon Press, 1993.
Johnson, B. *A World of Difference.* Baltimore, MD: Johns Hopkins University Press, 1987.
Kimball, A.S. 'D-Ciphering Dupin's Fac-simile Signature: The Infanticidal

Implications of a "Dessein si Funeste."' *The Edgar Allan Poe Review* 6 (Spring 2005): 20–36.
Kristeva, J. *Black Sun: Depression and Melancholia.* Trans. Leon S. Roudiez. New York: Columbia University Press, 1989.
- *The Kristeva Reader.* Ed. Toril Moi. New York: Columbia University Press, 1986.
- *Powers of Horror: An Essay on Abjection.* Trans. Leon S. Roudiez. New York: Columbia University Press, 1982.
- *Revolution in Poetic Language.* Trans. Maragaret Waller. New York: Columbia University Press, 1984.
Lacan, J. 'Seminar on "The Purloined Letter."' Trans. Jeffrey Mehlman. In John P. Muller and William Richardson, eds, *The Purloined Poe: Lacan, Derrida and Psychoanalytic Reading,* 6–54. Baltimore, MD: Johns Hopkins University Press, 1988.
LaCapra, D. *Soundings in Critical Theory.* Ithaca, NY: Cornell University Press, 1989.
LaValva, R. *The Eternal Child: The Poetry and Poetics of Giovanni Pascoli.* Chapel Hill, NC: Annali d'italianistica, Inc., 1999.
- 'Ritorno a Calypso.' *Romance Languages Annual* 6 (1994): 283–8.
Lawrence, D.H. *Studies in Classic American Literature.* Garden City, NY: Doubleday, 1953.
Leopardi, G. *Canti.* Ed. Fernando Bandini. 9th ed. Milan: Garzanti, 1988.
- *Poesie e prose.* Vol. 1. Ed. Mario Andrea Rigoni and Rolando Damiani. Milan: Mondadori, 1987.
Lepschy, A.L. 'Carolina Invernizio's *Ij delit d'na bela fia* and *Storia d'una sartina.*' *Italian Studies* 34 (1979): 93–104.
- 'The Popular Novel, 1850–1920.' In Letizia Panizza and Sharon Wood, eds, *A History of Women's Writing in Italy,* 177–89. Cambridge: Cambridge University Press, 2000.
Liimatta, K. 'Impressionismo di parole e suoni nella poesia di Pascoli.' *Italian Culture* 17 (1999): 61–75.
Lombroso, C., and G. Ferrero. *Criminal Woman, the Prostitute, and the Normal Woman.* Trans. and intro. Nicole Hahn Rafter and Mary Gibson. Durham and London: Duke University Press, 2004.
- *La donna delinquente, la prostituta e la donna normale.* Turin and Rome: L. Roux, 1893.
- *The Female Offender.* New York: Philosophical Library, 1958.
Lydenberg, R. 'Freud's Uncanny Narratives.' *PMLA* (October 1997): 1072–86.
Mazzoni, C. 'Is Beauty Only Skin Deep? Constructing the Female Corpse in Scapigliatura.' *Italian Culture* 12 (1994): 175–87.

Moi, T. 'Men against Patriarchy.' In Linda Kauffman, ed., *Gender and Theory: Dialogues on Feminist Criticism*, 181–90. Oxford: Basil Blackwell, 1989.

Moroni, M. 'Estetismo/modernismo in Italia. Soggetto panico, soggetto dietro il siepe, soggetto pubblico: D'Annunzio, Pascoli, Palazzeschi.' *Quaderni d'Italianistica* 15 (Spring–Autumn 1994): 61–74.

Nava, G. 'I *Canti di Castelvecchio*: Simbolo o allegoria?' In *Giovanni Pascoli: Poesia e poetica. Atti del Convegno di studi pascoliani*. Rimini: Maggioli, 1984.

– 'Il mito vuoto: L'ultimo viaggio.' *Rivista Pascoliana* 9 (1997): 101–13.

'La struttura dei *Poemi conviviali*.' In Mario Pazzaglia, ed., *I* Poemi conviviali *di Giovanni Pascoli: Atti del Convegno di studi di San Mauro Pascoli e Barga*, 233–48. Florence: La Nuova Italia, 1995.

Orlando, F. 'Costanti tematiche, varianti estetiche e precedenti storici.' In M. Praz, *La carne, la morte e il diavolo nella letteratura romantica*, vii–xxi. Florence: Sansoni Editore, 1996.

– 'Letteratura e psicanalisi: Alla ricerca dei modelli freudiani.' In *Letteratura italiana: L'interpretazione*. Vol. 4: 549–87. Turin: Einaudi, 1985.

– *Towards a Freudian Theory of Literature*. Trans. Charmaine Lee. Baltimore, MD: Johns Hopkins University Press, 1978.

Ovid. *The Metamorphoses*. Trans. Horace Gregory. New York: Viking, 1958.

– *Metamorphoseon Libri XV*. New York: Arno Press, 1979.

Pardo Bazán, E. '*The White Horse' and Other Stories*. Trans. Robert Fedorchek. Lewisburg, PA: Bucknell University Press, 1993.

Parkin-Gounelas, R. *Literature and Psychoanalysis: Intertextual Readings*. New York: Palgrave, 2001.

Pascoli, G. *La befana e altri racconti*. Ed. Giovanni Capecchi. Rome: Salerno, 1999.

– *Convivial Poems*. 2 vols. Trans. Egidio Lunardi and Robert Nugent. Plainesville, OH: Lake Erie College Press, 1979.

– *Il fanciullino*. Ed. Giorgio Agamben. 3rd ed. Milan: Feltrinelli, 1996.

– *Myricae*. Ed. Franco Melotti. Milan: Rizzoli, 1994.

– *Opere*. Ed. C.F. Goffis. 2 vols. Milan: Rizzoli, 1970.

– *Poemi conviviali*. Ed. Giuseppe Leonelli. Milan: Mondadori, 1996.

– *Poesie: Volume primo*. Ed. Augusto Vicinelli. Milan: Mondadori, 1997.

– *Selected Poems*. Ed. P.R. Horne. Manchester: Manchester University Press, 1983.

– *Tutte le opere di Giovanni Pascoli*. Milan: Mondadori, 1952, 1971.

Pascoli, Maria. *Lungo la vita di Giovanni Pascoli*. 2 vols. Milan: Mondadori, 1961.

Pasolini, P.P. *Antologia della lirica pascoliana*. Turin: Einaudi, 1993.

Pazzaglia, M. *Pascoli*. Rome: Salerno, 2002.

– 'Pascoli e la morte.' *Zeta: Ricerche e documenti sulla morte e sul morire* 19 (June 1997): 11–22.

Pellico, S. *Prose e poesie.* Florence: Salani, 1965.
Perugi, Maurizio. 'James Sully e la formazione dell'estetica pascoliana.' *Studi di filologia italiana: bulletino dell'Accademia della Crusca* 42 (1984): 225–309.
Petrarch, F. *Petrarch's Lyric Poems: The* Rime Sparse *and Other Lyrics.* Trans. and ed. Robert Durling. Cambridge, MA: Harvard University Press, 1976.
Petrucciani, Mario. *Emilio Praga.* Turin: Einaudi, 1962.
Petrucciani, Mario, et al., eds. *Materiali critici per Giovanni Pascoli.* Rome: Edizione dell'Ateneo, 1971.
Plato. *Five Dialogues.* Trans. G.M.A. Grube. Indianapolis and Cambridge: Hackett Publishing, 1981.
Poe, E.A. *The Complete Works of Edgar Allan Poe.* Ed. James A. Harrison. 7 vols. New York: AMS Press, 1965.
Pollock, L.A. *Forgotten Children: Parent-Child Relations from 1500–1900.* Cambridge: Cambridge University Press, 1983.
Praga, E. *Poesie.* 1969.
Praz, M. *Romantic Agony.* Trans. Angus Davidson. London: Oxford University Press, 1970.
Robertson, P. 'Home as a Nest: Middle Class Childhood in Nineteenth-Century Europe.' In Lloyd deMause, ed., *The History of Childhood,* 407–31. New York: The Psychohistory Press, 1974.
Rossi, P. 'I fiori del male: Giovanni Pascoli.' *Romance Languages Annual* 4 (1992): 348–52.
Salinari, C. *Miti e coscienza del decadentismo italiano.* Milan: Feltrinelli, 1960.
Scarano, E. *Dalla* Cronaca bizantina *al* Convito. Florence: Vallecchi, 1970.
Shelley, M. *Frankenstein, or The Modern Prometheus.* Ed. M.K. Joseph. Oxford and New York: Oxford University Press, 1992.
Shelley, P.B. *Shelley's Poetry and Prose.* Selected and edited by Donald H. Reimann and Sharon B. Powers. New York and London: Norton, 1977.
Sommerville, C.J. *The Rise and Fall of Childhood.* Beverly Hills, CA: Sage Publications, 1982.
Spackman, B. *Decadent Genealogies: The Rhetoric of Sickness from Baudelaire to D'Annunzio.* Ithaca, NY: Cornell University Press, 1989.
Sully, J. *Studies of Childhood* (1896). *Significant Contributions to the History of Psychology,* Vol. 3. Ed. Daniel N. Robinson. Washington, DC: University Publications of America, 1977.
Tarchetti, I.U. *Fantastic Tales.* Trans. and ed. Lawrence Venuti. San Francisco: Mercury House, 1992.
– *Fosca.* Turin: Einaudi, 1971.
– *Paolina: Misteri del Coperto dei Figini.* Milan: Mursia, 1994.
– *Passion: A Novel.* Trans. Lawrence Venuti. San Francisco: Mercury House, 1994.

- *Tutte le opere*. Ed. Enrico Ghidetti. 2 vols. Bologna: Cappelli, 1967.
Tennyson, A. 'Ulysses.' In Alexander W. Allison, ed., *The Norton Anthology of Poetry*, 402–3. 3rd ed. London: Norton, 1983.
Tessari, R. 'L'immagine della morte nell'opera di Tarchetti e nella Scapigliatura.' In *Convegno nazionale su Igino Ugo Tarchetti e la scapigliatura*. San Salvatore Manferrato: Comune, 1979.
Tessari, R., ed. *La scapigliatura: Un'avanguardia artistica nella società preindustriale*. Turin: Paravia, 1975.
Todorov, T. *The Fantastic: A Structural Approach to a Literary Genre*. Trans. Richard Howard. Cleveland, OH: The Press of Case Western Reserve University, 1973.
Tolliver, J. *Cigar Smoke and Violet Water: Gendered Discourse in the Stories of Emilia Pardo Bazán*. Lewisburg, PA: Bucknell University Press, 1998.
Toschi, P. *Invito al folklore italiano. Le regioni e le feste*. Rome: Studium, 1963.
Truglio, M. 'Giovanni Pascoli's Ventriloquized Female Voices.' *Romance Review* 8 (1998): 29–37.
- 'Strangely Familiar: The Uncanny Poetics of Giovanni Pascoli.' *The Romanic Review* 97 (2006): 231–54.
Vazzana, S. *La struttura psicologica dell'opera pascoliana*. Rome: Editrice Ciranna, 1974.
Virgil. *The Eclogues*. Trans. Guy Lee. London: Penguin Books, 1988.
Weber, S. *The Legend of Freud*. Expanded edition. Stanford, CA: Stanford University Press, 2000.
- *The Return to Freud: Jacques Lacan's Dislocation of Psychoanalysis*. Trans. Michael Levine. Cambridge: Cambridge University Press, 1991.
Weinapple, F. 'La "via crucis" del Pascoli.' *Lingua e stile* 27 (June 1993): 287–300.
Winter, S. *Freud and the Institution of Psychoanalytic Knowledge*. Stanford, CA: Stanford University Press, 1999.
Wordsworth, W. *The Oxford Authors: William Wordsworth*. Ed. Stephen Gill. Oxford and New York: Oxford University Press, 1990.
Wright, E., ed. *Feminism and Psychoanalysis: A Critical Dictionary*. Cambridge, MA: Blackwell, 1992.
Yaeger, P. 'Toward a Female Sublime.' In Linda Kauffman, ed., *Gender and Theory: Dialogues on Feminist Criticism*, 191–212. Oxford: Basil Blackwell, 1989.

Index

abortion, 11. *See also* infanticide
Achilles, 64–5
adult sexuality, origin of, 122
agency, 169n50, 183n47. *See also* identity
Alexander the Great, 78–9, 80, 81
Altheae (in Ovid's *Metamorphoses*), 99
anatomists and the socially dispossessed, 165n13
anthropometry. *See* Lombroso, Cesare
Arrighi, Cletto, 24, 165n1
auto-eroticism, 123–4

Bahktin, Mikhail, 184n61
Bataille, Georges, 20
Baudelaire, Charles: 'Une Charogne,' 167n35
Boito, Arrigo: 'L'alfier nero,' 36, 39–40, 167n33; 'Case nuove,' 51, 53–4; 'Lezione d'anatomia,' 30, 51–3, 53–4, 74; 'Una mummia,' 51; 'Re Orso,' 31–2, 36
Boito, Camillo, 24; 'Un corpo,' 30, 171–2n57
Bosis, Adolfo de, 125
Brooks, Peter, 45
burial alive, fear of, 50–1

Capuana, Luigi: 'Un vampiro,' 84, 90–2, 176–7n18
Carducci, Giosuè: 'Nevicata,' 177–8n31
castration anxiety, 49
childhood, history of, 107–9
children: cruelty of, 109, 119; sexuality of, 179–80n13. *See also* Freud, Sigmund, Works: *Three Essays on the Theory of Sexuality*
children's literature and *scapigliatura*, 25
Cixous, Hélène, 9, 27–8
Collodi, Carlo: *Pinocchio*, 25
compromise formation, 71
Convito, Il (journal), 80
criminal anthropology and atavism, 90–2. *See also* Lombroso, Cesare
Crookes, William, 139, 187–8n4

D'Annunzio, Gabriele, 80; *L'innocente*, 85, 86
Dante: *Il Convivio*, 80; *Inferno* XIV, 142, 144–5, 150; *Inferno* XXVI, 65, 69, 70; *Purgatorio* XV, 178n31; *Purgatorio* XXII, 151
Darwin, Charles, 141, 188n10
DeAmicis, Edmondo: *Cuore*, 25

death, 27
Derrida, Jacques, 127
difference, 113. *See also* otherness; sexual difference
Donne, John: 'The Ecstasy,' 31
double. *See* narcissism; vampirism

Eco, Umberto: *La misteriosa fiamma della regina Loana*, 163n40
Eden, Garden of. *See* golden age, myth of
Eros, 14, 44–5
Eurydice (in Ovid's *Metamorphoses*), 3

family as primary model, 115–16
father, figure of, 6–7. *See also* Pascoli, Ruggero
Felman, Shoshana, 35, 38
fetish, 21
Foscolo, Ugo, 26
Freud, Sigmund: on auto-eroticism, 123–4; on castration anxiety, 49; on children's sexuality, 179–80n13 (*see also* Freud, Sigmund, Works: *Three Essays on the Theory of Sexuality*); on the cruelty of children, 109, 119; on the fear of burial alive, 50–1; on the incestuous desire of the infant, 164n51; on infantile amnesia, 121–2; and the interpretation of dreams and jokes, 33; and literature, 16, 169n48; and the Medusa figure, 23, 43; on memory and repression, 116–17; on the nuclear family as primary model, 115–16; on the origin of adult sexuality, 122; on the separation of sexuality and reproduction, 123–4; and the uncanny, 7–9, 15–16, 35, 49, 73, 161n9. Works: 'The Aetiology of Hysteria,' 164n54; *Beyond the Pleasure Principle*, 7, 45, 160; *Civilization and Its Discontents*, 32–3; *The Ego and the Id*, 33; 'Family Romances,' 146; 'Femininity,' 118, 146, 181n27; *Future of an Illusion*, 135, 136–41; *Jokes and Their Relation to the Unconscious*, 16, 171n57; *New Introductory Lectures on Psychoanalysis*, 177n22; 'Screen Memories,' 117–18, 120; *Three Essays on the Theory of Sexuality*, 12, 13, 107, 109–10, 111–12, 113, 121–2; *Totem and Taboo*, 116; 'The Uncanny,' 16, 47–8, 63–4, 69, 76, 157, 161–2n10, 164n49

ghosts, 27–8, 29
golden age, myth of, 142–5, 155–6, 189n14
Gothic and psychoanalysis, 33–4
Graf, Arturo, 77–8, 80; 'L'altro viaggio di Ulisse,' 65, 70
Gramsci, Antonio, 181n28

Haeckel, Ernst, 141, 188n11
Hesiod: *Erga*, 142–3, 145; *Theogony*, 145
Homer: *The Odyssey*, 65, 66, 71–2
Horace: 'Carmen saeculare,' 142, 144, 148–9
horror, 32

identity, 31, 42, 49, 50. *See also* narcissism; vampirism
illness, 35–6, 39
incestuous desire of the infant, 164n51
individuality. *See* identity
infanticide, 11, 83–4, 85–6, 89–90, 93–4. *See also* abortion
infantile amnesia, 121–2

Invernizio, Carolina, 11, 84; and a bourgeois readership, 87–9; 'La fine di un Don Giovanni,' 88; *Ij delit d'na bela fia*, 85, 175–6n5; 'Razza maledetta,' 85; *Storia di una sartina*, 85, 86–90, 94, 175–6n5

Jackobson, Roman, 35

Kristeva, Julia, 16–17, 46, 76, 132, 160, 168–9n46, 174–5n23, 187n3

Lacan, Jacques, 33
Leopardi, Giacomo, 110, 141, 180n16; 'La ginestra,' 130; 'Nella morte di una donna fatta trucidare col suo portato dal corruttore per mano ed arte di un chirurgo,' 170–1n54; 'Il passero solitario,' 54–6, 172n59
Lombroso, Cesare, 11, 84, 86, 89–90, 94, 102–3

Manzoni, Alessandro: *I promessi sposi*, 25–6
maternal. *See* mother, figure of
maternal body. *See* mother, figure of
maternal phallus, 23
Medusa, figure of, 23, 43
Meleager (in Ovid's *Metamorphoses*), 99
memory: and desire, 122; and poetry, 116–17; and repression, 116–17
metonymy and metaphor. *See* Lacan, Jacques
monstrosity, 78
mother, figure of, 20–1, 37, 49–50, 53–4, 65, 77, 83–4, 89–90, 187n3; and self-annihilation, 6; and the uncanny, 50. *See also* abortion; infanticide; maternal phallus

mourning, resistance to, 59, 61, 100
mouth, image of, 20–2. *See also* voice as sign of presence

narcissism, 76
Narcissus, 76
nationalism in the thought of Giovanni Pascoli, 113–15
necrophilia, 27
nest, image of, 4, 23, 81, 95, 172–3n7. *See also* family as primary model

occultism. *See* spiritualism
Odysseus. *See* Ulysses
origins, 3, 9, 11, 12, 23, 85–6, 92, 105, 106. *See also* criminal anthropology and atavism; family as primary model; nest, image of
Orpheus (in Ovid's *Metamorphoses*), 3
otherness, 29, 31, 34–5, 112–15; and Italy, 34
Ovid, *Metamorphoses*, 3, 99, 189n14

Pascoli, Giacomo, 58–9
Pascoli, Giovanni: concept of the *fanciullino*, 13, 59, 61, 81, 106, 110, 111, 119, 120, 122–3, 131, 185n68 (*see also* Pascoli, Giovanni, Works: *Il fanciullino*); on the feminine, 131, 185n67; and the Freudian uncanny, 7, 46, 157–8; on the fundamental goodness of nature, 130; and the Gothic, 20; on the innate goodness of man, 119–20; on language and desire, 132–3; and morality, 119, 135–6; and the nuclear family as primary model, 115–16 (*see also* nest, image of); and otherness, 113–15; on poetry, 116–17, 122–32, 135–6, 180n21 (*see also* Pascoli,

Giovanni, and the concept of the *fanciullino*; Pascoli, Giovanni, Works: *Il fanciullino*); and the 'pre-grammatical' use of language and Freud's 'pre-genital' phase of sexuality, 123–4; and the prehistory of consciousness, 63; and the return of the repressed, 19; on romantic and erotic love, 130–2; on sleep and dreaming, 190n31; and the task of the poet, 116; and Virgil's *Ecloga* IV in epigrams, 149–50; works in Latin, 61–3. *See also* Pascoli, Ruggero; Vincenzi, Caterina Allocatelli. Works: 'Abbandonato,' 95; 'Antìclo,' 71–3, 131; 'La buona novella,' 152–5; *Canti di Castelvecchio*, 58; 'La cavalla storna,' 58; 'Ceppo' (poem), 95–100; 'Il ceppo' (short story), 11, 85, 94, 100–6; 'La cetra di Achille,' 64–5; 'La civetta,' 19–20; 'Creature,' 94; 'Dialogo,' 133; 'Digitale purpurea,' 14; 'L'era nuova,' 12, 16, 135, 136–41, 142, 146–9, 152; 'L'etèra,' 73–7; *Il fanciullino*, 12, 62–3, 107, 110–11, 116–17, 135–6, 141, 180n16 (*see also* Pascoli, Giovanni, and the concept of the *fanciullino*); 'Fides,' 94; 'Gelsomino notturno,' 13, 14, 105; 'Gog and Magog,' 16, 68, 77–82; 'La grande prolitaria si è mossa,' 113–15; 'In ritardo,' 59, 60–1; 'Minerva oscura,' 142; 'Morto,' 94–5; *Myricae*, 18, 58, 128–9, 132, 133; 'Orfano,' 59, 95, 177–8n31; 'Il passero solitario,' 54–6; *Poemi conviviali*, 7, 11, 18, 63, 64, 65, 125, 152, 162–3n22; 'Il poeta degli Iloti,' 145; *Primi poemetti*, 125; 'Siamo sette,' 58, 59–60, 61, 69, 82; 'La siepe,' 4, 161n3; *Sotto il velame*, 142, 150–1; 'La tessitrice,' 26–8; 'Il tuono,' 184–5n64; 'L'ultimo viaggio,' 63, 65–71, 81, 126, 131, 145; 'La via ferrata,' 14; 'La voce,' 20–3, 58; 'X agosto,' 4, 58, 104, 161n5

Pascoli, Luigi, 58–9
Pascoli, Margherita, 58–9
Pascoli, Ruggero, 4, 58–9, 129, 130, 134
Pasolini, Piero Paolo, 127
Pellico, Silvio, 84
Petrarca, Francesco, 130, 133–4
Plato: *Phaedo*, 74; *Symposium*, 80
Poe, Edgar Allan, 166n19. Works: 'Annabel Lee,' 21; 'Bernice,' 21; 'The Black Cat,' 169n51; 'The Cask of Amontillado,' 169n51; 'The Fall of the House of Usher,' 169n51; 'Ligeia,' 31; 'The Murders in the Rue Morgue,' 120–1; 'The Tell Tale Heart,' 87
poet as child, 110. *See also* Pascoli, Giovanni, and the concept of the *fanciullino*; Pascoli, Giovanni, Works: *Il fanciullino*
poetry: and religion, 136–41; and science, 136
Praga, Emilio, 24, 168n45; 'A un feto,' 30–1, 52
psychoanalysis: and religion, 136–41; sociopolitical critique of, 128; and subjective vs objective truth, 182n38. *See also* Freud, Sigmund, and the uncanny

Radcliffe, Anne, 34
Rousseau, Jean-Jacques, 108

Saussure, Ferdinand de, 40
scapigliatura, 11, 20, 24, 25, 28–30, 33,

34–5, 45, 46–7, 74, 83, 165n11, 171n57
self. *See* identity
sexual difference, 44
sexuality and reproduction, 123, 124
Shelley, Mary: *Frankenstein* and the Freudian unconscious, 120, 121
Shelley, Percy Bysshe, 117
spiritualism, 139, 177n22
Stoker, Bram: *Dracula*, 32
sublime, 168n40

Tarchetti, Igino Ugo, 11, 24, 25–6, 165n7. Works: 'Composition VI' of *Disjecta*, 26–8; 'I fatali,' 32; *Fosca*, 29, 32, 36–9, 40, 43; 'Lake of the Three Lampreys,' 48–9; 'La leggenda del castello nero,' 32, 42–3; 'La lettera *u*,' 36; 'Memento,' 41–2, 43–5, 53, 167n35; 'Osso di morto,' 29, 30; *Pensieri*, 42–3; 'Sognai,' 50, 56; 'Lo spirito nel lampone,' 29. *See also* burial alive, fear of
Tennyson, Alfred, Lord: 'Ulysses,' 65, 69
Thanatos, 14, 44–5

Ulysses, 12, 63, 65, 145, 174n19
uncanny: and the ambivalence of origins, 106; and castration, 10; and infanticide, 83–4; and the maternal body, 51; and Pascoli's concept of the *fanciullino*, 10; and *scapigliatura*, 83. *See also* Cixous, Hélène; Freud, Sigmund, and the uncanny; Freud, Sigmund, Works: 'The Uncanny'; Pascoli, Giovanni, and the Freudian uncanny

vampirism, 29, 36, 37, 38, 166n16, 176–7n18; and Christ, 32
Verga, Giovanni, *Storia di una capinera*, 55–6
Vico, Giambattista, 110, 141, 180n16
Villani, Giovanni: *Chronicles*, 77
Vincenzi, Caterina Allocatelli, 58–9, 97
Virgil: *Ecloga IV*, 142, 143–4, 148–50, 173n8
Vitrioli, Diego, 61–2
voice as sign of presence, 72–3. *See also* mouth, image of

womb. *See* mother, figure of
women in late-nineteenth-century Italy, 92–3. *See also* infanticide
Wordsworth, William: 'Intimations of Immortality,' 61, 65–6; 'We Are Seven,' 58, 59, 60, 82